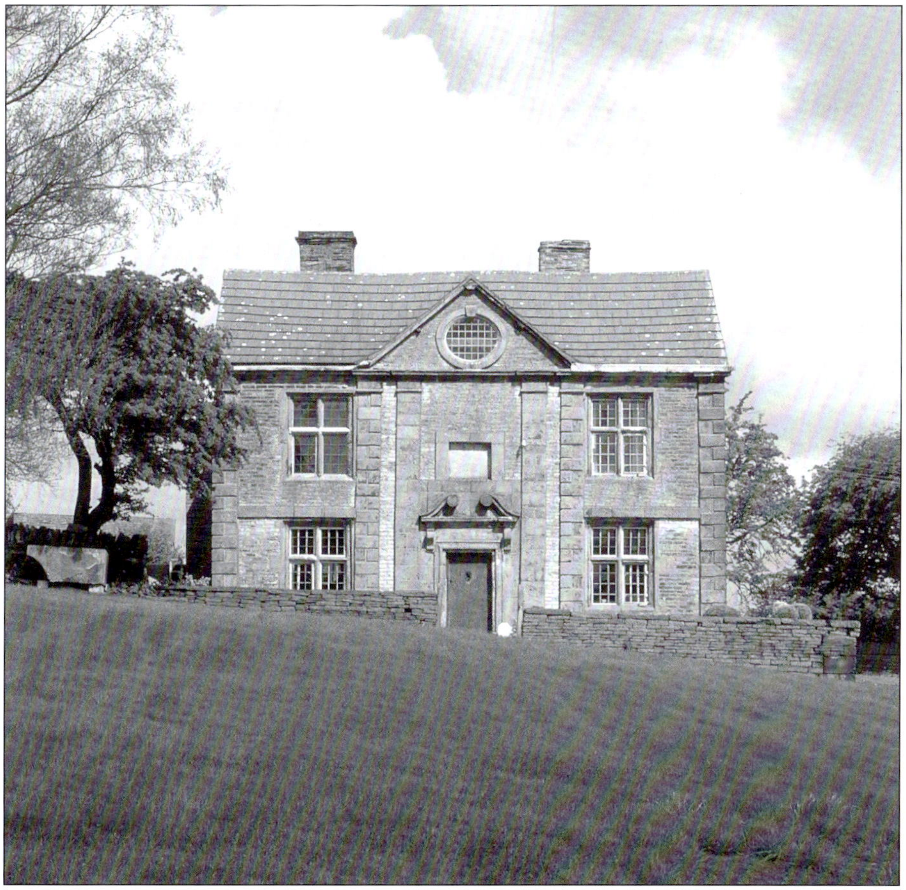

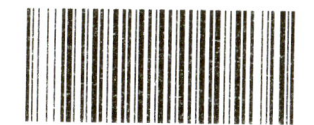

To my family:
wife Susan, children Christopher,
Stephanie and Peter
and
to the memory of my father,
Ronald Albert Miller
1928-1977

HISTORIC HOUSES IN LANCASHIRE

The Douglas Valley
1300–1770

Garry Miller

HERITAGE TRUST FOR THE NORTH WEST

Garry Miller has asserted his right to be identified as the author of this book.

All rights reserved. No part of this publication may be reproduced, stored in a retrieval system, or transmitted in any form by any means, electronic, digital, mechanical, photocopying or otherwise, without the prior permission of the author and copyright holder.

All photographs and illustrations by the author, unless otherwise stated.

Published by the Heritage Trust for the North West Ltd., Pendle Heritage Centre, Park Hill, Barrowford, Nelson, Lancashire. BB9 6JQ.
Registered Charity Number 508300.

The Trust is very grateful to the Paul Mellon Centre for Studies in British Art and the Marc Fitch Fund for grants towards the publication costs.

Printed by Printoff Graphic Arts, Nelson, Lancashire.

© Garry Miller, 2002.

ISBN: 0-948743-05-0

Frontispiece: Stone Hall, Dalton, an early classical house of c1700-1710.

List of Contents

Author's Foreword		vi
Foreword by Dr. R.W. Brunskill		ix
About the Author		x
About the Heritage Trust for the North West		xi
Introduction		xiii
I	Houses in the Landscape	15
II	The Medieval Legacy: Timber Framed Buildings 1400-1630	35
III	Houses of the Gentry 1570-1620	57
IV	Houses of the Yeomanry 1600-1720	87
V	The Zenith of Classicism 1720-1770	123
VI	The Fabric of Traditional Buildings	137
VII	Exterior Elements and Ornament	149
VIII	Interior Elements and Ornament	163
Inventory of Houses in the Douglas Valley		175
Glossary of architectural terms		207
Index		209

Author's Foreword

More than 20 years ago, as a young student of architecture, I began gingerly to knock upon the doors of various 17th and 18th century houses in the heart of what is one of Lancashire's most beautiful, but least publicised, localities. In those distant moments, the idea of what has ultimately become this book was first conceived.

I have been fortunate to have the help of a great many people without whom this book would never have been possible. Here I will attempt to convey my thanks, but do so feeling that whatever I say will be painfully inadequate in expressing my debt of gratitude.

Firstly, this work would never have made it into print without John Miller (no relation), Director of the Heritage Trust for the North West, who had the vision to take on board this new and ambitious project. Those already familiar with the work of the Trust will know of its role in preserving and maintaining some of the region's finest buildings and through the medium of this book their activities will hopefully be appreciated by a much wider audience. We envisaged that the book would trace the development of pre-industrial houses in a specific area of Lancashire and relate the buildings to the people who occupied them and the circumstances in which they were built. Furthermore, the approach should be one that even those with little or no specialist knowledge – other than a fundamental interest in period buildings – would appreciate, in order to promote the subject to its widest extent. This book is the reality of that vision. The Douglas Valley (the generic term I have chosen for the area between Chorley, Wigan and Ormskirk) was selected because its buildings have received little attention despite their quality and diversity, and considerable numbers survive despite the spread of urbanisation.

Tangibly, the vision also became reality thanks to the Trust's design team, who provided support and ideas at each stage of the project and ultimately created a successful marriage of text, photographs and artwork. The Trust also assisted by means of its library, which was a valuable provenance of rare illustrations of vanished buildings. All this, however, would have been impossible without the generous financial support from the Paul Mellon Centre for Studies in British Art and the Marc Fitch Fund.

Elsewhere, many individuals and organisations assisted in their own specialist fields and my appreciation to each of them now goes on record.

Nigel Morgan, friend and colleague for many years, was a constant source of assistance, inspiration, advice and encouragement. He gave invaluable critical analysis on each of the chapters and freely made available his perceptive research on the Lancashire gentry and the 1664 Hearth Tax, which proved of great value to my own interpretations of these subjects; for all this I stand considerably in his debt. I would also like to thank Dr. Ron Brunskill, for very kindly agreeing to write the foreword to this book and for his very generous comments. Also, to Alan Bennett, President of the North Craven Building Preservation Trust, for his interest and support.

Alan Crosby's work on landscape history also made enlightening reading and helps to place the buildings in the context of their surroundings. He also provided useful comments and put at my disposal his work on the landscape history of Blackrod.

Wigan Heritage Service supplied photographs of demolished buildings from their archives and Kath Brogan of Wigan Borough Council's conservation department kindly supplied information concerning Dower House, Ince. Lancashire County Record Office assisted with the plans of Lathom House and the Will Lathom drawings of historic buildings; I am grateful in particular to Neil Sayer for drawing my attention to the description of Birchley Hall in 1778. David Smith of Adlington allowed me to use his photographs of Adlington Hall and Rigby House Farm. Photographer Gary Taylor of Bolton, another long-standing friend and colleague, gave valuable technical advice. Miss Hilton of Club House Farm, Shevington, provided the C19 photograph of that building and more information besides.

I am grateful to Mrs Suzanne Steedman, who coped good-humouredly with my handwritten notes (of varying degrees of illegibility) and converted them into typescript more perfect than ever I could have achieved.

And of course the entire project would never have left the starting blocks without the co-operation of the owners and occupiers of the buildings themselves. The fact that the vast majority of households I approached welcomed my interest is a positive sign of their regard for the piece of history they occupy. The warmth of the reception given to me, and hospitality frequently offered, was much appreciated, as was the time they gave up to allow me to conduct what were frequently long and complex surveys. Space means I must thank them all collectively, with the exception of several whose assistance stands out. Mr and Mrs Gilmore of Douglas Bank Farm, Upholland, were extremely patient with my numerous efforts at obtaining a satisfactory cover photograph which does justice to their fine building. Janet and David Cole of Holt Farm, Coppull, drew my attention to this significant property and provided me with their own research material. The Speakman family of Johnson's Farm, Upholland, have welcomed me on many occasions over the past

20 years. Mr and Mrs Bothamley and Mr Hesketh and Mrs Greenwood of Kirklees Hall were patient during my many visits to record this complex building. Mr Martin Ainscough, chairman of the Ainscough Group, kindly allowed me to survey their headquarters at Bradley Hall and Chris Burke patiently accompanied me. Mr Bill Ainscough of Harrock Hall and Mr Roy Watson of Smith's Farm, Dalton, kindly allowed me to use in this book my earlier research into these buildings conducted on their behalf. To all the other owners, thanks must go anonymously but it is none the less sincere. I owe it to them to mention here that all these buildings are private property and thus their privacy must always be borne in mind by readers.

Lastly, I will end on an appeal to readers to draw to my attention any errors and omissions in order to correct them in future editions.

GARRY MILLER
September 2002

Foreword by Dr. R.W. Brunskill

Most people associate South Lancashire with industry and the crowded cities and towns in which it is located, yet much of this part of the county is in fact rural in character. A major component of this character is the traditional domestic architecture, about which Garry Miller has written so admirably.

Regional studies such as this of the Douglas Valley depend on a widespread survey of the region as a whole, coupled with detailed studies of individual houses of interest or significance.

Here, there are plans and photographs in abundance of houses representing different social levels, different forms of construction, different details of interior design and external appearance, developments of different periods and the differences which come from different locations. All this is given its social context – the role of the locally important landowners is examined along with that of the ordinary farmers. The houses of the gentry are put in their setting, just as the farmhouses are related to the changing role of the yeomanry. At the same time, the choice of building materials and the change in construction from timber-framing to stone and brick is clearly set out and illustrated.

At a time when the whole country seems to be in danger of being covered in concrete, it is encouraging that Garry Miller has been able to demonstrate how strong is the rural character and how fortunate it is that so many historic houses, built for people of varying social levels, survive for study and appreciation. It helps the process of appreciation that Garry Miller has provided such a well-founded and superbly-illustrated volume. To many people, South Lancashire is associated with George Formby, Wigan Pier and various fashionable football clubs. These all deserve their fame, but in a quieter way, the traditional houses deserve some fame too.

It is a pleasure to be associated with this book and I am sure that all readers will share this pleasure.

R.W. BRUNSKILL

About the Author

Garry Miller has been fascinated by historic buildings since he was a boy. In the past 30 years he has surveyed, photographed and recorded in detail many hundreds of houses and farm buildings in Lancashire, Cheshire, Cumbria and Yorkshire. He is also editor of the long-established Lytham St Annes Express newspaper. Garry lives in Lancashire and is married with three children.

About the Heritage Trust for the North West

The Heritage Trust for the North West is a registered Building Preservation Trust and was established in 1978 as a charity and company limited by guarantee. Under its former name, Lancashire Heritage Trust, it has rescued and restored many buildings of architectural interest at risk in Lancashire. Many of these are open to the public on a regular basis.

In 1996 the Trust merged with the former North West Buildings Preservation Trust (a Trust with similar aims) and enlarged its remit, as required by the Charity Commission, to cover the North West of England. To reflect this, the Trust is now developing projects in Manchester, Liverpool and Cumbria.

The Trust seeks to find new appropriate uses for historic buildings and encourages good design and craftsmanship. It has retained some of the buildings it has restored deriving rental income from them. Others are open to the public forming a network of historic places to visit. Pendle Heritage Centre, in Barrowford, East Lancashire, now celebrating its 25th Anniversary in 2002, is the Trust's flagship project, attracting over 100,000 visitors per annum.

Introduction

This book aims to investigate more than 500 years of rural houses in a specific area of Lancashire. The area selected is what can broadly be termed the Douglas Valley – the area between the towns of Chorley, Wigan and Ormskirk, through which the River Douglas flows from its source in the West Pennine Moors on its journey to the Ribble estuary near Preston.

Today much of this area is built up, but until the Industrial Revolution it was predominantly rural. The fact that considerable prosperity existed among its communities is indicated by the number of fine manor houses and farmhouses that have survived from the pre-factory era. In the analysis that follows we will use the evidence from two sources – that of the buildings themselves and also contemporary documents associated with them.

Together they combine to create a picture of how these houses were planned, constructed and used and – most importantly – who built them and how they could afford to. An inventory of 145 buildings surveyed is included in the book, in alphabetical order of the townships in which they occur. Each house has been given a reference number, and in the main text this appears in brackets after the name of the building.

CHAPTER I

Houses in the Landscape

From its beginnings in the West Pennine Moors close to the summit of Winter Hill, the River Douglas cuts a meandering route through much of south-west Lancashire on its westward journey to the coast. On its progress the river has carved a narrow valley through an outcrop of low hills between the towns of Chorley, Wigan and Ormskirk which form a transition between two extremes of landscape – the stark Pennine foothills to the east and the flat mosslands of the low-lying coastal plain.

For early settlers this intermediate zone offered an environment more amenable than the moors and mosslands, where physical conditions imposed great constraints upon agriculture and settlement. Consequently from medieval times onward a relative prosperity existed among the rural communities of the Douglas Valley: and tangible, primary evidence are the fine houses surviving from the late 16th to the early 18th centuries. They are silent witnesses to the fact that their occupants had amassed sufficient wealth to generate the building of substantial homes of unprecedented standard. These houses were built throughout the area and within a definite time span, indicating they were not just individual occurrences but collectively products of a distinct phenomenon: a wave of building – or rather, rebuilding – activity which affected entire sections of the rural community, transforming at the same time their way of life and the appearance of the countryside they lived in.

Across the chasm of several centuries, these buildings present many questions to the present-day onlooker. For whom were they built? Where was the money found to build them? What governed the choice of building materials? What were the rooms used for? And how aware and influenced were these inhabitants of an isolated and culturally backward county by changing fashions and styles in art and architecture nationally?

Well, as witnesses, perhaps the buildings are not that silent after all. The structures themselves, in their architecture, layout and decoration, can provide many answers either individually or in comparison with their contemporaries. Other information

Pl. 1
Looking across the Douglas Valley, from Parbold Hill to Ashurst. Today, the remnants of the thick woodland cover it held in medieval times are still clearly visible.

can be found through the documents associated with the houses and their owners. In the chapters that follow, both sets of evidence will be used to compose a picture of the circumstances that generated this of building and the houses it produced. First: the landscape in which they are set and the people who occupied it.

THE AREA AND ITS HOUSES

The geology of Lancashire has produced two landscapes within one county. Along the coastal zone, left behind by the retreat of the sea, the low-lying mossland belt stretches north from Liverpool to the Ribble estuary near Preston and beyond into the Fylde. In sharp contrast is the angular wilderness of the Pennine moors which encircles the Manchester conurbation in the southeast and extends north to form a physical boundary with Yorkshire before merging with the Cumbrian fells.

Between these extremes, the hills of the Douglas Valley form a western offshoot from the Pennines, intruding sharply into the coastal plain in a roughly triangular formation. But unlike the eastern backdrop of Winter Hill where the Douglas has its source, the landscape here is of a gently-rolling scenery, formed by underlying carboniferous sandstones rounded off by a thick covering of boulder clay left by retreating glaciers at the end of the Ice Age. The course of the river itself was carved by melting ice. From Winter Hill it meanders south through a narrow, steep-sided upper valley north of Blackrod and then towards Wigan, where – ignoring a low-lying mossland belt to the south at Ince – it makes a sharp turn northwestwards through higher ground. Here, the area's most spectacular scenery is produced as the valley widens out, terminating in the prominent hills of Parbold and Ashurst on either flank which form an abrupt end to the upland mass. Thereafter the ground falls to a wide floodplain north of Newburgh – once beneath sea-level after the melting of the ice sheets – through which the Douglas meanders northwards to finally discharge into the Ribble at its estuary near Tarleton.

Ashurst and Parbold are distinctive landmarks representing the differing nature of the landmasses which define the river valley. The latter (120m) rises above the valley's steep-sided northern slope where in places the sandstone is capped by outcrops of more resistant millstone grit, the rock which underlies much of the Pennines and contributes to a harsher landscape. North of Parbold the ground rises further to a cluster of smaller hills crowned by Harrock at 157m, then falls back eastwards to an almost plateau-like surface with the hill of Coppull the highest point at 93m. East of Wigan the ground rises sharply towards Aspull, Haigh and Blackrod with heights of up to 156m as a prelude to the West Pennine Moors beyond.

The southern landmass culminating at Ashurst (170m) presents a more rounded picture. Its qualities were admired centuries ago: on July 5, 1663, the husbandman farmer and diarist Roger Lowe of Ashton-in-Makerfield marvelled at the 'most gallant prospect' the view offered from here.[1] Ashurst forms the most northern extremity of a clearly-defined ridge running south-eastwards through Tower Hill at Upholland (146m) to Billinge Hill, at 179m the highest point in the area. Just south of Billinge is the outlying hill of Crank (79m) at Rainford which marks the southern termination of the uplands and descends to a wide mossland belt at its base stretching westwards to the coast.

Pl. 2
The highest point of the hills that flank the Douglas Valley is Billinge Hill at 179m, which rises behind Guild Hall, an early yeoman's house initially of 1629, built close to where the ground descends to meet the mosslands.

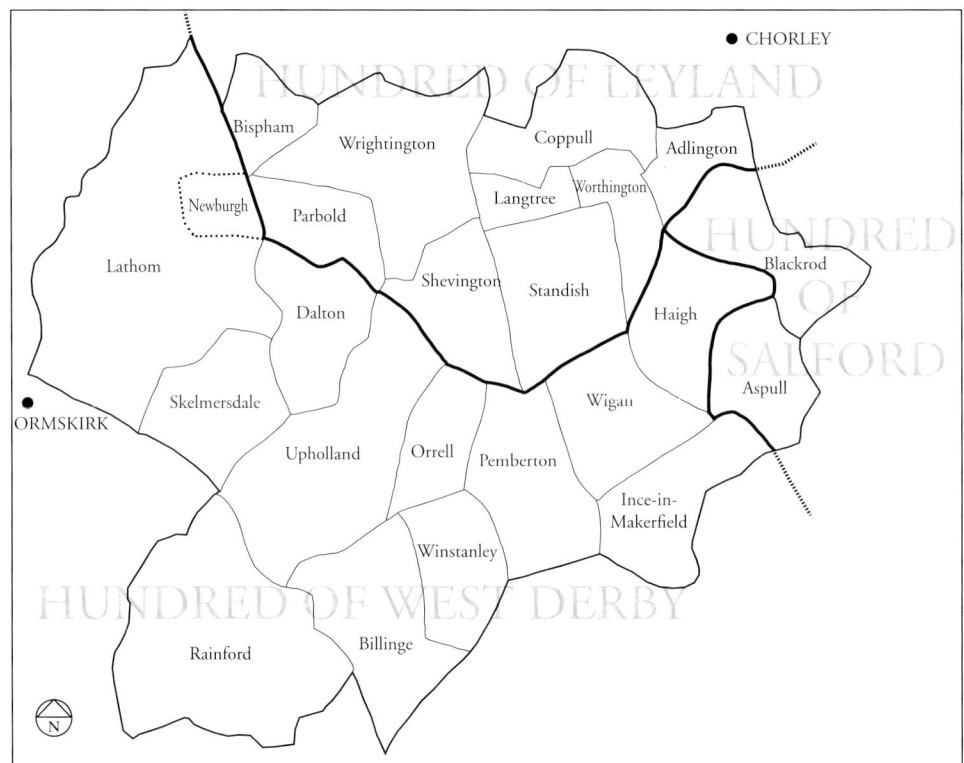

Map 1
The Douglas Valley:
Townships and Hundred
boundaries.

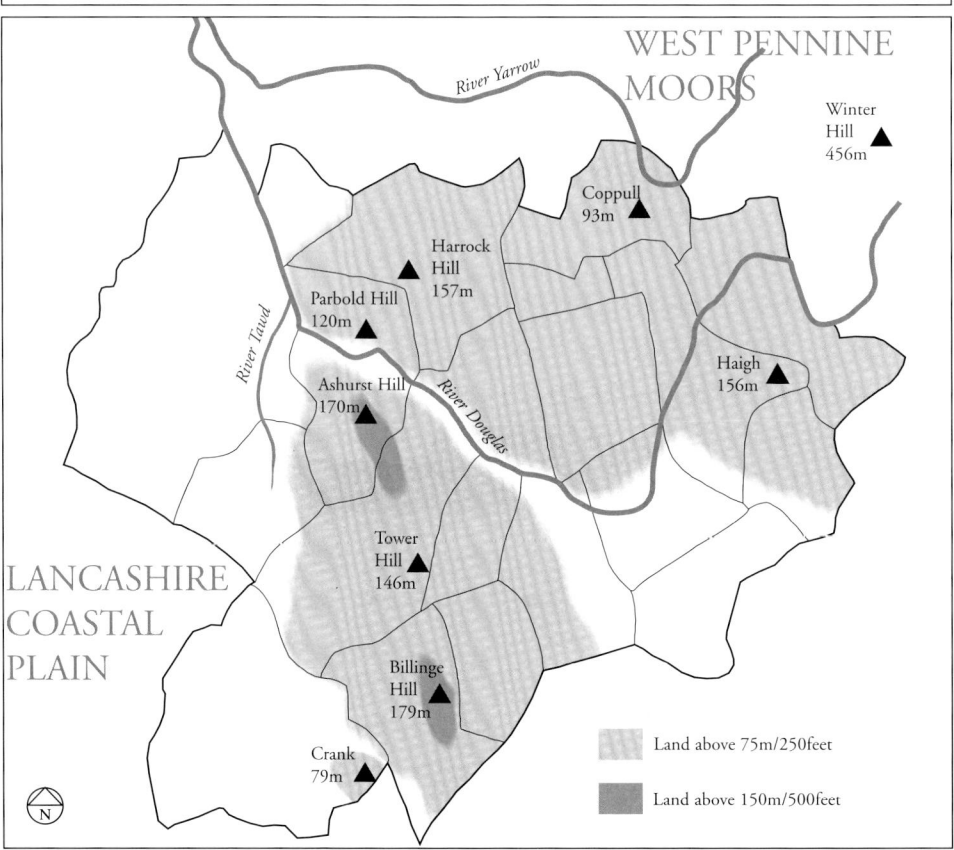

Map 2
The Douglas Valley:
Relief and drainage.

The landscape of the valley and its surrounding hills has many contrasts. To the north the picture is still largely rural, and in Wrightington, Coppull, Worthington and Adlington in particular, ancient houses stand in an ancient landscape of rolling, wooded hills criss-crossed by hedgerows, presenting a picture little changed from the time they were built. But further south the area is heavily built up around Wigan, a town ancient in itself and described in 1536 as 'as big as Warrington but better builded.'[2] This urban perspective extends westwards towards a town with more modern origins, Skelmersdale, built in the 1960s at the foot of Ashurst Hill to accommodate Merseyside overspill and swallowing some of the area's finest countryside in Dalton and Upholland in the process. Destroyed too were some of its finest buildings: others, like those in the former farming village of Elmers Green, Dalton, now survive fossilised within modern housing sprawl.

The houses of Elmers Green are, like so many others in the area, no longer working farms: the agricultural economy of the past three decades is one in which the small farmer has struggled to survive, and in many cases lost. Their lands sold, the houses have exchanged their centuries-old role as workplaces for a new one as desirable country homes for businessmen and the professional classes. Many have benefited from tasteful restoration by owners justly proud of their piece of the region's heritage. Others, thankfully a minority, have for one reason or another escaped salvation and after ending their working days have declined into disuse and ultimately dereliction and destruction.

Each of these houses is a thread in a fascinating tapestry of life which existed before the industrial revolution changed the complexion of the area. What makes the

Pl. 3
Lyme Tree House, a ruin on the western slope of Billinge Hill, is a tragic picture of a farm that has escaped salvation. A fine but now eroded doorway, inserted in the C18 into an earlier structure, declares this was once an important building.

buildings of the Douglas Valley so appealing is the diversity they present. Much of this comes from the fact that just as the landscape is a transitional one between Lancashire's lowlands and uplands, so the houses reflect a convergence between lowland and highland building styles, more noticeable than in any other part of the county.

Being an upland area, the majority of houses in the Douglas Valley are of stone. In this way they are akin to the houses of the Pennines, but the softer stone of the valley lends a mellowness not found in the houses further east. But shades of the lowland zone can be seen too in the brick houses found generally around the area's fringe where the ground descends to meet the plain. In the lowlands, the stone is concealed beneath a thick covering of clay which makes brick synonymous with buildings in these areas. However, many brick houses of the Douglas Valley are far more substantial than anything to be found in the coastal plain, where generally the poorer agricultural land could not generate sufficient wealth to create comparably fine buildings. The end result is that the Douglas Valley has some of the finest 17th and early 18th century rural houses in the whole of Lancashire. Before we begin to look at the buildings in detail we must first turn to the source of the wealth that generated them, and the sections of society that possessed it.

AGRICULTURE AND SETTLEMENT

At the time of Domesday, what we now know as Lancashire was remote, backward and uncivilised. It was so inconsequential that no name was given to it: the area was merely the land 'between the Ribble and the Mersey,' with its more northern extremities included within Yorkshire. The coastal plain was inhospitable mossland, the eastern reaches inhospitable moorland.

The intermediate zone of the Douglas Valley, though more tractable, was largely covered by a blanket of woodland. Records show that in the C12 and C13 both flanks of the Douglas Valley were well-wooded, the cover extending north to Wrightington and southwards along the Ashurst-Billinge ridge where it seems to have been especially dense in the Dalton area.[3] In the east too there are references to woods in Worthington, Langtree and Shevington. The legacy of this is still detectable today: physically, in the views of hills such as Harrock and Ashurst (plate 1), where trees still figure prominently in the landscape; and nominally through houses such as Upper Wood Farm, Standish (105) and Prior's Wood Hall, Dalton (45) which all bear testimony to the previous character of their surroundings.

Clearance of the woodland began in pre-Conquest times and accelerated during the C12 and C13 as a growing population put increasing pressure on the land. This

Pl. 4
Crawshaw Hall, with its stone-clad solar wing of early C16 date, stands above the river on a site that has even earlier origins. It was the seat of the Worthington family, who owned this part of the manor of Adlington from the C14.

frenetic period of activity is reflected in the many place names which incorporate the elements *-ley* and *-hurst*, both of which refer to woodland clearance. We therefore have Bradley (as in Bradley Hall) in Langtree, Tunley and Fairhurst in Wrightington, Ashurst and Elmers (probably originally *Elmhurst*) Green in Dalton, Gathurst in Orrell and Hawkley in Pemberton. On an even more localised level, many field names are found to incorporate the word 'ridding', a technical term for clearance usually associated with the C12-C14.

The earliest sites to be colonised were probably on the valley slopes, out of danger of flooding, and upon sheltered hilltop locations: in both the defensive nature of the location would be a primary consideration as early medieval society was a troubled one where the risk of invasion or lawlessness was ever-present. The locations of several manorial houses reflect these considerations, occupying sites of much earlier origin than the structures themselves. Parbold Hall, Parbold (88) stands near the summit of the hill with a commanding view across the valley, a house C17-C18 in date but home to the Lathom family who acquired the manor in 1242. Similarly Crawshaw Hall, (3) a fragment of an early C16 house in the upper valley at Adlington, was the seat of the Worthington family who acquired this part of the manor in the C14. Further north, Coppull Hall, Coppull (31) lies just below the plateau summit on a site formerly moated, as were many in the east of the area (see below, p23-24).

The impression left upon the landscape by the clearance of the woodland is one that is strikingly evident even today. The hills on both sides of the river possess all the qualities of an 'ancient landscape', with irregular fields bounded by ditches and hedgerows, a complex network of roads and lanes, all interspersed by patches of remaining woodland in locations unsuitable for cultivation. Against this background a farming economy developed in which both crop-growing and stock-rearing played important roles. Arable farming could be practised here with greater ease than upon the mosslands or Pennine foothills and consequently the townships of the Douglas Valley formed part of a broad swathe of central Lancashire which has been identified as the county's main crop-producing district in the medieval period.[4] However there were limitations. The Lancashire climate is such that the only crop that could be grown in any quantity was oats. Wheat was cultivated, but on a limited basis; even in 1795 oats remained the principal crop.[5]

The best arable land in the Douglas Valley lay at the foot and lower reaches of the Ashurst/Parbold landmasses where the soils were lighter and better-drained. At higher level, conditions made crop growing more restricted and instead these hills were largely used for grazing as part of an extensive seasonal stock-moving system involving movement of cattle from lower townships to these locations and perhaps beyond into the Pennine foothills.[6] Evidence of this is found in the place-name 'green' which occurs in many areas around the Ashurst-Billinge ridge – Elmers Green, Birch Green, Fosters Green, Goose Green for example – which indicates a patch of roadside grazing land. Also the occurance of the name 'moor' – as in Holland Moor, Shevington Moor, High Moor (Wrightington) and Coppull Moor – denotes the presence of rough grassland used for common grazing.

The pattern of woodland clearance had a direct effect on the settlements that evolved, resulting in a landscape of few nucleated but many isolated farms hacked piecemeal fashion out of the tree cover. The only town was Wigan, the commercial focus of the area, which sprang from a Roman settlement at this bend of the Douglas and was granted a charter in 1246 and a market 12 years later. Elsewhere the only noteable settlements were to the north at Standish and to the west at Upholland – both centred upon ancient churches. A further nucleus lay at Newburgh to the

Pl. 5
Evidence of communal farming is suggested by the nucleated settlement of Elmers (originally Elmhurst) Green at the foot of Ashurts Hill, Dalton. There are several C16 - C18 farmsteads, such as Yew Tree House of 1679 and 1710, surviving around a green which would have been used for grazing (foreground).

Pl. 6
Coppull Moor and a view unchanged for centuries: the stock oval and pond were part of a medieval farming system involving Coppull Hall and nearby Holt Farm.

northwest, which – as the name implies – was established in the C14 as an embryo market town; ultimately it failed to grow. Here, as in other nucleated settlements, a communal farming system existed among the farms grouped around the centre which would have made it easier to grow crops such as wheat, which demanded an annual cycle of rotation. By contrast, isolated farms had to be primarily self-sufficient, another reason why oats became Lancashire's principal crop, because it could be grown by a single farmer in a single season.

However, in places extensive co-operation existed between isolated farmsteads. Upon the slopes of Harrock Hill in Wrightington, two oval medieval enclosures, shared by several surrounding farms and defined by encircling lanes and hedgebanks, have been identified.[7] The northern oval was arable in nature with one of the farms being North Tunley (137), the early C17 house of the yeoman Rigby family but clearly with much earlier origins. The southern oval was pastoral and used by South Tunley (139) and South Tunley Hall (140), homes of the Wilson and Halliwell families; Tunley is referred to as early as 1332 so the system was probably in place by then. A similar double-oval system has also been identified at the hamlet of Walthew Green in Upholland.[8] Further east at Coppull, a stock oval is shared by the manor house, Coppull Hall (31) and nearby Holt Farm (33)[9] and a shared arrangement over grazing on High Moor at Wrightington may have existed at gentry level between the halls of Harrock (134), Fairhurst (133) and Parbold (88).[10]

The prosperity within this medieval agricultural economy provided the foundation for the substantial houses built by subsequent generations. Contemporary physical evidence for this affluence exists in the number of moated sites in the area: 21 in all, with a marked concentration in the east around Wigan.[11] Moats began to be constructed as a defensive measure during the political unrest of the mid-C12 and their popularity reached a height in the period 1200 to 1325, when – in a more stable society – they became a manifestation of wealth and status. Thereafter their use declined during the C14 and they became outdated and restrictive by the Tudor period. Several of the earliest surviving houses are found upon moated sites: Peel Hall, Ince (56) and Kirklees Hall, Aspull (9) both cruck-framed structures probably of the late C14-early C15, were formerly encircled by moats which have now been destroyed. A spectacular and rare example of a moat still wet surrounds Gidlow Hall at Aspull (7), a C15 house reconstructed in 1574 upon a site that may be C13.

A further symbol of early affluence was the granting of borough status to Wigan in 1246, indicating the presence not only of a concentration of population but also a concentration of wealth. This is further reflected in taxation records, which show that from the C14 to the C16, the Hundreds of West Derby and Leyland – within which most of the townships of the Douglas Valley lie – were the most heavily-taxed in Lancashire,[12] an indication of the prosperity that resulted from more favourable conditions which allowed a mixed and buoyant agricultural economy to develop. Records also show an increase in the amount of pasture land during the C15,[13] as throughout England animal husbandry became increasingly important to meet the demands of a rising population. In some areas of England great hardship was caused as common arable land was enclosed to create pasture but in south-west Lancashire this upheaval with the shift towards a capitalist farming system did not materialise as common fields were few in number anyway. Those involved in pastoral farming on

Pl. 7
The Gidlow family are recorded as freeholders in Aspull from 1291. The moat that survives around their hall, a C15 structure rebuilt in 1574 and 1840, may date from that time.

the uplands flanking the Douglas Valley would clearly have prospered, which goes some way towards explaining the appearance of substantial houses – such as Harrock, Fairhurst, Parbold and Coppull halls (133; 134; 88; 31) in the following century.

RURAL SOCIETY: GENTRY AND YEOMANRY

Prior to the Industrial Revolution, dependence upon agriculture was the one element linking all levels of what was a highly-structured society within which the fundamental division was ownership/non-ownership of land. This had its origins in the medieval feudal system, in effect a social pyramid of vertical dependancies with the king at its apex and peasants at its base. Those who held land were as a condition bound not only to perform servile labour on their lord's estate but also – as feudalism revolved around military power in a turbulent society – take up arms upon the battlefield for him as well.

The local unit of feudal power was the manor, the territory owned by a lord within which justice and land transactions were administered. Following the Conquest, Lancashire was divided into six 'Hundreds', large administrative regions which in turn were subdivided into manors. The manors were held by a lord who was himself a tenant, either directly of the king or of a nobleman who in turn held directly from the crown. Land within the manor was divided into that of the lord – the demesne – and that which he rented out to tenants. In certain cases, manors were subdivided with several lords each owning a portion: an example is Billinge, which by 1212 had 'long been divided' into three parts.[14] Religious institutions were landowners too. For instance, the Knights of St John of the Hospital (an order which originated in the Crusades) held lands in Wrightington and Parbold since the C13.[15] Their tenure, along with that of other religious bodies, ended abruptly with Henry VIII's dissolution of the monasteries and their lands were sold off to supporters of the king.

By the C16, feudalism had broken down and a capitalist, class-based society something akin to our own had evolved with boundaries drawn more or less by wealth. The substantial houses that appear from the late C16 suggests that within this society existed a considerable degree of affluence. But in reality it would appear that the resources to build to this superior standard were in the hands of certain privileged sections of society only, who together represented a minority of the rural population. The houses that survive from the late C16 to the early C18 are connected with the upper levels of society; specifically two groups identified by very generalised, class-based terms: the gentry and the yeomanry. The structure of both was complex: within each were various sub-classes along a scale determined by social standing and material prosperity. And the boundary between the gentry and the yeomanry was a vague,

Pl. 8
From Lathom House the Stanleys ruled as virtual kings. Little remains of that glory: the building was destroyed in the Civil War and its C18 successor has too experienced destruction by a C20 society that ought to have known better. Just the western service block remains.

subjective frontier open to speculation and interpretation.

Precisely what constituted gentry status in the C16 is probably as difficult for us to define now as it was at that time. As a class, the gentry – in the broadest sense of the term – were somewhat thin on the ground. It has been calculated that in Lancashire of the 1560s, there was just one gentleman to every 800 people.[16] At the absolute pinnacle of this class were the Stanleys, Earls of Derby, who from their seat at Lathom House, Lathom (66) ruled like virtual kings before its destruction during the Civil War. At various times in the C16 and C17, the Stanleys owned either all or part of the manors of Upholland, Coppull, Bispham, Lathom, Dalton and Skelmersdale, all within the Douglas Valley, as part of their vast territories in Lancashire and beyond. They were gentry in the most refined sense: beneath them were several strata of this class, descending into a somewhat indistinct interface with the upper levels of the yeomanry.

The Stanleys were a family without equal in the area and their influence radiated not just regionally but nationally. The area's other gentry shone with lesser magnitude and exercised power on a more parochial scale. These were the families who owned the manors which the Stanleys did not: most prominent were the Standishes of Standish (103), Bradshaighs of Haigh (52) and the Lathoms of Parbold (88), all of whom had who held their territories for several centuries. Beneath them in turn came a further, more localised, stratum. Certain manors had been subdivided, with families of consequently lesser status each owning a portion: families such as the Rigbys of Harrock Hall in Wrightington (134), the Haydocks of Bogburn Hall in Coppull (29) and the Houghtons of Kirklees Hall in Aspull (9).

Below these families was a grey area in which the lower gentry merged with the

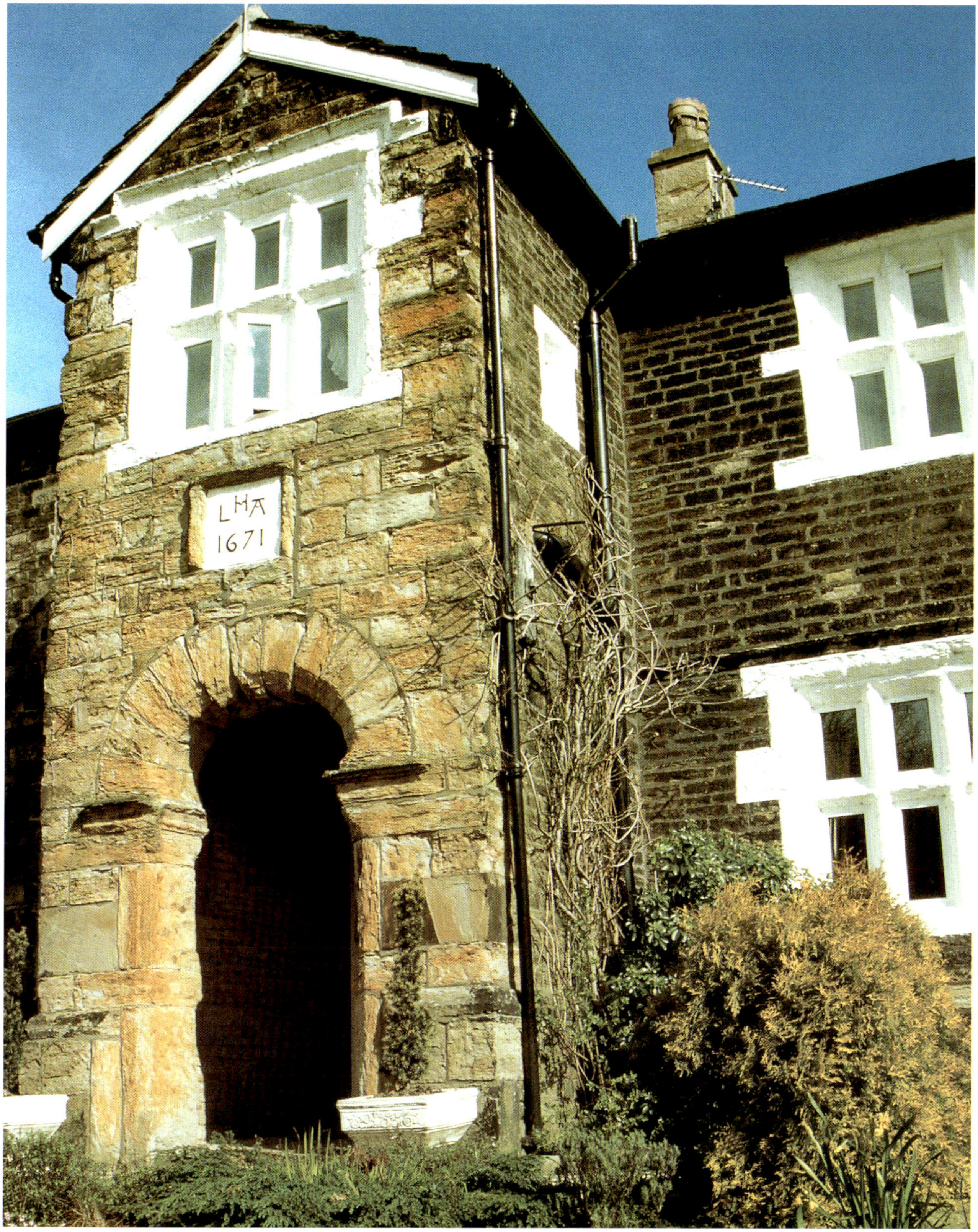
L HA
1671

upper ranks of the yeomanry. The yeomen were a middle class of capitalist farmers who had evolved out of the decline of feudalism to become an important sector of society by the late C16. Numerically they were more abundant then the gentry: the title an aspirational one indicating a farmer of superior status, above that of the ordinary 'husbandman'. Yet there were also those among the yeomen who, without the benefit of ancient lineage or manorial lands, saw themselves in a more elevated light and boldly styled themselves 'gentlemen'. As this title carried no strict definition it could easily be assumed by any ambitous yeoman who percieved the criterion as being wealth. In the case of certain individuals the situation was as ambiguous for contemporaries as it is today. A case in point is Robert Walthew (d. 1676) of Walthew House, Pemberton (90) who was descended from a blacksmith but amassed considerable wealth through real estate and moneylending and left goods amounting to more than £474 at his death. Walthew, along with seven other self-styled 'gentlemen', was forbidden from using either that title or 'esquire' by Sir William Dugdale at his heraldic visitation of Lancashire in 1667. However in other respects the government indirectly acknowledged Walthew's standing for they readily squeezed money out of him for military purposes. Despite an appeal, he was forced under the Militia Act in 1662 to finance the equipping of one horseman, a levy imposed upon those whose income exceeded £500 per annum. The others who contributed were manorial lords Thomas Bankes of Winstanley Hall (124) and Thomas Ashurst of Ashurst Hall, Dalton (34) so Walthew was clearly on a par with them financially.[17] Another illustration of this uncertainty over status is provided by Lawrence Halliwell of Halliwell's Farm (115), Upholland, High Constable of the Hundred of West Derby in 1667. He is intially referred to as both yeoman and gentleman in the Upholland parish registers of the 1660s, before the latter rank is applied with consistency among its pages.

The yeomanry too had its heirarchy, with some distinctions based upon the tenure by which land was held. The most privileged position was that of the freeholders. Their origins were as medieval 'free' tenants who were exempt from performing agricultural services for their feudal lords and had the right to hand down their lands to their heirs. Therefore they enjoyed absolute security and as a result their families were frequently long-established. The gentry held the core of their estates by freehold also, and accordingly some of the wealthiest yeomen may have used their freehold status to bolster their own claims to be gentry. In fact in the list of freeholders drawn up in 1600,[18] (map 7, p89) the majority of the names subscribed have the abbreviation 'gen' appended, which has led to the belief that freeholders generally were considered to be of gentry rank.[19] This is not necessarily the case. Although some were indisputably of gentry status, it is probable that others were merely wealthy

Pl. 9 *(previous page)* Gentleman or yeoman? The builder of Halliwell's Farm, Lawrence Halliwell, was initially described as both in the Upholland parish registers: but this powerful porch of 1671 would have played a vital part in his process of self-gentrification.

yeomen given this title out of a clerical sense of respect. But whatever the circumstances, it is beyond dispute that the freeholders represented an elite.

An equally-priveleged section of the yeomanry comprised those who held their lands by copyhold, an ancient form of tenure almost as advantageous and secure as freehold. This was so-called because transactions were made via the local manor court and the tenant owned a copy of the court roll (record of proceedings) in which the terms were documented. Copyholders were sucessors to medieval villeins, who under the feudal system were 'unfree' tenants holding their lands in return for agricultural services. Eventually these services were translated into a monetary equivalent or 'quit rent' paid annually. As these had been fixed in time immemorial, inflation had rendered the amounts concerned purely nominal by the C17. Copyhold tenure had several forms. It could be held upon lives – three being the norm – a term of years or by inheritance, the latter offering hereditary rights of succession to the eldest male heir and thus also allowing the formation of long-established yeoman families. This tenure had other advantages: copyhold land could be bought and sold and in Upholland, and possibly other manors, copyholders could sell materials such as stone, coal and timber found upon their estates.[20] Copyhold Farm, Wrightington (131) of 1659 reflects in its name this form of tenure, which still was legal right up until 1926.

Nationally, from the C16 on copyhold began to be replaced by leasing. Leaseholders – or 'tenants-at-will' – were in many respects at a disadvantage with terms and entry fines (a fee payable at the beginning of the lease) very much at the landlord's discretion. However, as the landlord-tenant relationship was a mutually-beneficial one, terms were normally kept fair and just: the tenant benefited from security and reasonable fines, and the landlord from a steady income and the improvement of his estate. This symbiosis is summed up by James Bankes of Winstanley Hall (124) in advice given to his son William in 1610: *'…In God's name take not too much rent nor yet too little, for a mean is the best, so shalt thou be best able to live.'* [21]

An indication of the almost generous nature of rental terms overall, in one manor at least, is found in the survey of Upholland by Parliamentary commissioners in 1653.[22] The report was commissioned with a view to the intended sale of the possessions of James, seventh Earl of Derby, after his execution for treason at Bolton in 1651. It reveals the annual income from Upholland's freeholders, copyholders and tenants came to £70. 0s. 4 d but because of the manor's value recommended a 'future improvement' to raise it to £571.1s.4 d. Such a massive increase – almost 400 per cent – is a striking comparison of how much the land was worth and how little the tenants paid for it.

These low overheads meant both gentry and yeomanry could reap the full benefit of their income at a time when prices for agricultural products was rising from the mid-C16. The area's mixed farming economy also meant they were insulated from market changes: grain prices fell steadily after 1650, yet animal product prices remained stable. And there were other sources of income: many gentry, and some yeomen, were involved in mining the coal which lay in the sandstone measures around Wigan; and money-lending and speculation in the form of bonds and specialities were practised by both class groups.

By the second half of the C17 clear evidence emerges that shows the prosperity of the Douglas Valley area established in medieval times had continued. This comes in the form of the Hearth Tax, which was essentially a tax on wealth as duty was paid on each hearth posessed unless the householder was declared exempt due to poverty.[23] In all parishes, the majority of households have just one hearth recorded: anything above this figure denotes affluence on a rising scale until one reaches the manor houses of Standish Hall (103) and Haigh Hall (52) which with a total of 17 each represent the highest in the area and a luxury unimaginable to the dwellers of single-hearth households. Yet even these pale into virtual insignificance beside the enormity of the 70 hearths recorded at Knowsley Hall, seat of the Stanleys after Lathom's destruction.

Analysis of the Ladyday 1664 returns for the 23 townships surveyed in this book reveals the area had almost twice the Lancashire average of houses with more than one hearth (map 3 above), a total of 39.7%, compared to a county average of 23%. In no

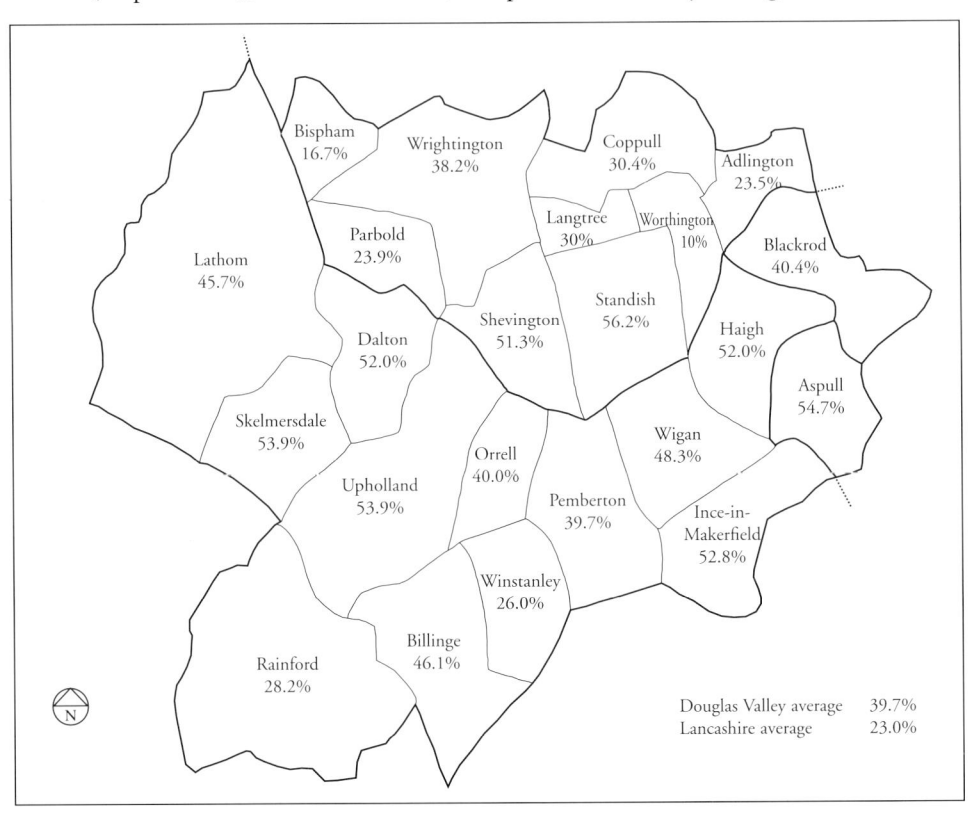

Pl. 10
Copyhold tenants were sufficiently well-placed to rebuild in the later C17. The name of Copyhold farm at Wrightington indicates the tenure at this isolated farm rebuilt by Oliver Halliwell and his wife Margaret in 1659. Pictured in 1981 before restoration.

Map 3
Multi-hearth houses in 1664. The map shows the percentage of households assessed on more than one hearth, Ladyday 1664.

other part of Lancashire is there a similar concentration of multi-hearth houses. In six townships – Aspull, Haigh, Ince, Shevington, Standish and Upholland – more than half the dwellings were multi-hearthed, their percentages some of the highest in the county and led by Standish at 56.2%. This underscores how advantaged the area was in comparison to the mosslands around the coast and the moorlands to the east, where the townships were dominated by single-hearth houses to a rate of over 90 per cent in some cases. Not even the area around Burnley, where some fine houses were erected in the late C16 and early C17 centuries on the back of an emerging textile industry, were there many multi-hearth houses as in the Douglas Valley – which on the basis of this, stands head and shoulders above anywhere else as the most prosperous region of Lancashire at this time. By the time these figures were being collated this had unmistakeably manifested itself physically, first in the new homes of the gentry and more recently in those of the yeomanry.

THE ERA OF REBUILDING

The houses that survive today are like pieces of a jigsaw: individual components which ultimately form a much wider picture. They illustrate an epoch of great change and advancement which lasted from the late C16 to the early C18 and generated widespread building activity in the Douglas Valley on a scale never before realised.

What occurred was part of a phenomenon of 'home improvement' which took place throughout the county from the late C16 to the middle of the C18, and is typified by the replacement of older, inferior and essentially medieval homes by new ones of superior standard. The phrase first coined to describe this occurrence was 'The Great Rebuilding'[24]; initially it was first considered to have taken place nationally between 1570 and 1640, but later research indicates a far more drawn out and complex sequence with different regions – even neighbouring localities – rebuilding at different times. Status, wealth, land tenure and building materials all became factors in a complex formula in which the rebuilt homes were the product of the equation.

The rebuilding in the Douglas Valley, as elsewhere, was an involved process. It began at gentry level in the 1570s and the wealthiest members of the yeomanry took up the initiative around 1600. Among this class however the movement did not achieve real momentum until the second half of the C17. By 1720 it had more or less petered out with those yeomen who had the ability to rebuild having done so. Then, as a postscript, we see a desire by the gentry to build once again, this time homes of an exceedingly refined nature: dignified classical country houses to replace the C16 and C17 structures which by then had become rapidly outdated.

The mechanism of rebuilding was complex too. It was not simply a matter of

Pl. 11
Yeoman prosperity as evidenced by North Tunley, Wrightington. The house, built possibly c1620 by the Rigby family, was one of the farms sharing a medieval arable oval upon Harrock Hill.

pulling old houses down and replacing them with the new ones, although frequently this was the case. Other houses were improved in several stages, presumably as money allowed, over a long period and by several generations. This, for example, accounts for the two datestones at Yew Tree House, Dalton (51): where yeoman John Crane added a wing to a pre-existing building in 1679, and his son Thomas carried out a more widespread remodelling in 1710. In some cases a new home was simply erected around the core of a much earlier one, thus fossilising the older building inside: a striking example of this being Dam House Farm, Langtree (58) which contains within an unpretentious exterior of c1700 the remains of a timber-framed hall of possibly two centuries earlier.

Table 1
Comparison of households recorded in 1664 Hearth Tax and surviving pre-1700 buildings, showing that only 7.3% of the C17 housing stock now remains. The majority of C17 buildings were insubstantial.

Township	Households 1664 (from hearth tax)	Pre-1700 houses now existing (listed/surveyed)	Survival rate
Adlington	47	3	6.3%
Aspull	108	4	3.7%
Billinge	76	6	7.8%
Bispham	24	3	12.5%
Blackrod	86	2	2.3%
Coppull	66	5	7.5%
Dalton	51	14	27.4%
Haigh	52	2	3.8%
Ince	36	1	2.7%
Langtree	40	3	7.5%
Lathom (inc. Newburgh)	171	10	5.8%
Orrell	30	4	13.3%
Parbold	42	3	7.1%
Pemberton	106	0	0%
Rainford	85	4	4.7%
Shevington	41	4	9.7%
Skelmersdale	70	0	0%
Standish	57	4	7.0%
Upholland	130	16	12.3%
Wigan	606	0	0%
Winstanley	54	1	1.8%
Worthington	20	3	15%
Wrightington	136	15	11%

Total 2,134   Total 107   Average survival rate 7.3%

Whatever form rebuilding took, the principal objective was the replacement of older, relatively insubstantial houses by superior ones of more lasting construction. This was largely achieved by a change in building materials from timber – universal throughout the medieval period – to stone and brick, although at first this was slow to take effect. But the rebuilding also had several important sub-texts. The versatility of the new materials meant houses could be planned and constructed in new ways and so great changes in lifestyle were set in motion. Thus the rebuilding saw a slow progression from households that were ordered along medieval lines to ones that are recognisably modern. This was augmented in the last quarter of the C17 by a growing trend away from Gothic-derived architectural details to concepts that were classically inspired as the Renaissance made a belated encroachment into the North. The end result was that the yeoman of 1700, standing back proudly to admire his newly-rebuilt house, had his foot on the threshold of the modern world; whereas his forefather of a century earlier had still been fixed firmly within the medieval one.

But rebuilding was not a process to be entered into lightly. It involved considerable expense and considerable disruption and two essential prerequisites: money and long-term security of tenure. The surviving buildings indicate that a substantial number of householders were able to achieve this position. Yet if one compares the numbers of households recorded in the 1664 Hearth Tax and the number of pre-1700 buildings that still exist, it will be seen that the buildings we see today represent only a fraction of the C17 stock with only an average of just 7.3% surviving (Table 1). The conclusion therefore is that the majority of the C17 buildings have disappeared, possibly because they were insubstantial in nature and therefore not products of the rebuilding.[25] Even if one allows for the destruction of 'permanent' homes with the passage of time, the figure still suggests the majority of the rural population – those below the level of the yeomanry – were not in a position to rebuild and therefore had to make do with medieval or post-medieval hovels. This shows that the wealth indicated by the Hearth Tax was not evenly distributed throughout society. The rebuilding, therefore, was largely a prerogative of the gentry and yeomanry and something which passed by society's lower levels, for they lacked the resources to provide homes that were durable enough to stand the test of time and last into the modern period.

The superior classes were more fortunate: yet despite the pains they took to reconstruct their derided medieval homes they frequently allowed some fragments of their earlier, pre-rebuilding houses to remain. Almost like ghost-hunters, we can now use those remains to reconstruct these vanished dwellings. So before we move on to examine the houses produced by the rebuilding, we begin by tracing the footprints of the houses it (almost) swept away.

NOTES

1. Diary of Roger Lowe, Chetham Society, vol XX, edited by W Sache, 1938
2. John Leyland, Itinery, VII, p47.
3. F Walker, 'Historical Geography of SW Lancashire before the Industrial Revolution', CS vol 103 (new series) 1939: p6.
4. HB Rogers, 'Land Use in Tudor Lancashire': Evidence of the Final Concords 1450-1558', Transactions of the Institute of British Geographers, 21 (1955).
5. John Holt, 'General View of the Agriculture of the County of Lancaster' 1795, p56.
6. Alan Crosby, 'The Landscape History of West Lancashire' (survey for West Lancashire District Council) 1993, revised 1994, sections 6.2, 6.8.4, 7.2.
7. Mary Atkin, 'Some Settlement Patterns in Lancashire', in 'Medieval Villages' (edited by Delia Hooke), Oxford University Committee for Archeology 1985, p171-185.
8. Audrey P Coney, 'Upholland, 1599-1633: A Community Study', unpublished MA thesis, Liverpool University (1989) p16
9. Alan Crosby, report on landscape history of Ellerbeck West proposed opencast coal site, 1989, p29-31.
10. Crosby, 'Landscape History of West Lancashire', section 7.5.
11. Information from Sites and Monuments Record, Lancashire County Council; also 'County Houses of Greater Manchester', Greater Manchester Archeological Unit, 1985.
12. Rogers, p48-49.
13. Rogers, p54-55.
14. Victoria County History of Lancashire, edited by William Farrer and J Brownbill 1911 (reprinted 1966) vol IV, p83.
15. VCH VI, p173.
16. BG Blackwood, in 'The Lancashire Gentry 1625-60: a Social and Economic Study' (D Phil Thesis, Oxford, 1973) identified 763 gentry families based upon the freeholders' list of 1600 (Record Society of Lancashire and Cheshire, vol 12, 1885).
17. J J Baggley, 'The Will, Inventory and Accounts of Robert Walthew of Pemberton', Records Society of Lancashire and Cheshire vol 109 (1965) p55-56.
18. J P Earwaker (ed) 'A List of the Freeholders in Lancashire in the year 1600' Record Society of Lancashire and Cheshire vol 12 (1885)
19. Blackwood, 'Lancashire Gentry' p5; J P Cooper, 'The Social Distribution of Land and Men in England, 1435-1700' Economic History Review, xx, No 3, p426.
20. Coney, Upholland 1599-1633, p51
21. 'The Early Records of the Bankes family at Winstanley,' edited by Joyce Bankes and Eric Kerridge, CS vol XXI 1973, p8.
22. 'Survey of the Manor of Upholland' April 1653, in Lancashire County Record Office, Preston.
23. The Ladyday 1664 assessment have been used as they also indicate those households declared exempt. Thanks are due to Nigel Morgan for making available his research on the county as a whole, which enabled the comparisons that follow to be drawn.
24. W G Hoskins, 'The Rebuilding of Rural England' in 'Provincial England' (1963)
25. In comparison, research by Nigel Morgan has shown a survival rate of 8.6% in the parishes of Croston and Eccleston to the north of the area, and 8.4% in the townships around Burnley and Colne. Again this was based upon 1664 hearth tax records set against surviving pre-1700 listed buildings.

CHAPTER II

The Medieval Legacy: Timber-framed Buildings, 1400-1630

In the middle ages, timber was the principal material from which domestic buildings throughout England were made. The thick woodland cover that existed across much of the country, the Douglas Valley included, made it plentiful and accessible. Stone, by contrast, was highly exclusive, used for the most prestigious buildings only: royal palaces, houses of the nobility, castles and churches. Gradually it achieved a wider circulation in the medieval period, where in cities such as Chester it was used from around 1200 onwards in the undercrofts of otherwise timber-framed buildings to minimise the ever-present risk of fire in narrow medieval streets. But in rural locations the dominance of timber remained unchallenged. Consequently in the Douglas Valley, as elsewhere, the homes of both lord of the manor and peasant farmers – although polarised on the social scale – were united by their means of construction, albeit with a distinct differentiation of quality and scale.

This long tradition continued into the C16. In 1539, the Tudor historian John Leyland, in his account of Morley's Hall at Tyldesley near Manchester (recently dated to around 1460[1]) refers to a timber-framed building, which he described as 'the usual type of construction for all gentlemen's houses in Lancashire'[2]. By this time however, the woodland cover throughout England, the Douglas Valley included, had been denuded to more or less its present extent. As a result the gentry and yeomanry turned increasingly to stone, and then brick: both of which had the ability to endow their houses with the prestige and longevity once reserved only for those at the pinnacle of medieval communities. These buildings therefore became the fashionable expression of a society celebrating its freedom from feudal bondage. But there was no sudden end to the timber legacy. The fact that just 7.3% of the 1664 housing stock now survives (as table 1 shows) is evidence that timber-framed buildings dominated the countryside throughout the C17 and into the following century. Thus the majority of the population lived in houses that were essentially medieval in derivation.

However some of these early timber dwellings have survived the passage of time,

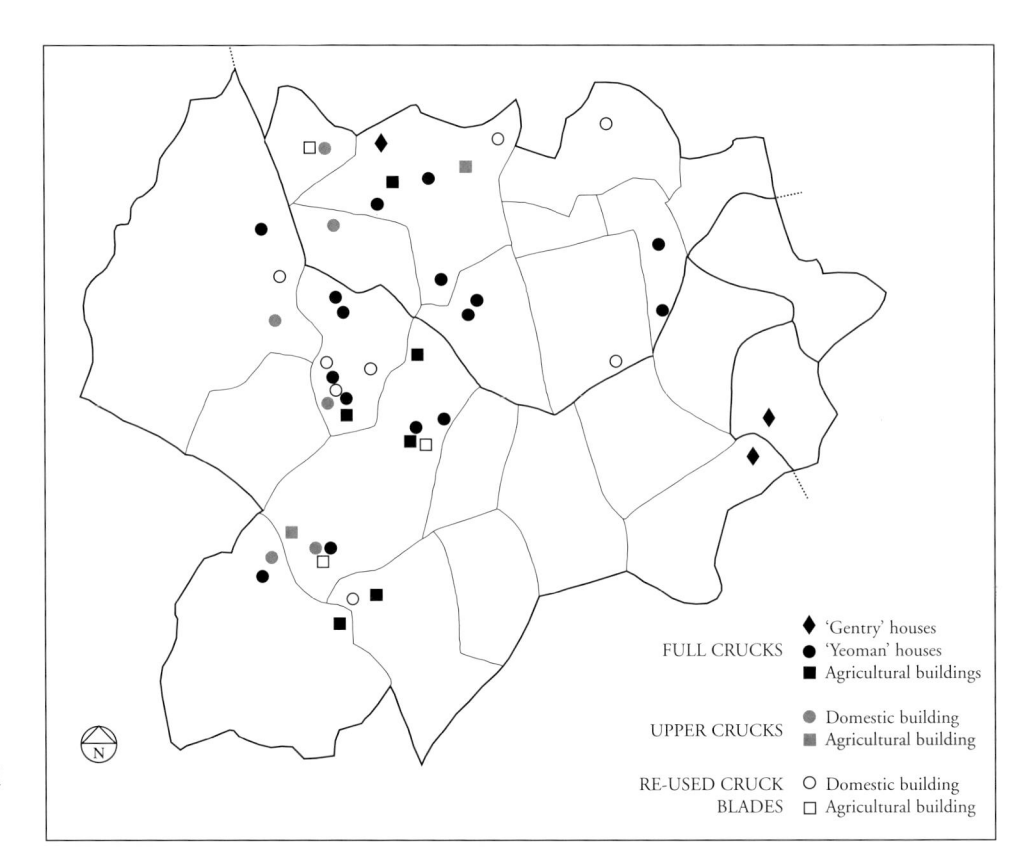

Map 4
Distribution of cruck-framed buildings in the Douglas Valley.

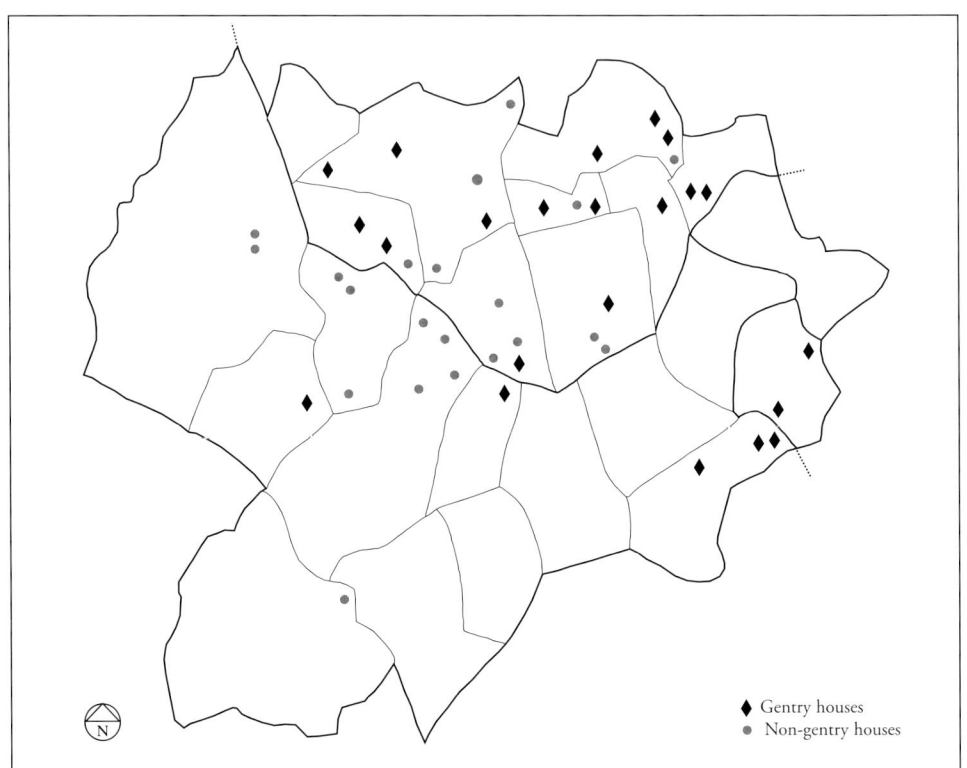

Map 5
Distribution of post-and-truss buildings in the Douglas Valley.

'fossilised' when subsequently modernised in the rebuilding of the C16 and C17 – and so enabling us to reconstruct with some clarity what they looked like. They are of two kinds: either cruck-framed or of post-and-truss construction. The two were radically different carpentry methods, which – despite elements of plan and room function that were common to both – produced houses of quite different appearance.

Crucks were big, shaped beams or 'blades', set into the ground or on a stone base and joined at the apex to form an inverted 'V' shape to carry the weight of the roof. They produced somewhat primitive, single-storey linear buildings which looked something similar to an upturned boat and the trusses divided the buildings into 'bays' or compartments. The outer walls – again timber-framed and often quite insubstantial – had no load to bear and were virtually freestanding. In contrast, post-and-truss buildings were made from a series of jointed frames through which the walls supported the weight of the roof via trusses. This method was superior and more flexible as it allowed the construction of buildings more than one storey in height. Crucks however had the longer pedigree, having been used by the gentry in Lancashire possibly since the late C13 (presumably continuing an ancient tradition for which we have no evidence); but they lost their prestige during the C14 and C15 when post-and-truss construction was endorsed by the county's major gentry. For a time in the late medieval period, both techniques existed side-by-side. Eventually however cruck construction was relegated to homes of lower status, where it continued in use into the C16, possibly beyond: so by this time, a man's standing could be judged by whether he built his home on crucks or used post-and-truss instead.

ELEMENTS OF THE MEDIEVAL HOUSE

Whether the houses were for lord or peasant, built of crucks or post-and-truss, certain components were universal. Most crucially, each had one main room which was pivotal to the function of the rest of the household. In gentry houses this was termed the hall: in lesser houses, those which ultimately housed the yeomanry, the housebody. The role was similar whatever the status: it was the largest and principal room where most of the everyday business of the household took place – cooking, eating, entertaining, and (perhaps in the case of servants) sleeping. The earliest surviving halls were products of cruck construction, and therefore single storey and open to the roof. But even after this method was surpassed, the tradition of this great open hall continued – very much as a status symbol. In medieval times it was probably the only heated room in the house. Before the appearance of chimney stacks (or their predecessors) in the later C16 the fire was made upon an open and the smoke allowed to drift out through a hole in the roof. This hearth was used also for cooking unless there was the luxury of a physically-separate kitchen, due to the fire risk, as some gentry households are known to have had (see page 83). Life therefore would have gone on amid a permanent haze of smoke, fumes and soot – conditions which, especially in the more cramped structures of lesser men, we would today find shockingly intolerable.

The hall had a dual role as the confluence of all the other functions of the house yet also acted as a hierarchical barrier by which they were separated. At one end – designated the 'upper' to underline its superiority – was sited the high table or 'dais' where the master took precedence when dining. Leading off the hall beyond this was the private room for the use of the family only, where the most valuable possessions would have been kept. In the medieval period, the name given to this room was the 'bower', but by the C17 the more familiar term 'parlour' was in general use. Servants, farm workers and the like were allowed thoroughfare into the hall, but the 'upper end' was strictly out of bounds without permission. Their territory lay at the corresponding 'lower' end of the hall, where rooms with a service function were situated: perhaps a kitchen (for food preparation rather than cooking, if this took place in the hall or a separate building) a buttery and a pantry. Usually there rooms were segregated from the housebody by an entrance passage running across the building from front to back, termed the screens passage in gentry houses (where a movable wooden screen was positioned to shield the hall from draughts from the entrance, as in the elaborate example at Rufford Old Hall, just north of our area) or

Table 2
Analysis of domestic full crucks recorded in the Douglas Valley.

Township	Building	Status	Presumed date M=medieval; PM = post-medieval	No. of Trusses	Scantling H = heavy; M = medium; L = light	Remarks
Aspull	Kirklees Hall	gent	M	3	H	Former central truss of hall has lower portion of blades removed; yoke with carved roundel; smoke blackening
Dalton	Blackbird's Farm	yeoman	PM	2	M	Trusses with collars at either end of housebody in house rebuilt C17 with two crosswings.
Dalton	Harsnips	yeoman	PM	1	M	Upper portion of blades replaced by C17 principal rafter truss during cladding; datestone 1667
Dalton	Lower House	yeoman	PM	2	L	Trusses at right angles suggesting wing; house clad C17-18
Ince	Peel Hall	gent	M	2	H	Central truss of hall arch-braced to collar. Smoke blackening on 2nd truss; wing C15-16
Lathom	White Cottages	yeoman	PM	3	M	Longhouse with former stable and shippon; possibly of 5 bays originally
Rainford	Hydes Brow Farm	yeoman	PM	1	M	Rebuilt 1703; evidence of outshut during cruck phase
Shevington	Calico Wood Farm	yeoman	PM	1	L	Within small house of early C18
Upholland	Bounty Farm	yeoman	PM	1	M	Rear wing added to cruck range c1667; evidence of outshut during cruck phase
Upholland	Lower Tower Hill	yeoman	PM	1	M	Lower portion of blades removed; clad 1684
Worthington	Black Lawyers	yeoman	M	3	H	Datestone 1617; demolished mid-1980s
Worthington	Manor House	yeoman	M	1	H	Arched-braced to collar; base of blades moulded; wing 1670.
Wrightington	Bannister Farm	gent/yeo	M	1	H	Another truss said to be concealed. Clad and extended C17-18
Wrightington	Higher Barn	yeoman	PM	1	M	Upper portion of blades replaced by C17 principal rafter truss during cladding

through passage (in lesser houses without the benefit of a screen).

The hierarchy within the medieval household therefore existed along its length. In conforming to this, these hall-houses were invariably linear in plan: each component taking its respective place and slotting into the next. This convention was so strong that its influence on house plans continued to be felt long after society had abandoned the open hall and its entourage. It spanned the two disciplines of timber-framing too, for the footprints of both cruck and post-and-truss buildings reflect identically the social structure within.

CRUCK CONSTRUCTION: DISTRIBUTION AND HIERARCHY

> *"…Little shanties of dwellings, with no room in them for the exercise of social and domestic decency; old, tumble-down, thatched cottages, with walls bending in and out in all directions…."* [3]

This was the description of cottages in Mawdesley, just to the north of our area, in 1872: cottages that were no doubt cruck-framed and by that time, synonymous with rural poverty and deprivation. By this time, crucks had long since ceased to be built but yet still clearly existed in some numbers; now objects of contempt and derision, but the relics of a long tradition that had began in the medieval period at the opposite end of the social scale.

The origins of cruck construction are lost in time: they are the most primitive form of building that has come down to us. Various dates for their beginnings have been put forward, from sub-Roman to C13: but certainly by the C14 they were in widespread use nationally at both gentry and peasant level. Today, surviving examples are found all over England and Wales – 3,054 were recorded in 1981[4] – but with the curious exceptions of the east coast and the south east. A further idiosyncracy is that they are generally associated with lowland rather than upland areas.

This pattern is repeated in Lancashire, where crucks are found throughout the coastal plain, eastwards into the Douglas Valley hills, but thin out towards the Pennines. In our area there is a total of 25 examples of 'true' crucks, of which 19 are in domestic buildings, the rest agricultural (see map 4). These are augmented by a sizeable number of cruck timbers salvaged and re-used in later buildings of non-cruck form, and a handful of the C17 derivative known as 'upper crucks'. All this suggest that crucks were at one time in common use, but examination of the map reveals an uneven distribution of the surviving examples. The majority are found in the west and north of the area, chiefly in Wrightington, Dalton and Upholland, with a particularly noticeable concentration at the former farming hamlets of Elmers Green and Fosters Green in Dalton, where out of 14 buildings of C16-early C18 date, five contain

Pl. 12
Crucks of heavy scantling revealed by the decay of Black Lawyers, Worthington. The fine quality of the timber indicates a non-gentry house of medieval date.

A-A1 Section through hall

B-B1 Section through service wing

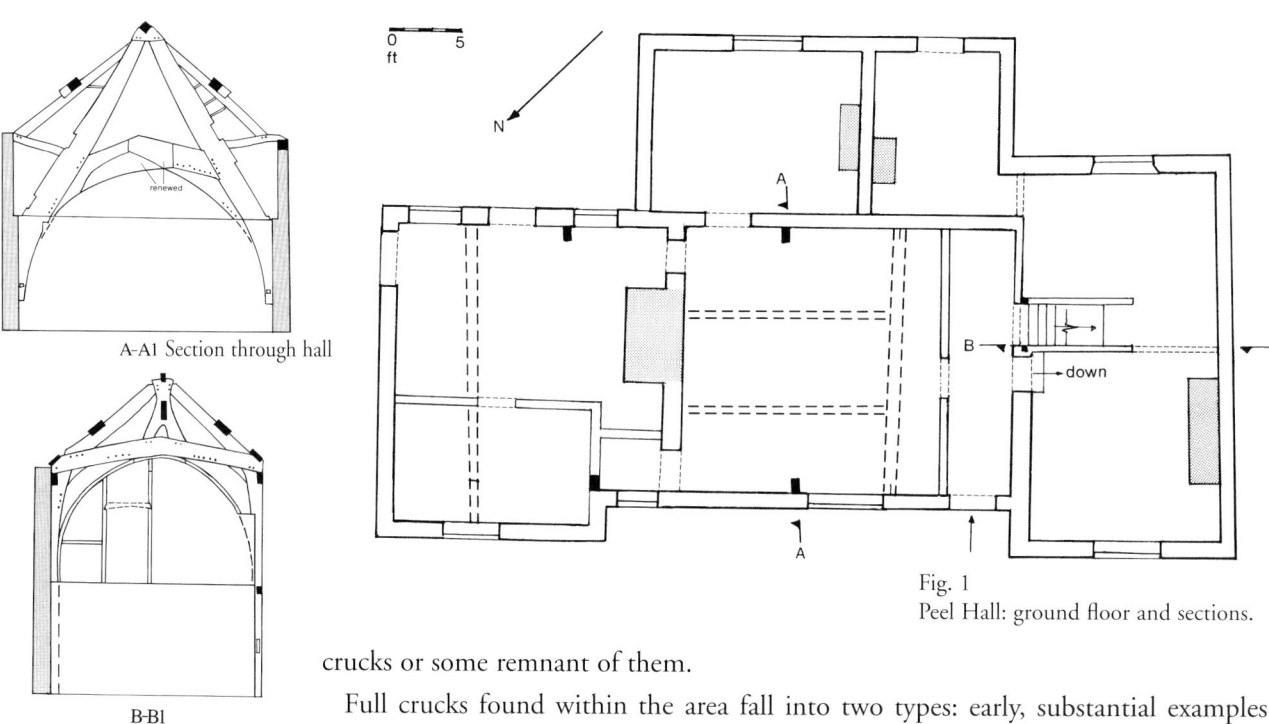

Pl. 13
Peel Hall, Ince, contains some of the finest crucks in Lancashire, at least C14 in date.

Fig. 1
Peel Hall: ground floor and sections.

crucks or some remnant of them.

Full crucks found within the area fall into two types: early, substantial examples erected by the gentry at the height of the technique and later, poorer examples built when the tradition was waning. The early examples date probably from the C15 or before. The later ones are probably C16 and are generally found within yeoman houses rebuilt in the C17-18. These later, 'yeoman' crucks are considerably more numerous, representing 15 out of the total of 19 full crucks recorded in the area.

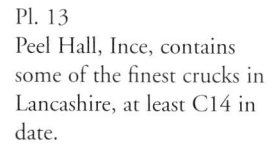

The gentry crucks display their superiority in both the quality of the timbers and the dimensions of the structures they created. Examples elsewhere in Lancashire have shown the manorial gentry were erecting houses upon crucks in the early C14, during a phase of building which peaked nationally during the years 1300 to 1325 immediately prior to the Black Death.[5] Two gentry examples in the Douglas Valley may belong to this phase: Peel Hall (56; figure 1) at Ince, and nearby Kirklees Hall (9; plate 14, figure 2) at Aspull. Both are substantial buildings with heavy timbers – suggesting an early date – producing structures each around 22 feet in height and 18 feet in width, which compare well with cruck halls built in Tameside, east of Manchester, and dated dendrochronologically to the early C14.[6] Clearly, only those in a privileged position could afford houses such as these, and in the cases of Kirklees its builders can be clearly identified to the Houghton family, sub-manorial freeholders within Aspull: a John, son of Thomas de Halghton, owner of two messuages plus land in Aspull in 1317, is the earliest record of this family.[7] Peel's history is uncertain, but it may have been the home of the Brown family, sub-manorial freeholders recorded in 1391. The early origin of both is confirmed by the moats which formerly surrounded them. From these examples it is reasonable to assume that cruck halls were standard accommodation for manorial lords in the area during the C14 and that there were many others which have now gone. Possibly another example of a gentry cruck structure exists at Bannister Farm, Wrightington. One truss survives from a substantial hall, possibly that of the Nelson family who rose to prominence and acquired the Fairhurst estate nearby around 1536-40 and thereafter built Fairhurst Hall (133) in the late C16. However this cruck is inferior in both quality and dimensions to Peel and Kirklees, suggesting a later date, possibly late C15 or early C16.

The quality of the timbers used at Peel and Kirklees would have contributed to their survival from so early a date, while those of lesser men were probably less resiliant to the onslaught of time. However, there is evidence that substantial crucks were being erected by men of non-gentry status possibly in the late C15 and early C16. Before its unfortunate demolition in the mid-1980s, the decay of Black Lawyers at Worthington (125) revealed three fine trusses of heavy scantling (plate 12) similar to those at Peel and Kirklees. In the C17 this was probably occupied by the Fisher yeoman family; it had a datestone of 1617, but the nature of the timbers makes one suspect they were medieval. Also in yeoman occupation (by the Jolly family) in the late C17 was the nearby Manor House (126; figures 3-& 4) also at Worthington, but this contains the solitary arch-braced truss of a substantial earlier building. The date may be the C15, as this was a tenanted farm which formed part of an endowment at Standish church referred to in 1483.[8] These show that although the gentry may have moved on from cruck construction by the beginning of the C16, it was still providing homes for important tenants.

By comparison, the poorer quality, plainer treatment and fragmentary survival of the crucks within the yeoman houses suggests they are later in date, C16 or perhaps

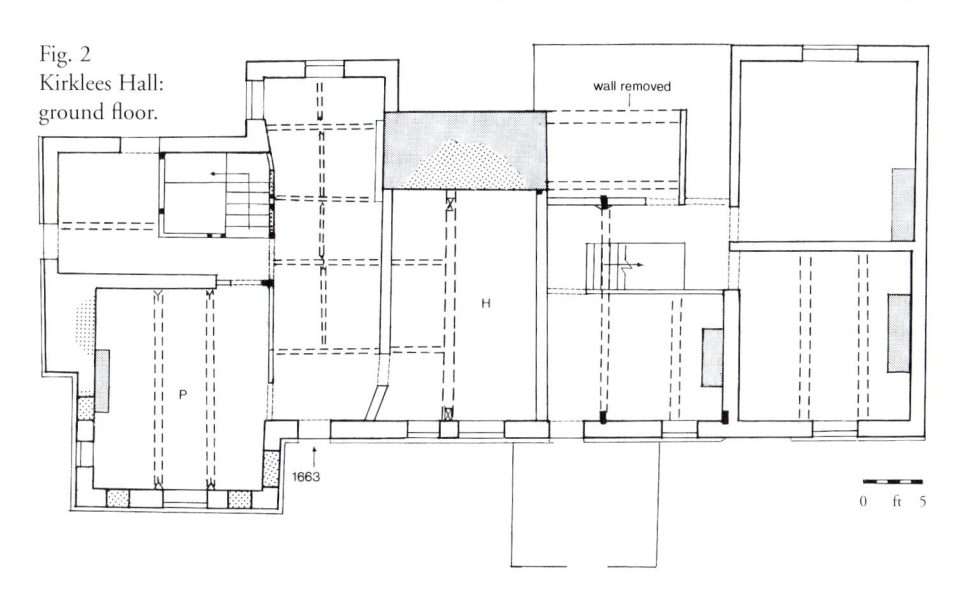

Fig. 2
Kirklees Hall: ground floor.

Pl. 14
Beneath a C17-C18 exterior, Kirklees Hall, Aspull, contains the remains of the cruck-framed hall, probably of late medieval date, of the Houghton family. They are recorded as freeholders from 1317 and the site was formerly moated.

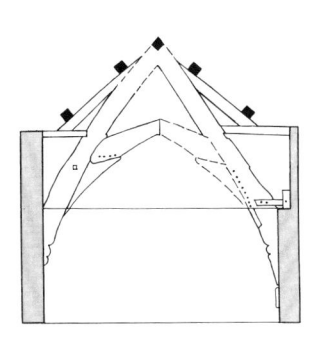

A-A1
Fig. 4
Manor House, section through hall showing fine arched-braced cruck.

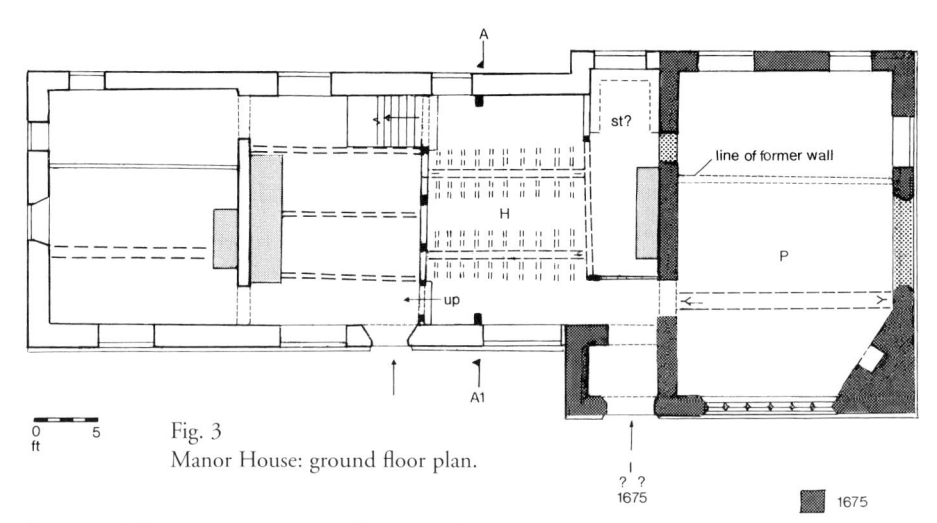

Fig. 3
Manor House: ground floor plan.

early C17. Their occurrence in houses of this class indicates many – if not most – yeomen occupied cruck houses before the rebuilding of the C17-early C18. Corroborating evidence is found in the Hearth Tax returns also. For example, the yeomen Thomas Ayscough of Lathom and John Stannanought of Dalton were both taxed on single hearths in 1664, suggesting their homes were of the cruck type: their sons rebuilt in 1690 (Jump's Farm, 65) and 1714 (Stannanought, 47) respectively. The latter even re-uses cruck timbers in its roof. A relative shortage of timber from the C16 may have meant poorer material frequently had to be pressed into service. The crucks at Lower House, Dalton (44) illustrate this in particular, being irregular in outline and of poor scantling measuring only 6 inches by 6 inches in places (figure 5). Because of their nature and extensive reconstruction during the rebuilding, none of these later crucks structures has remained as intact as Peel (or Black Lawyers before its demise) so generally their presence today is instead restricted to a sole surviving cruck or some truncated portion of it (see Table 2).

CRUCK HOUSES: FORM AND FUNCTION

The layout of cruck houses was essentially very simple: a central hall dividing bays at either end housing private and service rooms. This is found at Peel and Kirklees. In both the central hall is two bays in length, totalling some 29 feet at Peel and 28 at Kirklees, the trusses themselves around 22 feet in height and 18 in width. Before their subsequent alterations, both would originally have been four bays in length, using five trusses in all.

In cruck houses the central truss of the hall was frequently given superior treatment. Its role was more than structural: it was prestigious, symbolising the status of the lord and could be admired by guests seated at the high table. At Peel this truss is distinguished by a cranked collar arched-braced to the blades[9] and for extra effect, this truss is more finely finished on the side facing the dais. This assumes, of course, that it was visible through the smoke of the open hearth: the apex of the trusses at Peel are heavily smoke-blackened, as is the central truss of the former hall at Kirklees. This too may have been arched braced, but the lower portion of the blades was removed when the hall was ceiled in the C16.

Beyond the dais at Peel, the bower lay in the upper bay and the truss at this end was closed to stop smoke infiltrating from the hall. A ceiling has been fitted in this bay, perhaps in the C16. Lofting of the upper end of cruck houses was a simple adaptation to provide extra space, possibly for sleeping. At the lower end of the hall a through-passage probably existed to divide it from the service bay that lay beyond. This was replaced by the present service wing, of post-and-truss construction, in the late C15-early C16. At Kirklees the situation is reversed. The lower bay remains, but the upper was replaced by a parlour wing c1600.

None of the non-gentry cruck houses are as complete. The closest was Black Lawyers (125) at Worthington where a range of at least three bays existed, possibly incorporating a single-bay hall. But the other example of a medieval tenanted cruck hall, Manor House at Worthington (126) shows two-bay halls also existed at non-gentry level. The evidence is a superb truss (the sole one remaining) with cranked, arch-braced collar – similar to Peel – which must have been central to a two-bay hall (figure 3). The smaller scale of this truss – height 19 feet, width 15 – indicates its later date and lower status, yet overall this must have been a significant building by virtue of the style of this truss and the moulding at the base of its blades.

The post-medieval trusses encapsulated within yeoman houses present an equally fragmentary picture. The likelihood too was that these followed the gentry precedent of a hall dividing upper and lower bays. This layout is found in similar-status cruck houses of the coastal plain, where many of this type have survived relatively intact.[10] They display upper ends – usually subdivided on the ground floor to create a parlour and buttery – with a loft above, a central open hall and a service bay beyond it. Some however have further bays beyond the service, with a non-domestic function: frequently a stable and a shippon. This is the true form of cruck 'longhouse' with accommodation for both man and cattle under the same roof, and at Newburgh where the uplands descend to meet the coastal plain we have the remains of a house of this type, White Cottages (82). This was originally much larger, as the domestic bays have been sheared off, but those that housed stable and shippon at the eastern end still remain. Therefore in its original form it may have stretched to five bays at least, typifying the low, straggling nature of these longhouses.

Crucks were restrictive. Not only did they lack an upper storey, they were difficult to adapt when pressure upon space increased. Generally the only way to create more

Pl. 15
Lower House, Dalton is a rare combination of a cruck framed wing (the upper one, on the left). The housebody was never ceiled; the lower wing is C18.

Fig. 5
Lower House, cruck at junction of range and upper wing.

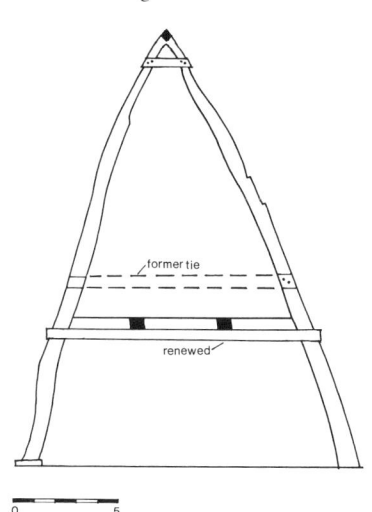

room was to add further bays, creating a longer, unwieldy structure. However evidence remains of attempts to get round these problems. One involved building 'outshuts', a low extension usually to the rear, under a swept-down continuation of the main roof in 'catslide' manner. Outshuts are also found rarely in post-and-truss buildings such as Draper's Farm, Parbold (86) of the early C17 and more frequently in stone or brick yeoman's houses of the later C17. The function was generally a storage or service one. The presence of outshuts in cruck houses at North Meols near Southport, north west of the Douglas Valley, was noted more than a century ago by Sidney Addy in his pioneering study of traditional buildings.[11] Although none survive in original timber-framed form in our area, there is evidence they were once there. At Hydes Brow, Rainford (92) there is an outshut in C18-19 stone to the rear of the possibly-C16 former cruck range. An absence of weathering on the timber-framed rear wall of this range suggests the outshut had always been present. Also, at nearby Bounty Farm, Upholland (109) a similar area of timber-framed rear wall shows a lack of weathering: indicating it must once have been concealed, and again an outshut provides an explanation. Both these houses are modest affairs in areas at the edge of the mossland (as is North Meols) so for men of limited means the outshut may have provided an economical alternative to the more expensive and disruptive option of building further bays.

A more radical solution was to build a crosswing at right angles to the main range. The concept of a hall flanked by wings at right angles containing private and service rooms was introduced by post-and-truss houses of the C14 and C15 (see below, page 49). This provided a compact solution to the alternative of a straggling linear arrangement. These houses appear to have cast some influence over those who continued to use crucks. Although rare, there are instances of cruck ranges with cruck-framed crosswings in Lancashire. In the Ribble Valley there is Dinckley Hall[12] and east of Manchester is Taunton Hall at Ashton-under-Lyne, Tameside[13], both gentry examples. In the Douglas Valley there is Lower House, Dalton (44), a yeoman example however: the W wing contains a cruck as does the main range. The quality of both is notably poor, suggesting this is a later example from the time when timber was becoming scarce, possibly late C16-early C17. By this time the idea of crosswings would have been fairly current so at Lower House we may see the builder following this trend with what limited materials were available. A rarity, perhaps: but as with the outshuts witnessed by Addy in the 1890s, there could once have been many more.

DECLINE OF THE CRUCK TRADITION

At the end of the day, these modifications offered only marginal improvement. Crucks died out because they were inflexible: they were a medieval creation suited to a medieval lifestyle, but when society advanced beyond that, they failed to cope and their days became numbered. Men required houses with more rooms and a system that created straggling, linear houses of one storey only ceased to be a practical alternative. Post-and-truss construction, alternatively, provided the chance to erect more compact buildings of two or more floors and from the C14 gradually gained acceptance in the upper strata of rural society.

So when did crucks become extinct? It was certainly not an overnight process. It appears post-and-truss framing had superceded them at manorial gentry level by c1500, on the evidence of examples we will discuss shortly. Just over a century later, wealthier yeomen were building new houses of this type also and significantly, some such as Giant's Hall, Standish (102; plate 46, figures 6 & 7) and Willow Barn, Wrightington (144) have roof trusses which re-use cruck blades. These are possibly from the buildings they replaced, a clear indicator of how crucks were regarded – at this level anyway – as obsolete by the early C17. Possibly though the system was still current below yeoman level at this time and beyond. Certainly on the coastal plain, and further north into the Fylde, cruck structures were still being built in the late C16 and early C17, so given the tradition of the area it is reasonable to assume this carried on at certain inferior social levels in the Douglas Valley at the same time. In agricultural buildings they may have lived on even longer, and there is some evidence to suggest that the crucks in the late C17 stone barn at Lower Tower Hill, Upholland (119) had originated from the house rebuilt in 1684.

Physical evidence of the decline of crucks comes later in the C17 with the appearance of a final variant of the technique. Called 'upper crucks', they are hardly crucks at all but really triangulated roof trusses – similar to those used in post-and-truss buildings – but with curved blades. These are supported upon a tie-beam and are used in conjunction with load-bearing masonry walls (see Chapter VI) and not timber-frame. The earliest upper crucks are found at Upholland in the rear wing added to the cruck range of Bounty Farm (109) probably of 1667, and an outbuilding at Manor House, Upholland (120) dated 1668. Their presence in humble buildings in a marginal area suggests that by this time and even at this level full crucks were considered redundant. Upper crucks again turn up in modest circumstances at Scythe Stone Delph Farm, Rainford (94; figure 8) of 1682, Manor Cottage, Parbold (87) of 1686 and Eccles House, Bispham (25) of 1700-1710. Surprisingly they also find favour in some rather more prestigious buildings. Their use at both Stone Hall, Dalton (48) and Lowe's, Newburgh (78, figure 9) of c1700-1710 is bizarrely at odds with the role these houses play as pioneers of the new classical style. Symbolically, Stone Hall and Lowe's represent the extinction of the cruck tradition. Yet the buildings it created were still widespread and remained in service for some time. The Hearth Tax returns of 1664 (map 3) provide clear evidence that crucks dominated the landscape, revealing an area where – despite being the most prosperous in Lancashire – 60% of houses were single-hearth, probably cruck-built, structures. So it becomes abundantly clear that these 'little shanties of dwellings' provided home to more than half the population. The accounts of eyewitnesses such as Hewitson show crucks in fact remained a visible part of the landscape even in the late C19. Despised and ridiculed by this time, they had provided a roof over the heads of those in society who had not the means to participate in the rebuilding so blatantly enjoyed by the gentry and yeomanry.

Fig. 6
Giant's Hall, section through wing, showing re-used cruck blades in roof truss.

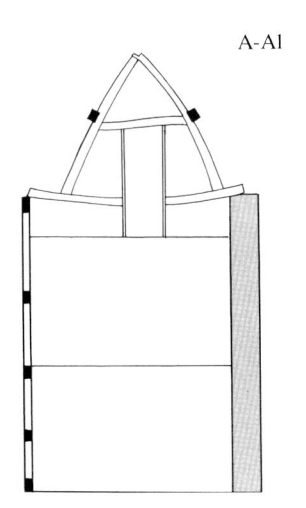

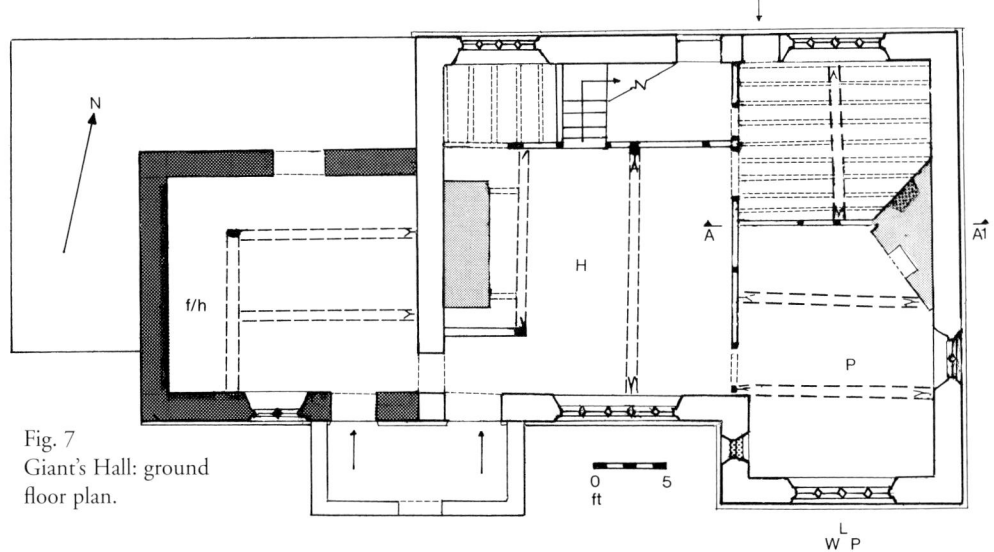

Fig. 7
Giant's Hall: ground floor plan.

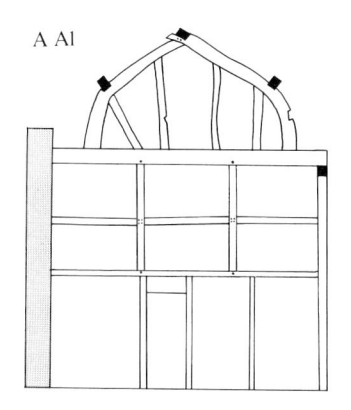

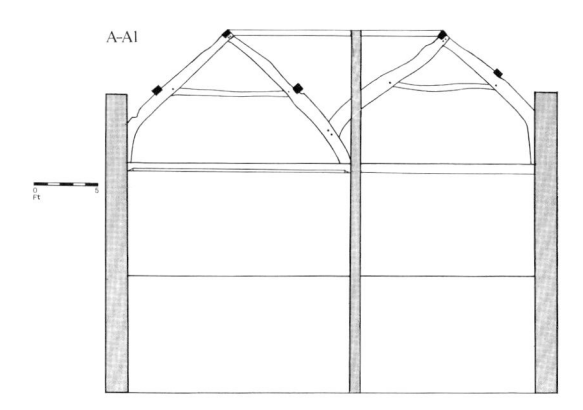

Fig. 8 (far left)
Scythe Stone Delph Farm, section through housebody showing upper cruck (for plan, see page 111).

Fig. 9 (left)
Lowes, long section showing unusual coupled upper cruck trusses.

POST-AND-TRUSS CONSTRUCTION

Although houses such as Peel and Kirklees represented the height of the cruck tradition, they also represented its watershed. Not long afterwards, new trends were being set with the appearance in Lancashire of major manorial houses built not upon crucks but using post and truss construction. First to appear was Baguley Hall, South Manchester, in the C14, followed the next century by other fine examples such as Smithills, Bolton, Ordsall near Manchester and Rufford just north of the Douglas Valley.[14] These prestigious buildings, built by important families of regional influence, began the breakaway from crucks and set the pattern for domestic building for the following two centuries.

These houses established new standards which at first were only within the reach of the major gentry, but subsequently others who were sufficiently well-placed and aware began to follow suit. Athough the cruck tradition was well-entrenched, the benefits of a construction system which created homes more than one storey in height were clearly obvious. By the beginning of the C16, gentry families in the Douglas Valley were investing in this type of superior accommodation which post-and-truss construction offered.

The resulting buildings were more durable than crucks, but more complicated and thus more expensive. Therefore they are generally associated with the better-placed members of society and this is borne out when one examines the distribution of post-and-truss buildings in the Douglas Valley (map 5). This demonstrates that more than half are of gentry status: out of 44 recorded examples, 22 (52 per cent) belong to this group. In comparison we have already seen that the majority of crucks are found in yeoman houses (map 4). The fact that fewer post-and-truss yeoman houses exist is partly accounted for by stone and brick quickly superceding this method early in the yeoman rebuilding.

Post-and-truss houses were, quite simply, 'boxes': a series of frames jointed together. Uprights called wallposts supported triangulated roof trusses which carried the

Table 4
Analysis of post-and-truss buildings in the Douglas Valley.

Pl. 16
Elements of fine timber framing: Bradley Hall, Langtree, showing detail of chamfered and stopped wallpost, braced to wallplate and supporting tie beam of truss.

Township	Name	Status	Date	Remarks
Adlington	Crawshaw Hall	gent	C15-16	Surviving solar wing of house of sub-manorial status; stone clad C16-17.
Aspull	Gidlow Hall	gent	C15	Stone house of 1574 containing arched-braced trusses of timber-framed C15 predecessor; moated site.
Aspull	Kirklees Hall	gent	C16	Cruck-framed range rebuilt c1600 and upper wing added; 1820s drawing shows decorative framing. Brick clad C17-18.
Coppull	Bogburn Hall	gent	C16-17	Brick house of 1663 containing substantial roof trusses and timber-framed earlier building.
Coppull	Coppull Hall	gent	C16-17	Remains of substantial manor house, brick clad C17; site possibly moated.
Coppull	Coppull Old Hall	gent/yeo	C16-17	Original form uncertain prior to C17-18 brick cladding.
Coppull	Holt Farm	yeoman	C16-17	Former open hall of non-gentry status, wing added ? early C17. Brick cladding c1700; ancient site.
Dalton	Felton's Farm	yeoman	C16-17	Fragment of house of uncertain form, stone clad C17-18.
Dalton	Holland's House	yeoman	C17	Wing and hall range, possibly c1608; clad in stone c1700.
Dalton	Lower House	yeoman	C17	Fragment of post-and-truss continuation/reconstruction of cruck-framed wing; stone clad C17-18.
Ince	Peel Hall	gent	C15-16	2-bay lower wing with kingpost truss added to C14 cruck hall; moated site; brick clad C17.
Langtree	Bradley Hall	gent	C15-16	Former open hall C15-early C16 with service wing of C1600; clad in brick C19.
Langtree	Dam House Farm	yeoman	C16	Late open hall, early C16, fossilised within brick rebuilding of c1700.
Langtree	Langtree Hall	gent	C16?	Substantial timber-framed manor house recorded in 1653 Commonwealth survey.
Newburgh	Lys Cottage	yeoman	C17	Range of early C17 brick clad 1691 when wing added at upper end.
Newburgh	Rose Cottage	yeoman	C16-17	Fragment of timber-framed house clad in stone C17-18; kingpost truss remains on external gable.
Orrell	Ackhurst Hall	gent	C17	Substantial hall range and wing, possibly c1618; stone clad extended later C17.
Parbold	Draper's Farm	yeoman	C17	Fragment of house of uncertain form, stone clad later C17.
Parbold	Parbold Hall	gent	C16?	Re-used fishbone trusses in attic of C17-18 manor house imply substantial timber-framed predecessor.
Rainford	Guild Hall	yeoman	C16-17	Timber-framed external wall surviving at rear of sizeable brick house of 1629.
Shevington	Coach House Farm	yeoman	C16-17	Housebody range and wing, stone clad and extended 1663.
Shevington	Club House Farm	yeoman	C16-17	Single-bay parlour wing added to earlier cruck-framed range.
Shevington	Crooke Hall	gent	1608	Fine manor house of hall range and flanking wings; demolished 1937.
Shevington	Gathurst Hall	yeoman	C17	3-bay linear house, brick clad late C17- early C18.
Skelmersdale	Sephton Hall	gent	C16-17	Timber-framed house of several periods, stone clad early C18; demolished.
Standish	Giants Hall	yeoman	C17	Housebody and wing, earlyC17; house clad 1675
Standish	Standish Hall	gent	1574?	Hall range with decorative framing, possible courtyard plan; demolished.
Standish	Upper Standish Wood	yeoman	C17	Crosswing, possibly added to cruck range; clad/rebuilt C17-18
Upholland	Johnson's Farm	yeoman	C15-16	Open hall, possibly aisled: stone wing added 1647; subsequent cladding.
Upholland	Knight's Hall	yeoman	C16-17	Wallposts of substantial house survive within 1716 rebuilding.
Upholland	Newgate Farm	yeoman	C16-17	Firehood and smoke bay surviving within stone house of 1707.
Worthington	Worthington Hall	gent	1577	Substantial manor house with decorative framing, altered c1700 and C20.
Wrightington	Fairhurst Hall	gent	C16	Substantial storeyed hall and flanking wings, brick clad C18.
Wrightington	Harrock Hall	gent	C16?	Minimal evidence of timber-framing within fine stone house of c1600.
Wrightington	South Tunley	yeoman	1622	Wealthy yeoman house, clad 1677 in brick; latest dated post-and-truss building in area.
Wrightington	Spring Bank	yeoman	C17	Fragment, possibly wing, of larger house, mostly stone clad C17-18.
Wrightington	Willow Barn	yeoman	C17	3-unit house of early C17 clad in brick c1660-1690.
Wrightington	Wrightington Hall	gent	C16?	Wing with decorative panels shown in drawing of 1820s.

purlins, and horizontal members called rails connected the wallposts to give the structure stability and strength. Within this framework a ceiling could be easily inserted. The result was a house of completely different form to cruck structures. Within, the hall was still single-storey but was flanked at either end by storeyed wings, the 'upper' containing private and the 'lower' service rooms. Life could now go ahead on two levels – a reflection of the vertical hierarchy found in society itself. The plan allowed a greater privacy by allowing the lord to distance himself from the busy thoroughfare of the hall. This he did by siting his own private room – termed the solar – on the upper floor of the upper wing, as far away from the hall as possible. With this, the gentry set a trend for first-floor living which was embellished further by the new houses they came to build in the late C16 and early C17.

As in cruck halls, the lower wing was usually separated from the hall by the screens passage, but sometimes a truss of special form acted as a dividing line. Called the spere truss, it embodied full-height and often decorative posts or 'speres' mounted inward of the outer walls, between which the movable screen could be sited. They helped to shield the hall from draughts from the entrance but also served as a physical and hierarchical barrier between it and the lower wing. This evolving plan of hall-and-crosswings has such impact that its influence lasted for the next two centuries. Even in the early 1700s – though the open had been long since abandoned – houses were still being modelled upon this layout, a telling indication of both its influence and the area's conservatism.

Pl. 17
Collar of arch-braced roof truss relocated in stair tower of Gidlow Hall, Aspull, indicating presence of substantial timber-framed hall of C15.

HALL-HOUSES OF THE DOUGLAS VALLEY

By 1500, gentry hall-houses had begun to appear in the area. Possibly the earliest – certainly the most substantial to survive – was Bradley Hall (57; figure 11-14) in the sub-manor of Bradley, within Langtree. What remains is the hall, originally of four narrow bays, with screens-passage. The upper wing has gone. It may have been of differing date: addition and subtraction of wings in the hall-house plan is a common phenomenon, as it was easier to rebuild a wing rather than the entire house. At the lower end however is a long service wing, of around 1600, which extends beyond the rear of the range and thus suggest the house may originally have been built around a courtyard. If so it was modelled on houses of the major gentry, which were invariably of courtyard plan: Smithills, Ordsall and Rufford are all of this type, and although later, so too may have been Standish Hall, Standish (103). At some 28 feet high, Bradley is appreciably taller than the 22 feet of Peel and Kirklees and the visual impact it created must have been considerable in a cruck-dominated countryside. The hall itself contains four tall narrow trusses of principal rafter type supported on heavy

Fig. 10
Bogburn Hall, section through housebody showing truss of heavy scantling from timber-framed phase prior to brick cladding (for plan, see page 110).

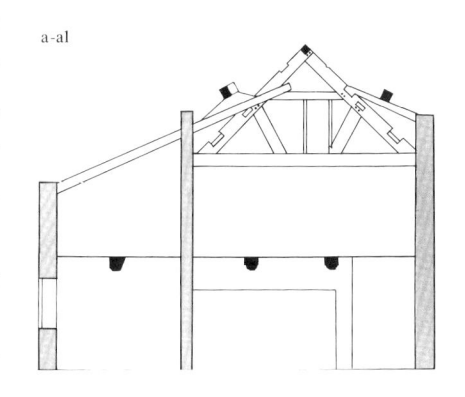

Pl. 18
Bradley Hall, Langtree. Victorian cladding conceals a fine post-and-truss manor house with former open hall, probably of the late C15-early C16 and service wing of c1600.

wallposts chamfered for decorative effect. What was formerly the central truss is, as in the tradition set by Peel, given extra distinction, with a cranked tie beam.

Evidence, albeit comparatively fragmentary, exists to show similar houses being built by other sub-manorial families elsewhere. At Crawshaw Hall, Adlington (3) the solar wing of the hall, with fine principal rafter roof trusses, is all that remains of a substantial house of the Worthington family with 14 rooms recorded in 1626. Within Bogburn Hall, Coppull (29; figure 10) are substantial roof trusses suggesting an important timber-framed structure was once present: possibly of early to mid C16 date, with a hall of two bays at least. At Gidlow Hall, Aspull (7) re-used roof trusses – including one of fine arched-braced form (plate 17, figure 37) – indicate the ghost of a C15 predecessor of some considerable size, with up to nine bays suggested by the carpenter's mark 'X' on one of the trusses. In a more modest development, a service wing of post-and-truss construction, with idiosyncratic kingpost roof trusses, was

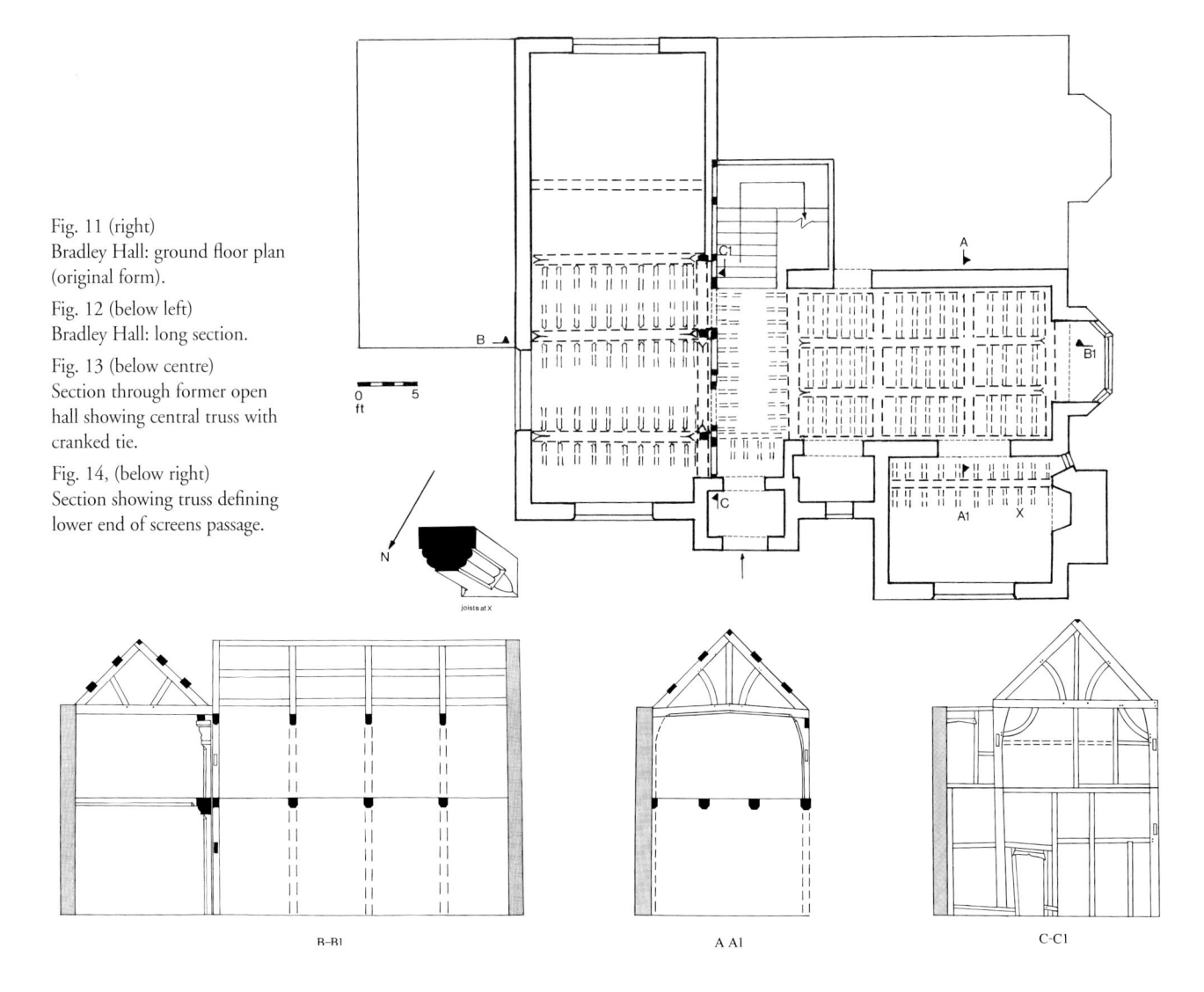

Fig. 11 (right)
Bradley Hall: ground floor plan (original form).

Fig. 12 (below left)
Bradley Hall: long section.

Fig. 13 (below centre)
Section through former open hall showing central truss with cranked tie.

Fig. 14, (below right)
Section showing truss defining lower end of screens passage.

B–B1

A A1

C–C1

added to Peel Hall (56) in the late C15-early C16 (figure 1).

All this investment in substantial post-and-truss hall houses points to a phase of rebuilding by the medieval gentry class occuring in the late C15- early C16 as peace resumed under the Tudors following the disruption of the Wars of the Roses. If minor gentry such as the Gidlows and Worthingtons were able to discard crucks or at least substantially improve upon them, then by implication their superiors at manorial level would have made this transition also. Therefore the new manor houses erected by families such as the Standishes of Standish (103), Worthingtons of Worthington (128) Lathoms of Parbold (88) and Bradshaighs of Haigh (52) in the late C16 may themselves have succeeded post-and-truss halls which in turn had replaced crucks. Earlier timber-framed fragments discovered inside both Parbold Hall (88) and Harrock Hall, Wrightington (134) may testify to this having occurred there. The gentry were sufficiently well-placed to rebuild their homes every few generations, so each structure may simply have been another stage in what could be seen as an ongoing sequence of improvement.

Evidence has recently come to light that suggests post-and-truss hall-houses were erected by families of non-gentry status, probably at a later date. Renovation at both Dam House Farm, Langtree (58) and Holt Farm, Coppull (33) uncovered open halls within the housebodies of what were externally buildings of c1700. At Dam House, an open principal rafter truss (possibly central in a two-bay hall) with a closed one to the north survives, braced to wallposts (figure 16). At Holt, a similar truss with evidence for bracing to wallposts occurs over the range to which a timber-framed wing was added in the early C17 (figure 15). The ceilings in both are later insertions. Both halls are

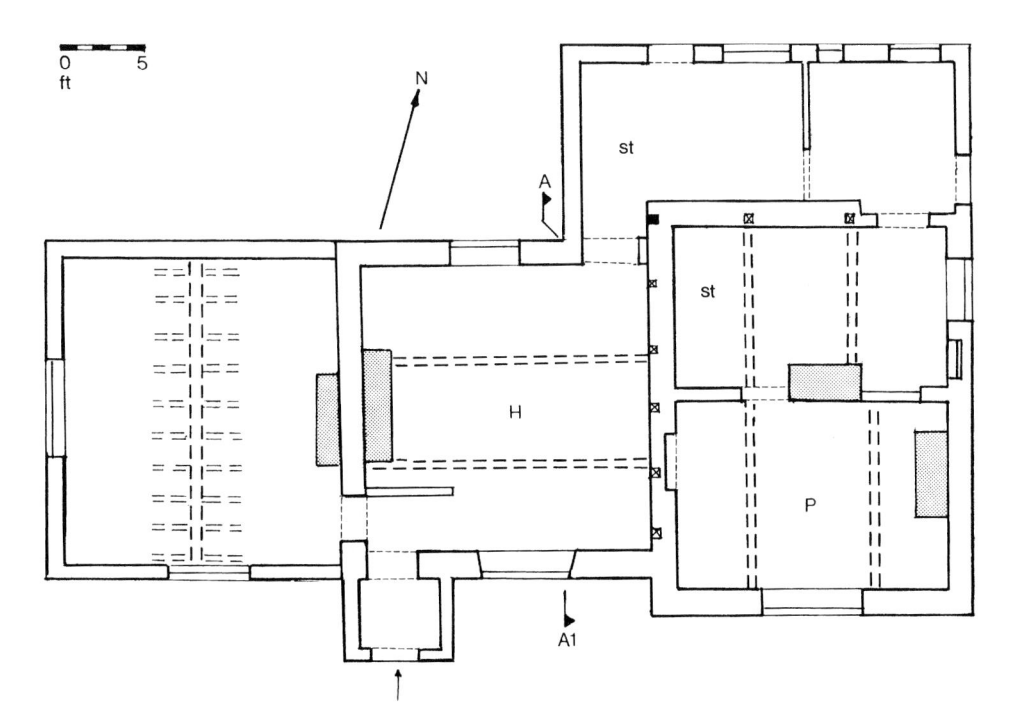

Pl. 19
Holt Farm: beneath the C18 exterior is a former open hall and added early C17 crosswing.

Fig. 15 (left)
Holt Farm: ground floor plan.

Fig. 16 (below)
Holt Farm, section through housebody showing truss from former open hall.

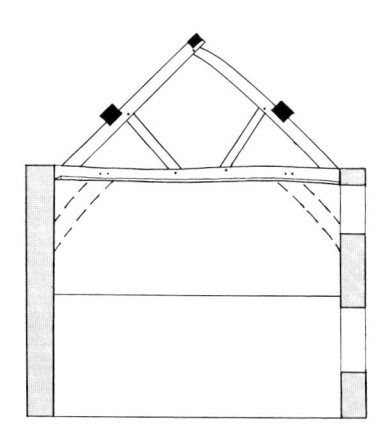

51

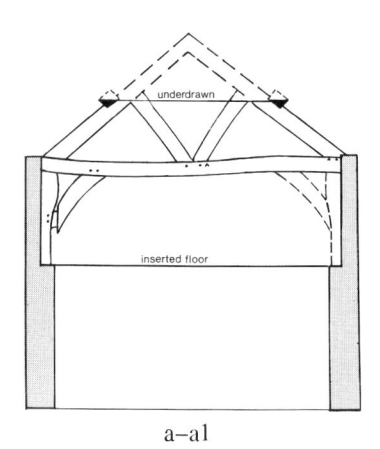

Fig. 17
Dam House, section showing truss of former open hall.

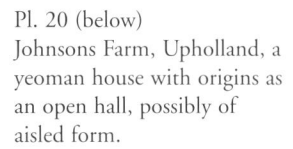

Pl. 20 (below)
Johnsons Farm, Upholland, a yeoman house with origins as an open hall, possibly of aisled form.

Pl. 21
Interior of housebody at Johnsons Farm, showing moulded uprights which may be spere truss or aisle posts.

diminutive in comparison to nearby Bradley (57), with heights of just 20 feet at Dam House and 22 at Holt. Neither have the appearance therefore of gentry houses and the indications therefore are that these were homes of wealthy tenants affluent enough able to progress from crucks to hall-houses at an early stage.

As to the date: they probably stem from the first half of the C16, before the demise of the open-hall tradition generally. That occurred in the mid to later C16, when changing lifestyles, with a requirement for more private accommodation, made the medieval hall obsolete and no longer a status symbol. Open halls ceased to be built after that time, and although houses in timber-frame continued to be built during the early stages of the gentry rebuilding their halls were ceiled to provide chambers above. Standish (103) and Worthington (128) of the 1570s both illustrate this point.

A further hall-house of probably late medieval origin exists, but is an enigma which merits some separate discussion. Johnson's Farm at Upholland (117, figure 18), although largely a C17 yeoman house, originated possibly as an open hall of aisled form. Aisled halls are a rarified version that originated in the late 13th century and at that time housed kings and nobility. They occur in southeast England and the Midlands where they were current until the C15: but also found in an unparallelled nucleus around Halifax in West Yorkshire, where they continued to be built into the C16 on the back of profits from a thriving local textile economy.[15] These buildings are so-called because of low extensions – the aisles – on either side of the hall space with the roof swept down over then in the manner of an outshut. The aisles are separated from the hall by an arcade composed of wallposts but as there is no partition, movement between the two

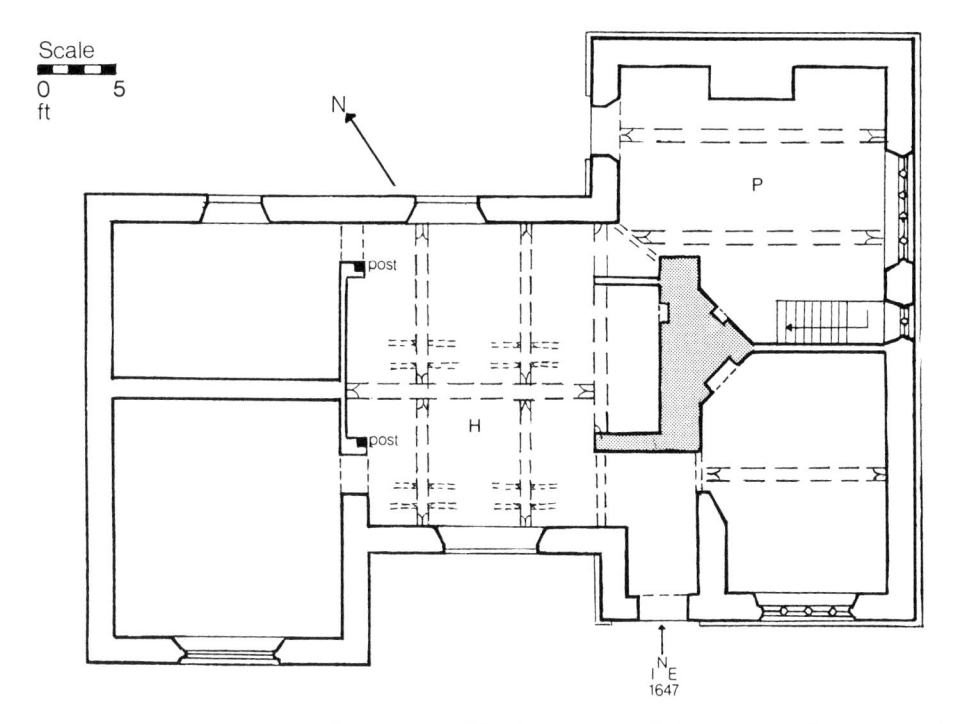

Fig. 18
Johnsons: ground floor plan.

is unrestricted. Examples of this type of building west of the Pennines have never been conclusively proved: Johnsons falls into that category.

The house (plate 20) consists of a low, stone-clad hall originally open but ceiled probably in the C16 with a parlour wing added 1647 by the Naylor yeoman family, and a service wing of later C17 date. At the lower end of the housebody what may be arcade posts, and the space between these and the outer walls suggests aisles on both sides. One of the posts is a C16 replacement, but the other is earlier and heavily moulded (plate 21). However all roof timbers above the ceiling have been renewed, so there is nothing more conclusive. Nevertheless, Johnson's ought not to be ignored: if it is not of aisled origin, then how else could the proportions of the hall be explained? It remains as one of a handful of buildings which offer some evidence that this superior type of hall-house once existed in Lancashire.[16]

DEMISE OF TIMBER-FRAMING

Timber-framed construction was obsolescent from the time when in the 1570s the first stone gentry houses made their debut. Although some of the earliest homes of the yeoman rebuilding – Giant's Hall, Standish (102), Willow Barn, Wrightington (144), Draper's Farm, Parbold (86) and Gathurst Hall (100) and Club House Farm, Shevington (97) for example – used this method in the early C17, stone was already making an impression upon the pattern of building. With timber becoming scarce, stone was seen as more lasting and prestigious, and represented the way forward.

Pl. 22
South Tunley, the last dated post-and-truss building: 1622. Drawing before 1950s reconstruction. (Mrs Riding).

We now find ourselves faced with a question similar to that posed by crucks. When did post-and-truss construction cease to be current? With crucks it was largely speculation, but in this case we have the more reliable evidence of datestones. The latest dated post-and-truss building is South Tunley, Wrightington (139; plate 22) where the date 1622 on the now rebuilt porch refers to the timber-framed house built by Thomas Wilson, and his wife. Shortly afterwards, in 1629, we have the appearance of a substantial yeoman houses in brick, Guild Hall at Rainford (91) a remodelling by James Naylor of the timber-framed house of his father William. These dates, plus the

Pl. 23
Fragment of a once-larger post-and-truss structure, now reduced to a cottage: Spring Bank, Wrightington.

increasing numbers of brick and stone houses appearing from this time on, give an indication of when the transition took place. As with crucks however, houses of post-and-truss construction were around for some time after the method became obsolete. Several yeoman examples – Giants Hall, Standish (102), Willow Barn, Wrightington (144), and Club House Farm, Shevington (97) – survived until the later C17 before being clad, which suggests that timber-frame was broadly acceptable up until this time. More elevated examples however, such as Standish Hall, Standish (102) and Crooke Hall, Shevington (98) retained their framing until they met their end this present century, probably by virtue of its superior nature. Yet others, much lower down the scale, demonstrate an often puzzling co-existance of timber-frame and masonry cladding which can really only be explained by a limited rebuilding due to limited resources. Rose Cottage, Newburgh (81) where a fine truss of fishbone form adorns the gable of an otherwise stone and brick building, and Spring Bank, Wrightington (141), a curious fragment of a once larger house, are two such examples.

CONCLUSION

The Douglas Valley, like the rest of Lancashire, had a long tradition of timber-framed building which lasted from the middle ages to the C17. Both forms of construction – crucks and post-and-truss framing – were practised, with crucks the older of the two. Their use was once universal: they formed the homes of the gentry from at least the C14 as demonstrated by Peel Hall at Ince and Kirklees Hall at Aspull; and of lesser men for much longer. In the same century however a new type of house was pioneered by the wealthiest of the county's families using post-and-truss framing. By the beginning of the C16 these hall-houses with storeyed wings were being built at sub-manorial level as structures such as Bradley Hall, Langtree, Crawshaw at Adlington and Gidlow at Aspull demonstrate. Timber-framed hall-houses of this type continued to be built throughout the C16, but from the 1570s the great open hall of medieval tradition was abandoned and the last generation of timber-framed houses had halls that were ceiled with chambers above.

Post-and-truss construction was the prerogative mainly of the gentry. Most of the surving houses belong to that group, but the first yeomen to rebuild also used this method in the early C17. Crucks however have survived most in houses usually of yeoman status; with the exception of several medieval gentry examples which represent the craft at its height. The remainder are probably C16-early C17 in origin. The Hearth Tax records reveal an overwhelming number of single-hearth dwellings in all townships. This tends to confirm the notion that the majority of the rural population including the yeomanry lived in cruck-built houses prior to the rebuilding.

The yeoman rebuilding made complete the transition to stone and brick as the principal materials of domestic building. The indications are that by the 1630s post-and-truss construction had been superseded in this way, but beneath yeoman level crucks survived and were commonplace until the late C19. The evolution of the upper cruck derivative in the late C17 suggests full crucks were obsolete among the yeomanry by this time, although in agricultural buildings their use or re-use may still have been acceptable.

We now turn our attention to the highly-complex rebuilding process which made the ancient tradition of timber-framing obsolete. The epicentre of the movement can be traced back to the 1570s in the homes of the gentry and from there its repercussions were felt throughout the next 150 years.

NOTES

1. Royal Commission on the Historical Monuments of England report. The house has a fine crown-post roof.
2. John Chandler, 'John Leyland's Itinery: Travels in Tudor England' (1993) p265
3. Anthony Hewitson ('Atticus'), Our Country Churches and Chapels, 1872.
4. N. Alcock 'Cruck Construction'. Council for British Archeology Research Report no 42, 1981.
5. Greater Manchester Archeological Unit, 'A Survey of the Cruck Buildings of Tameside', 1998. Dendrochronology shows four cruck houses of either manorial or tenanted status dating from this time. They are (felling dates in bracks): Apethorn Fold, Hyde (c1242); Newton Hall, Newton (c1315); Taunton Hall, Ashton-under-Lyne (c1315-20); Woodfield Farm, Ashton-under-Lyne (c1338).
6. GMAU, 'Tameside', 1998.
7. VCH IV, p121.
8. Rev T C Porteus, 'History of Standish', 1927, p225-7.
9. A similar arched-braced truss at Taunton Hall, Ashton-under-Lyne is dendro-dated to c1315-20. GMAU, 'Tameside', 1998, p49.
10. The houses mainly used here for background material are: 107, School Lane, Haskayne, Downholland, Moss Farmhouse, Ince Blundell, Adamson's Farm, Eaves, near Preston, Rhododendron Cottage, Treales, near Kirkham (all surveyed by Garry Miller, 1987) and Scotch Green, Goosnargh (surveyed by Garry Miller and Nigel Morgan)
11. S O Addy, The Evolution of the English House, Social England Series, 1898, p43-44.
12. Department for Culture, Media and Sport, list of buildings of special architectural or historic interest, Ribble Valley district.
13. GMAU, 'Tameside', 1998, p34-37.
14. A similar manor house, but on a smaller scale, is Alston Old Hall at Longridge in the Ribble Valley, built by the Houghton family probably in the mid-C15. (Surveyed by Nigel Morgan, Garry Miller and Margaret Pannikar, 1990).
15. Colum Giles, Rural House of West Yorkshire 1400-1830, RCHME, 1986, p27-36; also
16. Eric Mercer, English Vernacular Houses, RCHM, 1975, p9-11, 14-16. Another is Fisherfield Farm, Spotland, in the Pennines above Rochdale, where one aisle only appears to have existed in an early C16 building clad in stone in 1692. (Surveyed by Garry Miller, 1991).

CHAPTER III

Houses of the Gentry 1570-1620

For those belonging to the gentry classes, it was almost a requirement in the late C16 and early C17 that they build a substantial new house to match their status. A spacious, imposing residence was deemed necessary to the gentry lifestyle: practically, to provide accomodation for a large household and entertaining guests, and, less tangibly, to create or augment the necessary image of social or political prestige. By the late C16, houses based upon the medieval open hall were no longer adequate for this role and needed to be replaced. From the 1570s we see this happening with the beginning of an intense period of rebuilding which created houses of revolutionary character throughout the area.

These houses symbolised the end of the medieval period and the beginning of the modern era, and were the products of tremendous social changes at large in Tudor England. A new order of society had emerged following the turbulence of the Wars of the Roses and the Reformation, one in which the nobility – viewed as a potential threat to an unsteady Crown – were supressed but beneath them a multi-layered strata of gentry flourished as the country at last found political and religious stability and economic prosperity in the reign of Elizabeth. What distinguished them from their medieval forebears was a more materialistic outlook in which money was lavished on temporal rather than spiritual needs. Resources which once would have supported the church were instead poured into the building of magnificent new homes: powerful and imposing in appearance (but no longer defensive in nature), spacious and comfortable inside. The pattern was set by the prodigious mansions built by the nobility during the second half of the C16. Palatial structures such as Longleat, Wiltshire, begun c1568, Burghley House, Northamptonshire, c1585 and Hardwick Hall at Derbyshire of the 1590s became the inspiration for countless homes of lesser standing. These houses were lasting monuments to the gentry at their zenith, symbolising their status, affluence and achievement. In certain cases they assisted relatively new members of the class in disguising a deficiency of pedigree behind a powerful façade. In more practical terms, the houses set standards of accommodation and construction never before achieved and their influence extended far beyond their class as they served as role models imitated by the yeomanry when they to began to rebuild later in the C17.

Although the gentry had the resources to renew their homes every few generations or so, this spectacular rebuilding of the late C16-early C17 is the earliest from which substantial numbers of houses survive. A major factor in this is the use of stone, which gradually displaced the traditional timber-framed construction methods and became synonymous with homes of the gentry, suggesting both permanence and nobility in a landscape dominated by inferior cruck-framed structures. The houses pioneered other crucial developments. Although in layout they largely retained the form of the medieval hall house, they contained halls which were no longer single-storey and no longer the focus of everyday household life. The declining importance of the hall was counterbalanced by the increased provision of private rooms for the family, reflecting a more cultured, refined lifestyle which distanced itself from the activity of the hall.

The houses dating from this period are all homes of prominent people in society, and therefore a considerable amount of information can be gleaned about them, not merely from the buildings themselves but also documentary sources. In all, 23 gentry houses have survived in the area under consideration – or have been documented if they haven't – from the period between 1570 and 1620 and the families who built and

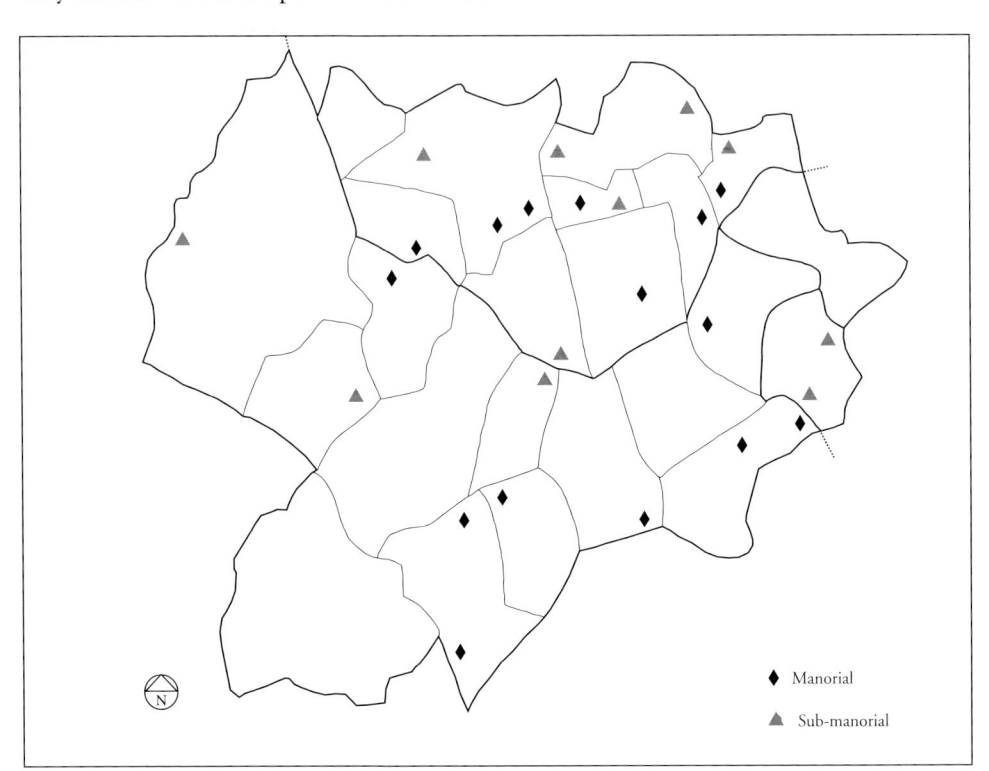

Map 6
Distribution of gentry houses, 1570-1620.

occupied them can each be identified (table 5). A relatively clear picture emerges therefore of the people who initiated and furthered the rebuilding and the timescale in which it occurred. At face value these houses appear as monuments to a gilded age in which the gentry thrived. But their significance is deeper than that. Equally they indicate that this class was undergoing a metamorphosis. Many of the established 'old gentry' were making way for newcomers, and it was these parvenu lords that propelled the rebuilding along - either directly through the fine homes they created or indirectly through the influence their homes came to exert.

WHO WERE THE GENTRY?

The composition of the Lancashire gentry in the late C16 was complex, with various divisions on a pyramidal scale. It is possible to simplify them into three broad categories: major, middle and minor. The major gentry were the county's pre-eminent landowners, whose influence extended regionally and sometimes was also of national significance. At the apex of the pyramid were the Stanleys, Earls of Derby, who had profited from their support for Henry VII at the battle of Bosworth in 1485 and were now the crown's representatives in the county. Beneath them were notable 'county' families such as the Molyneux of Sefton – second wealthiest after the Stanleys – the Heskeths of Rufford, the Houghtons of Hoghton Tower and the Shireburnes of Stonyhurst. All in the C16 still exercised great power, inherited from their warlord landowner forebears and diluted only marginally by the fact that the country was now at peace. In the process of government, they were key players as their support was crucial in political, financial and military terms.

Representing the middle gentry were landowners on a smaller scale, those who were sole owners of individual manors. In this area the Standishes of Standish, Bradshaighs of Haigh, Gerards of Ince, Lathoms of Parbold, Langtrees of Langtree and Worthington of Worthington fall into this category. All were long-established, since the C13 at least. Their antiquity was frequently displayed by the fact they took their

Pl. 24
The extravagance of gentry houses occasionally translated into funerary monuments: this is Edward Wrightington of Wrightington Hall in Standish Church.

surnames from the district they held, and more tangibly through the moats which stood around some of their homesteads. A further indication of their importance is the title 'armiger' – meaning esquire, and an entitlement to bear a coat of arms – given to them on the 1600 freeholders list,[1] distinguishing them from the average 'gentleman' within their manors, they still retained a feudal supremacy, exercising complete jurisdiction over local administration, justice and land transactions through the manor court over which they or their stewards presided. The influence of the most important of these manorial lords extended further afield. Who they were is tellingly revealed by the map of Lancashire drawn up for Lord Burghley in 1590.[2] Those landowners of strategic importance to the government – politically, militarily

Table 5 Analysis of surviving or recorded gentry houses.

Township	Name	Family	Title[1]	Status[2]	Tenure	1593 lay subsidy L=lands G=goods	Date	Building material	No. of hearths 1664	Remarks
Adlington	Allanson Hall	Allanson	gent	sm	freehold	L£1.0.0	1618	brick/timber-frame	4	LaterC17 wing added to rear; service end demolished
Aspull	Gidlow Hall	Goodlaw	gent	sm	freehold	L£1.0.0	1574	stone	-	Rebuilding of ?C15 timber framed house remodelled 1840; moated
Aspull	Kirklees Hall	Houghton	gent	sm	freehold	L£1.0.0	lateC16	timber-frame	-	Parlour wing added to ?C14 cruck hall-house; moated site
Billinge	Birchley Hall	Anderton	gent	m	freehold	–	1594	stone	16	Sstone-built manor house copied by Winstanley and Bispham
Billinge	Bispham Hall	Bispham	gent	m	freehold	L£1.0.0	c1600	stone	12	Identical to Birchley; substantial additions of early C17
Coppull	Chisnall Hall	Chisnall	armiger	sm	freehold	L£5.0.0	c1600	stone	7	Truncated and remodelled c1800; moated site nearby
Coppull	Coppull Hall	Dicconson	—	sm	freehold	G£5.0.0	C16-C17	brick	10	Addition to earlier, probably timber-framed manor house
Dalton	Ashurst Hall	Ashurst	gent	m	freehold	L£3.0.0	C17?	stone	10	Modernised; gatehouse 1649
Haigh	Haigh Hall	Bradshaigh	armiger	m	freehold	L£17.0.0	c1605-1612	stone	17	Rebuilding modelled on Birchley Hall; further rebuilt c1700 and 1827-1840
Ince	Ince Hall	Brown	gent	sm	freehold	L£14.0.0	c1601	timber-frame	5	Rebuilt following fire 1854
Langtree	Bradley Hall	Standish	armiger	m	freehold	L£1.0.0	c1600	timber-frame	5	Additions to C15-C16 hall-house possibly on courtyard plan; moated
Lathom	Blythe Hall	Blackleach	gent	sm	freehold	L£1.10.0	C16-C17	stone?	4	Remodelled C19; extended 1920s
Orrell	Ackhurst Hall	Leigh (from1616)	—	sm	freehold	—	c1618	timber-frame	4	Rebuilt in stone 1686
Parbold	Parbold Hall	Lathom	armiger	m	freehold	L£6.0.0	c1600	stone	-	Addition to earlier (?timber-framed) house; rebuilt late C17 and 1740s
Pemberton	Hawkley Hall	Molyneux	gent	sm	freehold	L£2.10.0	early C17	stone	10	Demolished; moated site
Shevington	Crooke Hall	Caterall	gent	sm	freehold	L£2.0.0	1608	timber-frame	6	Demolished
Skelmersdale	Sephton Hall	Sephton	gent	sm	freehold	L£1.0.0	late C16	timber-frame	7?	Demolished
Standish	Standish Hall	Standish	armiger	m	freehold	L£20.0.0	c1574	timber-frame	17	Demolished; addition of late C17 and 1740; poss. courtyard plan; moated
Winstanley	Winstanley Hall	Bankes(from1595)	armiger	m	freehold	—	c1596?	stone	14	Rebuilt late C18-earlyC19; moated site of earlier hall nearby
Worthington	Worthington Hall	Worthington	armiger	m	freehold	L£5.0.0	1577	timber-frame		Service end rebuilt c1700; upper end rebuilt C20
Wrightington	Fairhurst Hall	Nelson	gent	sm	freehold	—	lateC16	timber-frame	5	Clad in brick C18
Wrightington	Harrock Hall	Rigby	gent	sm	freehold	L£1.0.0	c1600	stone	6	Additions of c1700 and alterations of C19-20
Wrightington	Wrightington Hall	Wrightington	armiger	m	freehold	L£2.0.0	C16?	timber-frame/stone	15	Demolished

1. In 1600 freeholders list.   2. M = manorial; SM = sub-manorial

and financially – were named upon it along with their houses. Represented are Edward Standish of Standish Hall (102), Richard Lathom of Parbold (88), Thomas Gerard of Ince (54), and Roger Bradshaigh of Haigh (52). They therefore were regarded as potentially crucial in the process of government. Effectively their support was expressed in monetary terms. As significant landowners, they found themselves forced to contribute to various subsidies and levies aimed at raising finance for the government or underwriting military campaigns. The Standish family, for example, were the second highest assessed in the Hundreds of Leyland (after the Heskeths of Rufford) in levies of 1574, 1588, 1593 and 1632 which also demonstrates they maintained a degree of financial stability throughout this period.[3]

Despite unrest and conflict during the medieval period, these families held on to their position – as the head of the local feudal society – with relative stability. A significant change in the composition of the middle gentry occurred in the late C16 however. Several of the 'old gentry' relinquished their manors and made way for families new to either their territories or the class. By 1581, a branch of the Anderton family – major gentry residing at Lostock Hall north-west of Bolton – acquired the manor of Birchley in Billinge from the Heatons, who had held it since the late C14 at least.[4] Around 1600, the Ashurst family, recorded earlier as sub-manorial landowners in Dalton, acquired the manor in its entirety.[5] The manor of Coppull also changed ownership at this time, the Rigby family of Burgh in Duxbury near Chorley, acquiring it from the Earl of Derby.[6] But the most remarkable newcomer was James Bankes, who effectively purchased gentry status with his acquisition of the manor of Winstanley. Bankes was a successful London goldsmith-banker who prospered further

Pl. 25
Winstanley Hall, possibly of around 1596, is not only testimony to the rise of James Bankes, who effectively purchased gentry status with his acquisition of the manor – but also to the new Elizabethan society in which this was possible. Depicted in 1817; from M Gregson 'Portfolio of Fragments Relating to the History ... of the County Palatine and Duchy of Lancaster' (1869).

Pl. 26
Minor gentry who held manors that had been subdivided, were also able to build powerful houses, as Hawkley Hall, Pemberton, demonstrates. Its owners, the Molyneux family, had been resident since the C13. (Wigan Heritage Service)

by establishing himself in Lancashire as a landowner, initially in Pemberton and then early in 1596 acquiring Winstanley from the family of that name who had held the manor since the mid C13 at least and were now 'selling up' due to financial difficulties. The displacement of an old gentry family by a parvenu graphically displays the extent to which society was changing in the capitalist economy that emerged following the breakdown of feudalism.

These families, whether old or new, enjoyed considerable influence as the sole owners of their manors. In contrast, other manors were divided into separate freeholds at an early date, allowing the emergence of several smaller landowners who acquired gentry status. It is this group of sub-manorial landowners who constituted the minor gentry of the C16 and early C17; table 5 shows a considerable number of these families existed and were able to rebuild at this time.

A hierarchy existed within their ranks also. The two most prominent families were the Rigbys of Harrock in Wrightington and the Chisnalls of Chisnall in Coppull. The former had held their estates since the C13, initially as tenants of the religious order of the Knights of St John of the Hospital, but following the dissolution they held directly from the Crown.[8] In 1557 their hall was described as a 'capital messuage'[9]; fragments of a timber-framed, perhaps C15-early C16 predecessor were unearthed within the present c1600 stone structure during its restoration.[10] The Rigbys' standing was on a par as that of the Standishes, Bradshaighs *et al* in the eyes of the government as they and their hall are indicated on Lord Burghley's map of 1590. Furthermore, Nicholas Rigby was a close associate of the Earl of Derby in the 1580s. The Chisnalls, meanwhile, were not singled out in this way but in another respect were denoted as ranking alongside their manorial peers. In the freeholders list of 1600, and consistently in other tax records after that, Edward Chisnall (d. 1635) is described as 'armiger', when the rest of the sub-manorial gentry are referred to as 'gentlemen'.[11] The family had held land in Coppull and Worthington since the C13, and their standing was doubtless increased by the fact that the lords of Coppull manor had been non-resident there since the time of Edward IV,[12] making them the largest local landowner in that township.

Less prominent landowners appear to have reaped the benefit of freehold status at an early date. As we have seen, the Worthington family acquired a portion of Adlington manor relinquished by the Duxbury family in the C14; their hall of Crawshaw (3) contains the remains of a fine solar wing of possibly early C16 date. Substantial houses belonged also to two Aspull families recorded as freeholders there in medieval times. Traces of a sizeable hall-house of C15 date belonging to the Gidlows (7) – freeholders in 1291 – bear witness to their prosperity, as do the crucks of the hall of Kirklees nearby, residence of the Houghtons who are first recorded in 1317. In Pemberton, another subdivided manor, the house of the Molyneux family who owned the Hawkley estate was described as a 'capital messuage' with demesne lands in the 1580s (89).[13] In 1664-5, this family were able to trace a pedigree back to the time of Edward I[14] and at the same time many of the other sub-manorial lords were able to record similar, if not quite so protracted, ancestry.

This class of gentry had its parvenu members too. The Nelsons acquired the Fairhurst estate in Wrightington around 1536-40[15]; before building Fairhurst Hall (133) in the late C16, their home may have been the cruck-framed hall which is now the core of Bannister Farm (129). In 1664, the family returned both a short pedigree and a coat of arms.[16] These were essentials at the lower end of the gentry scale where the interface with the upper yeomanry was characterised by many pretenders to gentility.

GENTRY PROSPERITY: ITS SOURCES

Although an extensive fortified mansion of the Stanleys existed at Lathom House,[17] this was destroyed during the famous siege of the Civil War. Therefore the houses that remain from the late C16 and early C17 for us to deal with are those of the middle and minor gentry.

The size and quality of these structures indicate their builders must have enjoyed considerable wealth in order to have built on this scale. Among them a general hierarchy evolves with those of the manorial gentry being generally more substantial than those of their sub-manorial counterparts. A common factor uniting both classes exists however. All those who rebuilt in the late C16-early C17 were of freehold status (table 5). Although not all freeholders in Lancashire were gentry in the strictest terms, they were in an advantaged position and in the Douglas Valley, as elsewhere in the county, this form of tenure appears to have facilitated the building of substantial houses at a relatively early date.

Contemporary records can provide evidence of the degrees of prosperity existing within the gentry at this time. In the late C16 and early C17 various 'subsidies' (ie. taxes) were imposed upon the wealthiest members of society in each township. Men were assessed on the value of their land or goods, and taxed upon whichever category was the greatest source of their income. In the case of the gentry, it was usually their lands. A useful indicator is the 1593 Lay Subsidy, coming as it does in the middle of the gentry rebuilding period.[18] The considerable variations it contains reveal a land-owning hierarchy reflecting the polarity between the middle and minor gentry families (see table 5).

The manorial lords were by far the highest assessed, with Edward Standish paying the most at £20. This reflects his extensive landholdings, which in 1611 were described as 28 messuages, a watermill and more than 630 acres in Standish alone with acres in neighbouring townships as well as the manor of Bricksworth in Northampton;[19] in 1577 Standish was described as supposedly 'a man of 500 marks yearly revenue and worth £1,000 in substance.'[20] The other prominent families, the Bradshaighs, Gerards and Lathoms paid less at £17, £14 and £6 respectively. On his death in 1623, Thomas Lathom was found to hold 470 acres in Parbold alone, plus a fourth part of the manor of Wrightington and 300 acres there, plus land in Newburgh and the reversion of the manor of Allerton near Liverpool, with 520 acres.[21] Another substantial landowner, James Bankes of Winstanley held 1,288 acres in that township, Billinge and Orrell at his death in 1617 as well as lands in Pemberton and the manor of Houghton at Winwick, north of Warrington.[22] Bankes had not yet acquired Winstanley in 1593 so paid only £2.6s.8d on his Pemberton estate in the lay subsidy. As to the sub-manorial landowners, their less-extensive estates are indicated in the amounts levied under the subsidy. Only the Catteralls of Crooke in Shevington paid more than £1. Yet the lands some held were still considerable: In 1606, Thomas Gidlow of Aspull owned 280 acres in Aspull and Ince along with 20 messuages and the 'capital messuage' of Gidlow Hall.[23]

Some of these landowners had increased their estates or otherwise benefited in the second half of the C16 from the sale of monastic lands under Henry VIII. Until the Dissolution, religious institutions held land in several townships. The Knights of St John of the Hospital, an order dating back to the Crusades, were landowners in Standish, Dalton, Aspull, Shevington, Wrightington, Parbold and Blackrod. The

Priory of Burscough also held lands in Lathom and Dalton and the Priory of Upholland was also a landowner. In the wave of iconoclasm that accompanied the Dissolution, trafficking in monastic lands became a respectable pursuit, the results of which were highly profitable to gentry with an eye for speculation. Elsewhere in Lancashire, one who amassed a fortune in this way was John Bradyll of Whalley, esquire, who in his will of 1575 stated he rose by 'byinge and sellinge of lands that I bought of King Henry the Eight'.[24] Locally, several families also pursued this line of business. On his death in 1623, Thomas Lathom of Parbold Hall (88) owned 20 acres of land, five of meadow and 15 of pasture in Parbold, 'late belonging to the Chantry of Dugles (Douglas)... late dissolved.'[25] Ex-Hospitallers property was also owned by Thomas Gidlow of Gidlow Hall, Aspull (7) on his death in 1606: a messuage plus 12 acres and the watermill in Aspull. These were now held of the king, at a rent of 12d, but were worth 20s per annum.[26] Another family who appear to have reaped some benefit of these dealings are the Rigbys of Harrock Hall (134) in Wrightington, tenants of the Hospitallers since the C13 at least. A rental of around 1540 shows the family paid 5s 6d for Harrock. The Hospitallers' territories in Wrightington were sold by the Crown in 1546. In 1557, the Rigby lands, now held of the king and queen, carried a total rent of 1s 4d.[27] Whatever transactions had occurred, they were clearly to the Rigbys' advantage, something also testified to by their substantial hall built c1600.

In the same vein, Tudor England had also created other opportunities for wealth and advancement. A society which no longer embraced miltary prowess as a respectable and profitable pursuit discovered alternative occupations that offered equally-encouraging prospects by less bloody means. For many it was the law. Throughout Lancashire, several monumental houses were built upon fortunes gained from the rising legal profession, among them Gawthorpe at Padiham near Burnley and Clegg Hall, Milnrow near Rochdale. The most outstanding exponent of this was Sir Gilbert Gerard, eldest son of James Gerard of the Hall of Ince (54), attorney-general to Elizabeth I and later Master of the Rolls. Gerard was also comissioner for the sale of Crown lands, and so was the means by which those who dealt in these commodities rose to prosperity. His own acquisitions included not only territories in Lancashire but further afield. His achievements were an inspiration to other gentry families who realised that education and speculation held the secret to amassing greater wealth then that won by their warrior-landowner forebears upon the battlefield.

Meanwhile other gentry families acquired more limited wealth by less spectacular, more traditional, means, relying on income from their lands both from rents and produce. All the gentry were heavily involved in agriculture, either on a purely subsistence level or to supply a wider market in addition to their own needs. A few surviving agricultural buildings provide tangible evidence of this. The finest is the cruck barn at Harrock Hall, which at seven bays is the largest structure of its kind in Lancashire:[28] its timbers are of heavy scantling and felling dates between 1562 and 1568 have been ascertained through dendrochronology.[29] A shippon was added at right angles in the early C18. It is reasonable to assume the Rigbys would not have been alone in owning agricultural buildings of this substance, and equally that their superiors at manorial level may have built barns that were even larger. Unfortunately none remain. Two other sub-manorial houses possess substantial barns, that at Gidlow Hall, Aspull (7) is possibly of C16 origin,[30] and that at Allanson Hall, Adlington (2) dated 1682. Extensive buildings elsewhere are indicated by contemporary documents. The Parliamentary survey of Parbold Hall (88) in 1653 recorded one new barn, comprising 'one faire range of building and six bays' and one other barn of two bays, both built of stone and roofed with 'slate' (here meaning sandstone flags).[31] At Fairhurst Hall, Wrightington (133) an oxhouse, stable and mill were recorded in the inventory of Richard Nelson in 1619.[32]

Probate records shed a degree of light on the agricultural practices of the gentry. Those surviving from the families building or occupying the houses in the early C17 mention both livestock and crops. Primarily these may have been for the consumption of the immediate household, but in certain cases inordinately large numbers of these commodities may suggest production on a commercial basis. One that stands out is the inventory of Richard Nelson, who was clearly an agriculturalist on a large scale.

As we saw in Chapter I, Fairhurst, along with the halls of Parbold and Harrock, may have shared grazing land upon High Moor in Wrightington. Whatever the case, Nelson had a notably large herd of cattle, 50 in all, which suggests stock being reared for a wider market. In comparison, his social superior, James Bankes of Winstanley Hall (124) had 29 in 1617[33] and Nelson's neighbours (possible business partners?) Thomas Lathom at Parbold[34] and Nicholas Rigby at Harrock[35] had 34 in 1623 and 28 in 1629 respectively. The herds of other landowners put these into perspective. Thomas Worthington of Crawshaw had 17 head of cattle in 1626,[36] and Edward Worthington of Wrightington 11 in 1613,[37] the same number possessed by Thomas Sephton of Skelmersdale in 1646. The latter examples suggest herds kept for purely domestic needs.

Similar variations occur in the amount of crops recorded. James Bankes had the largest amount: £96.13s. 4d was the value of his 'corn growinge upon land' in 1617. Such an amount would suggest commercial activity, but it appears that around 1610 Bankes decided to grow only sufficient corn to meet the needs of his own household due to high labour costs.[38] The value of Richard Nelson's crops were considerably less, but again were higher than those of his counterparts elsewhere. In 1619 he owned 13 acres of oats (valued at £32) seven of barley (£20) and two of beans (£4) and further evidence of extensive arable involvement were his 'five yoke of oxen' needed to draw the ploughs. Nicholas Rigby's inventory records 10 acres of oats and two of barley (together worth £31) and seven acres of hay at £9. Smaller amounts elsewhere may reflect smaller households. Thomas Sefton in 1646 had oats valued at £9, corn, barley and wheat at £5 and wheat on the ground at £6; along with £5 of barley stored in the parlour chamber and 20 bushells of winnowed oats at £1.[39] Thomas Worthington of Crawshaw had £10 of corn and hay plus £3 in 'wheat growing'; Edward Worthington of Worthington just five-and-a-half acres of corn at £5 and half-an-acre of wheat at 50s. These inventories all bear out the dominance of oats in the crop system. Thomas Sefton's comparatively large amounts of wheat however are explained by his land being at the base of the Ashurst-Billinge ridge where the ground is better-drained and more fertile. Wheat is tellingly absent from the inventories of Nelson, Lathom and Rigby upon the hills on the opposite side of the valley.

The gentry were not merely agricultural landlords however. They were also industrialists: indirectly, by promoting the various tradesmen such as nailors, potters, blacksmiths and tanners who were among their tenants; and directly through an emerging new industry upon which all these specialists depended. Extensive coal measures lie within the sandstone formations that sculpt the landscape of the Douglas Valley and by the first half of the C16 they were being mined. At the forefront of this exploitation were the gentry who owned and worked most of the collieries around the Douglas Valley in the C16-C17: their opportunism helped not only to finance the building of fine houses but also laid the foundation of the industry for which the county would later become renowned.

Pl. 27
Profits from coal helped to finance the rebuilding of Haigh Hall in the early C17, where imposing bay windows dominated the structure. This view is of 1826, the year before the start of a long-running reconstruction.
(LCRO DP291/20)

Its beginnings however were a very fragmented affair. Before 1700, fewer than 20 collieries – mostly with short working lives – were in operation at any one time on the south-west Lancashire coalfield.[40] There were two concentrations: around Wigan and at Prescot, to the south-west and outside our area. Those around Wigan were grouped on the hills on both sides of the Douglas Valley and between 1590 and 1689 collieries were known to have existed at Pemberton, Winstanley, Orrell, Shevington, Haigh, Aspull, Blackrod and Adlington as well as within Wigan itself. The gentry profited considerably from the increasing demand for coal during the C16 and C17. Domestic heating and cooking probably represented the principal market, a considerable segment of which were the multi-hearthed houses of the gentry themselves. The Bankes family in 1679 took more than 47 tons from their pits for use at Winstanley Hall (124)[41] where 14 hearths were recorded in the 1664 Hearth Tax. This provides a yardstick by which the consumption of other gentry homes can be judged, ranging from Standish (103) and Haigh (52) halls – with 17 hearths each, the largest numbers assessed in 1664 – to those of Allanson (2) Blythe (62) and Ackhurst (84), with four hearths only in that year.

The domestic market however widened considerably during the C17 with the appearance of multi-hearthed houses of the yeomanry in widespread numbers. As we have seen already in Chapter 1, the Douglas Valley had almost twice the Lancashire average of houses with more than one hearth in the 1664 Hearth Tax (39.7% compared to 23%). This must have been a significant factor in the development of the embryonic coal industry. In addition, the industrial market was also expanding, both in the immediate locality and beyond. In 1601 the Gerard family of the Hall of Ince (54) supplied cannel coal from their Aspull colliery to tradesmen in Lancashire '& elsewhere'.[42] Several pockets of these industries had formed in and around the Douglas Valley by 1600 and flourished during the C17. Blacksmiths were probably the most numerous but there were other specialists. Nailmaking was quite widespread, taking place at Standish, Blackrod, Billinge and Winstanley; a particular concentration lay further east at Chowbent near Atherton. Pottery developed at Rainford and by 1600 glassmaking further west at Bickerstaffe. Wigan itself was a growing manufacturing town by the mid C16 and a further market was opened up in 1590 when embargoes on coal exports were lifted in Liverpool.

Coal was therefore a profitable business to be in and clearly it made a financial contribution to the gentry rebuilding. However, much earlier than this some were already renowned for the wealth obtained from mining. The Bradshaighs of Haigh Hall (52) had so distinguished themselves in this respect that the Tudor historian John Leyland in 1539 commented: 'Mr Bradshaw has discovered much cannel, a substance like sea cole on his land, and this has proved very profitable for him'.[43] Some of these profits would have helped finance the rebuilding of the hall in the early C17. Coal may have also contributed towards the rebuilding of Winstanley Hall (124), for James Bankes' grandson subsequently derived an income of £100 per annum from mines on his lands.[44] The Bispham family of nearby Bispham Hall (13) at Billinge were colliery-owners also.[45] Both of these houses were substantial, trendsetting structures which may have been made affordable by the results of their owners' mining activities. The presence of mining-related equipment in their inventories indicate a degree of involvement by other gentry families. 'Coal carts' occur in several: Edward Worthington of Worthington Hall (128) and Nicholas Rigby of Harrock (134) each had three; Richard Nelson of Fairhurst (133) and Thomas Lathom of Parbold (88) each had two. Nelson furthermore had a 'turner for a coal pit'. The fine houses built by all of these families testify that profits from coal played a key role in the gentry rebuilding.

At the same time, another industry for which Lancashire would become renowned was emerging elsewhere. Textiles, either directly or indirectly, helped in the same way as coal to finance the building of fine houses in the county's northeast, the area centred on Burnley and Colne.[46] In the inventories of the Douglas Valley gentry, as well as its yeomanry (see below, page 96), there is some evidence of similar domestic textile production but not enough to show that anything on a commercial scale existed. Equipment and cloth are recorded in the inventories of several minor gentry members. At Bogburn Hall, Coppull (29) John Haydock in 1620 had two looms plus three yards of grey russett cloth worth £3 and kersey wool (a coarse fabric) plus yarn totalling £3.2s.10d.[47] In 1633, John Blackledge of Blythe Hall in Lathom (62) owned two spinning wheels plus flax yarn and a web of cloth.[48] Thomas Lathom of Parbold in 1523 had no spinning wheels but an unusually large number of sheep – 58 in all – which suggests he may have provided the raw material to be spun elsewhere. Clearly textile manufacture was taking place in the area but on a distinctly more limited basis than in the county's northeast and therefore is unlikely to have achieved the same significance as a source of finance for the building of substantial houses.

In addition to agriculture and these embryo industries, finance for new homes may have been obtained from another source. Evidence of a seemingly complex network of financial dealings can be found in the inventories of the gentry. These are described under the terms 'debts', 'bonds' or 'specialties'. Debts would appear to be either money loaned or credit offered to an individual, bonds and specialties were investments designed to accumulate money through interest. The amounts involved were frequently considerable. Former goldsmith-banker James Bankes in 1617 had debts owning to him worth £293, 33% of the total value of his inventory (£866 12s 10d). In 1629 Nicholas Rigby of Harrock had £340 in bonds, 53% of the £638 5s 6d of his inventory. At a later date, and somewhat spectacularly, Thomas Bispham of

Bispham Hall, Billinge (12) had in 1678 £680 – 70% of his inventory total of £965 7s 6d – as 'debts owed by specialties'.[49] In his will, he states he has money at interest which was hoped to provide £300 apiece for his five younger children. Others had more complex arrangements. John Haydock of Bogburn Hall in 1623 was owed a total of £167 11s 5d (39% of his inventory total of £432 6s 2d), of which £98 15s 10d was by specialty, £1 1s 7d 'by note' and other debts totalling £54 14s 0d. Money appears to have been loaned to people of both greater and lesser standing. Of the £120 owed to Richard Nelson of Fairhurst in 1619, £50 was each owed by Thomas Lathom (of Parbold Hall) and Richard Halsall esquire of Croston, the rest by individuals whose names have no such ring of prominence. At the end of the day it is hard to say exactly what contribution these transactions made to the building plans of the gentry, but the profits raised would either directly or indirectly contributed to the degree of wealth which spawned their substantial houses.

THE GENTRY REBUILDING: TIMESCALE AND MECHANISM

The mechanism by which the gentry replaced their medieval houses was complex, involving several varied processes. In terms of timescale, the dates on the surviving houses (table 4) indicate a period of activity – beginning in the 1570s and complete by 1620 – which saw the construction of substantial new homes. This mirrors the building activity which was occurring elsewhere in Lancashire at that time. In the northeast of the county, the prodigious major gentry houses of Stonyhurst in the Ribble Valley (1590s)[50] and Gawthorpe, Padiham, near Burnley (1600-1605)[51] are the products of this phase along with several middle gentry homes in the Burnley area of similar or earlier date.[52] On the relatively disadvantaged coastal plain, the rebuilding there was led by houses such as Moor Hall, Aughton, of 1566,[53] Downholland Hall of c1600[54] and Carr House, Bretherton of 1613,[55] all houses of middle gentry status.

However it is possible that before these all-new homes appeared, preliminary improvements were made to pre-existing buildings as a prelude to the wider rebuilding movement. These stem from the fact that the open hall and its open hearth were obsolete by the middle of the C16. The new houses that appeared from the 1570s onward all had halls fitted with ceilings to provide a chamber above. However, the ceiling-in of open halls may already have begun before this time. Several former open halls have survived to show evidence of being ceiled in advance of improvements dating from the subsequent main stream phase of rebuilding. The cruck halls of Peel Hall, Ince (56), Kirklees Hall, Aspull (9) and Bannister Farm, Wrightington (129) each had ceilings inserted before their upper ends were rebuilt as crosswings in the late C16-early C17. The beams carrying the ceilings at Peel and Kirklees have roll-

Pl. 28
The insertion of a ceiling in the former open hall at Bannister House, Wrightington, was an event of such importance that the builder placed a shield and his initials upon the spine beam.

mouldings of the late C16, but that at Bannister is more intricately moulded in the manner of the mid-C16 and is remarkable for a plaque with the initials TN (possibly Thomas Nelson) again in the style of the mid to late C16 (plate 28). If we assume that all these families had taken the initiative to do away with their open hall by the 1570s, so too must have the others who then subsequently went on to build all-new houses at a later date. Another piece of evidence is found in the will of Roger Catterall (LRO WCW 1602) of Crooke Hall, Shevington (98) which refers to the 'chamber over the hall', indicating the latter was ceiled by 1602 – before the house was subsequently rebuilt in 1608.

A further significant step which probably occurred at the same time as the ceiling-in of the halls was the installation of chimneys in place of open hearths. At Kirklees the two processes clearly were simultaneous as the main beam carrying the inserted ceiling is supported on the stack at that end. Both this and Bannister are fitted with a type of stack which became in subsequent decades a distinguishing feature of the halls of the gentry. This was the lateral hearth, located on the rear wall of the hall which performed two subliminal roles other than the primary function of providing heat. Firstly its location emphasised the importance of the hall – and by inference that of the family also – and indicated that the upper and lower ends retained their

Pl. 29 Standish Hall at Standish, of around 1574, was the earliest timber-framed house of the gentry rebuilding and displayed elaborate decorative panels.
(Wigan Heritage Service)

Pl. 30 (below) Fragment of another fine early timber-framed building: Worthington Hall, Worthington, of 1577.

medieval functions. Secondly, its use for heating only denoted that the family were affluent enough to have a heated kitchen elsewhere to do the cooking. By contrast, yeomen did their cooking upon the hearth in the housebody, which was placed axially and therefore had to perform a dual role. An axial stack, for instance, was inserted at Peel, suggesting the house had declined from gentry to yeoman level by the late C16. Lateral hearths therefore were a status symbol, without which a gentry house would be incomplete – although there are cases where its use was mimicked by aspiring members of the yeomanry.

Compared to these improvements, a total rebuild was a more drastic course of action. To embark upon it required not only finance but security: yet several families in the 1570s took this route and paved a way for others to follow. Interestingly, the pioneers of this rebuilding were placed at various stages along the scale of the gentry heirarchy. It comes as no surprise that around 1574 Edward Standish, the area's foremost landowner, rebuilt his hall of Standish, now sadly demolished (102; plate 29). But the benchmark set by this family was quickly followed by a less prominent member of the middle gentry when in 1577 Edward Worthington rebuilt the manor house of the township (120; plate 30).

Though both these buildings helped to establish standards that subsequent houses would follow, both were notably conservative in retaining timber-framed construction despite stone houses emerging elsewhere in Lancashire at that time. It was left to a man of lesser standing – but far greater vision – to endorse the use of stone, the material which symbolises the aspirations of the rebuilding. Stone construction was pioneered by Thomas Gidlow, member of the family who had been freeholders in Aspull since the C13. The elaborate datestone upon their rebuilt C15 hall house (7, plate 31) shows this achievement came in 1574; around the same time as Edward Standish was still relying on timber, Gidlow showed himself to be way ahead of his conservative peers. Shortage of timber was not the reason: at his death in 1606 he still owned 20 acres of woodland. Reasons of prestige must underly Gidlow's choice to build in stone. His family were clearly prospering at the time – a coat of arms was granted in 1581[56] and Gidlow was appointed coroner of Wigan in 1586[57] – and he may have wished to symbolise their 'renaissance'. Under the influence perhaps of the fine stone houses beginning to appear elsewhere at this time, Gidlow must have realised that the use of this new and prestigious material considerably advanced the image of gentility – and enhanced the reality.

But despite this innovation, gentry houses continued to be built in timber until the second decade of the C17 at least. They included the substantial halls of Fairhurst (133) at Wrightington, Ince (also known as Peel Ditch, 55; plate 33) and Crooke at Shevington (98; plate 32) dated 1608 as well as additions to Bradley Hall, Langtree

(57) and Kirklees Hall, Aspull (9). Other timber-framed gentry halls which probably dated from this period – but all now demolished or subsequently rebuilt – were Adlington (1), Wrightington (145), and the Hall of Ince (54, plate 34). The latest use of this material at gentry level may be Ackhurst Hall, Orrell (84) probably 1616-18. But the future was written in stone: and in the 1590s a powerful group of houses appeared which became templates for not just this class but the homes of the yeomanry which were yet to come. Probably the first was Birchley Hall of 1594 (12; plate 36) home of the Anderton family who in themselves were long-established gentry but relatively new to this manor within Billinge. At their seat at Lostock Hall near Bolton, the main branch of the family had shown considerable foresight by constructing a stone gatehouse with early (albeit incorrect) classical details as early as 1563.[58] At Birchley, the use of the mellow local sandstone added a dignity and presence to the building that timber could never have achieved. With its tall, symmetrical five-gabled façade, Birchley is virtually an icon of the Elizabethan gentry house. The depth of the impression it created is evident in the way it was subsequently emulated. Probably its earliest imitator was Winstanley Hall, Winstanley (124; plate 25) where the grandeur of Birchley cannot have failed to impress James Bankes, who had acquired the manor a short time afterwards. With his London connections, Bankes would have been well aware of architectural progress and would have appreciated the advances Birchley had made. Bankes probably rebuilt the hall of Winstanley to celebrate his acquisition, creating what was essentially a larger version of Birchley and using stone – in the manner of Thomas Gidlow – to further the gentrification of his family.

Pl. 31
A far-sighted decision gave Gidlow Hall, Aspull, the distinction of being the area's first dated stone building. This drawing of 1826 shows in the foreground what appears to be a now-removed service wing at the N end. (LCRO DD290/34)

Pl. 32
More conservative families still opted for timber-frame construction. Crooke Hall, Shevington, was already outmoded when it appeared in 1608.
(Wigan Heritage Service)

Pl. 33
The township of Ince formerly had two timber-framed halls. Ince Hall (or Peel Ditch) presented a symmetrical five-gabled façade before its destruction by fire in the 1850s. This sketch by Will Lathom dates from the 1820s.
(LCRO DP 291/2)

Pl. 34
The Hall of Ince conversely presents a more rambling picture in this view.
(from Philips, 'Old Halls of Lancashire and Cheshire', drawn in 1822-24, pub. 1893.)

Among the established gentry, Birchley exerted a strong influence too. A virtual replica was built by the Bispham family, lords of another of the manors within Billinge, when they rebuilt their hall c1600 (13; plate 35). Further east at Haigh, the contracts for the rebuilding of the hall (52) in 1605-12[59] clearly indicate it was modelled upon Birchley: Roger Bradshaigh had married a member of the Anderton family. But independent of Birchley's influence, fine stone houses began to materialise elsewhere and the first decade of the C17 saw the appearance of the substantial halls of Harrock at Wrightington (134) Parbold, (88) Hawkley in Pemberton (89; plate 26) with evidence for a similar structure at Chisnall in Coppull (30). Singularly and collectively they confirmed that stone was the accepted material for houses of this class.

Despite being innovative in other respects, these homes were essentially updated versions of the hall-houses of the later medieval period. Although some, such as Standish Hall at Standish (102) and Bradley at Langtree (57) may have retained the courtyard plan inherited from an earlier phase, the majority of houses produced during the gentry rebuilding perpetuated the layout of a central hall flanked by one or more wings containing private of service rooms.

They fall into two basic categories. The first are 'all new' houses which were a complete rebuilding resulting in a homogeneous structure retaining little or nothing of its predecessor. Bispham Hall (13), Winstanley (124) and probably Birchley (12) fall into this type. Needless to say this was an ambitious and costly exercise possible only if extensive funds were available and perhaps justified only if the existing structure was beyond redemption. The second type are 'improved' houses where additions were made to medieval structures which were in part retained. This 'staggered rebuilding' took two forms: new halls added to pre-existing service wings and new wings added to pre-existing halls. As we have seen, the addition, subtraction and replacement of crosswings is a relatively common phenomenon in late medieval houses (such as the service wing added late C15-early C16 to Peel Hall, Ince, 56); wings are rarely of the same date as the halls to which they relate. It is somewhat surprising to find that some of the most substantial gentry halls of the period were grafted on to seemingly-inferior earlier remnants. Yet this was the case at Worthington (128) of 1577 and both Parbold (88) and Harrock (134) of around 1600. In all of these cases halls and upper wings were added to earlier service ends. At Worthington the evidence is a closed truss above the 1577 hall range where it meets the service end (the latter rebuilt c1700), thus implying replacement of a pre-1577 structure. At Harrock (figure 20) three doors in the screens passage denote the presence of a service wing yet the masonry shows the c1600 rebuilding did not extend beyond this point.[58] At Parbold the 1653 Parliamentary surveyors found the 'new building' added to an older range containing kitchen and buttery.[59] In the two latter examples it is almost certain that the older wings were timber-framed and visually therefore the uncomfortable marriage of these and the new stone edifices must have verged on the bizarre. Such incongruity may seem puzzling. But, as we will see, the emphasis in the rebuilding was upon increased domestic comfort and therefore the hall and upper

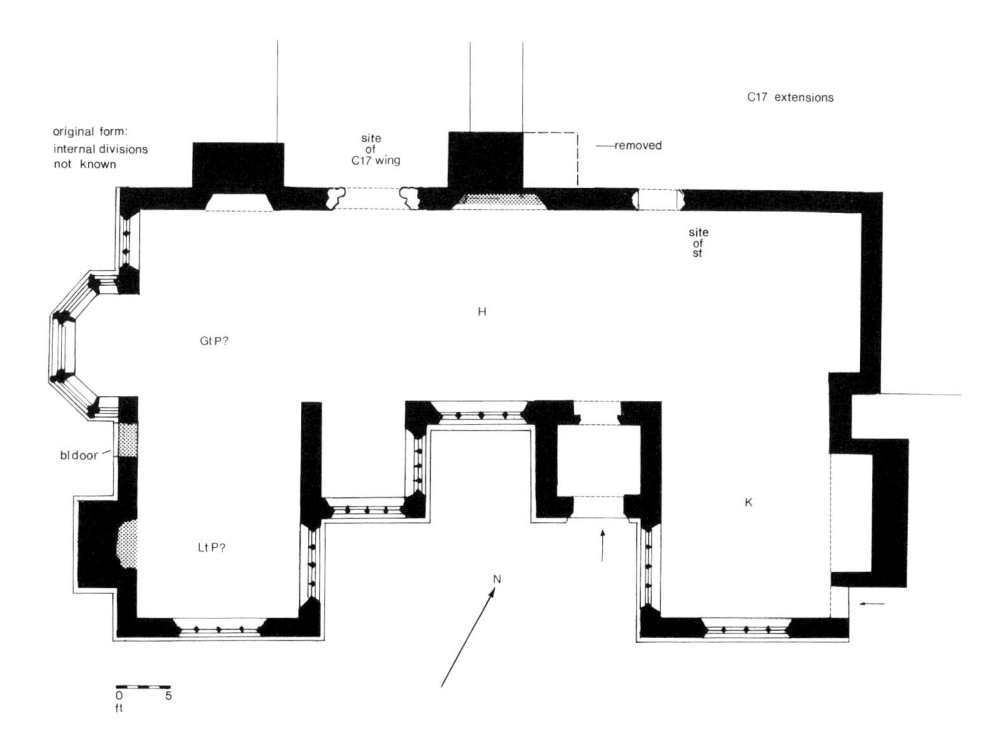

Fig. 19
Bispham Hall, ground floor plan.

Pl. 35 (below)
Strength, determination and clarity are all displayed by the façade of Bispham Hall, c.1600.

ends took priority. It is possible that these service ends were relatively new and in a reasonable condition. Yet, that at Parbold was 'very much ruinated and ready to fall down' when surveyed in 1653.

The same drive for domestic improvements generated the building of new upper wings onto pre-existing halls. Among the yeomanry this became common practice in the C17, where most of the houses upgraded in this way appear to have been cruck built. Gentry examples however are rare. The most obvious is Kirklees Hall, Aspull (9) where a sizeable timber-framed wing was added in the late C16 to the cruck hall which had probably been ceiled earlier. Nearby at Peel Hall, Ince (56) a short upper wing was similarly added to this cruck hall in the early C17, yet probably the building had fallen from gentry status by this time. This limited improvement, involving the retention of cruck halls which were already long-outmoded, is a form of conservatism which probably had its explanation in a lack of sufficient funds to finance a more comprehensive rebuilding.

PLANS AND APPEARANCE

These plans ultimately governed the external appearance of the houses but during the rebuilding there was an emerging consensus that this situation ought to be reversed. The essentially medieval plan of hall-and-crosswings tended to produce a building asymmetrical in appearance. This was because the screens passage entrance lay at one end of the hall, and the wings themselves may have been of differing date or size, or there may have been one wing only. Form in these buildings was therefore secondary to function. This is evident in the facades of Worthington Hall of 1577 (128) and Crooke Hall, Shevington (98) of 1608, where symmetry is impossible because of the off-centre entrance to the screens passage and Kirklees Hall, Aspull (9) because of the added wing.

However, there was an emerging trend in the late C16 for form to override function. This was the result of the first stirrings of the Renaissance in Lancashire, which expressed itself in the introduction of classically-inspired architectural details – as opposed to Gothic – and the desire for an ordered, symmetrical façade. The major gentry of Lancashire ushered this movement along, with classical decoration correctly applied at the gatehouse of Stonyhurst of the mid-1590s, and perfect symmetry in the façade of Gawthorpe, Padiham, built 1600-05 and also the smaller but nonetheless powerful Clegg Hall, Milnrow, near Rochdale, of c1610. At the same time, several members of the middle gentry gave an early endorsement to the classical trend with facades that were planned with almost total symmetry in mind. First to achieve this in the Douglas Valley was Birchley Hall at Billinge in 1594 (12), which balanced all

Pl. 36
Dated 1594, Birchley Hall acted as the template for innovative gentry houses of the period.
(Wigan Heritage Service)

its elements behind a five-gabled symmetrical front of a pattern adopted both locally and further afield in the late C16. The aim, on a smaller scale, was identical to that of Longleat, Burghley and Harwick: to symbolise wealth and power. The central hall was flanked by projecting wings of equal size with short projections in the inner angles, that at the lower end being the porch and the corresponding one marking the dais end of the hall. The entire composition, three storeys high, conveys resolution, strength and dignity. Shortly afterwards it served as the template for Winstanley Hall – essentially a larger version – and thereafter for Bispham Hall also (figure 19). Elsewhere in Lancashire the five-gabled façade found favour at other substantial gentry houses such as Hacking Hall of 1607 at Billington in the Ribble Valley[62] and Staley Hall, Stalybridge of the C16-C17.[63]

The evolving desire for symmetry was such that attempts were made where houses were only partially rebuilt. This is apparent at Harrock Hall, Wrightington (134; plate 37, figure 20) where a hall range and upper wing were added c1600 to a service wing retained from its predecessor. Central to the hall range is a fine full-height bay window with matching porches at either end: the lower accessing the screens passage, the upper (a C19 rebuilding but almost certainly a copy of the original) apparently offering independent access to the parlour wing. Of course the entire structure would have lacked overall balance by the disparity between the old and new builds, but the significance is that the Rigbys – one of the most prominent of the minor gentry families – had recognised and were emulating a concept already endorsed by their superiors.

Classical forms of decoration, by contrast, remained largely ignored. Instead, styles

Pl. 37
Despite being grafted on to an earlier service wing, Harrock Hall still achieved symmetry and strength in its appearance.

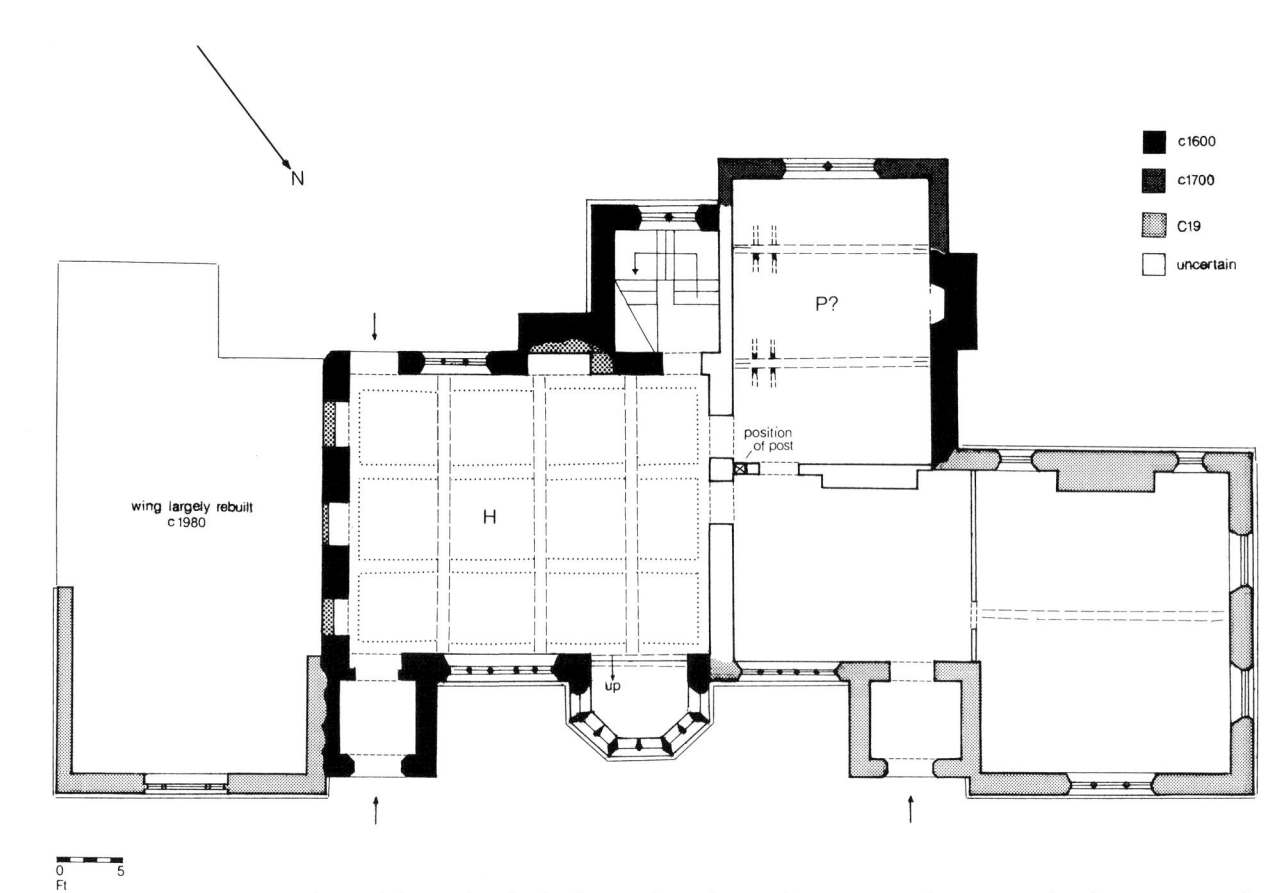

Fig. 20
Harrock Hall, ground floor plan.

derived from the final phase of Gothic architecture – the Perpendicular – persisted long, producing doorways with four-centred (or 'Tudor') arched heads and mullioned or mullioned-and-transomed windows with individual hoodmoulds above. A concession to the slow realisation of classicism comes c1600 in the appearance of a new type of doorway at the halls of Bispham (plate 35) and Harrock (plates 37,96). Here the entrance to the porch is in the form of a semicircular and upon moulded responds. This type clearly became synonymous with gentry houses as it had many imitators throughout the C17 and beyond among the Douglas Valley yeomen who obviously aspired to better things.

ROOMS AND THEIR FUNCTIONS

Behind these façades subtle changes were evolving to affect the way in which life in the household was ordered. The new gentry houses were well-provided with private rooms, reflecting the growing desire for this type of accommodation and the corresponding decline of a medieval lifestyle centred on the hall.

The hall however retained its traditional place physically – if no longer socially – as the centre of the building, and although no longer single storey remained the largest room of the household. At Bispham (13) the hall occupies an area some 30 feet in width and 18 feet in depth. At Parbold the width of the hall in the rebuilding of c1600 is uncertain, but it appears to have been notably deep at around 21 feet, suggesting an unusually large room overall. In 1653 the room was described as 'paved with smooth stone', indicating the floor was flagged as most other halls would have been. Furthermore, the west end of the hall was 'wainscotted'; that is, decorated with wooden panelling, which again would probably have been typical of other houses.[64]

From outside the hall was distinguished by having the biggest and best windows. Nowhere is this more apparent than at Harrock (134), where the Rigbys maximised the use of glass as a status symbol. Its hall, measuring some 30 feet wide by 22 feet deep, was lit not only by a grid of mullioned and transomed windows but also a full height bay window as an extravagant centrepiece (plate 37). But judging from the evidence of inventories, behind these dignified facades the halls appear as sparsely-furnished rooms probably reserved only for occasional use in receiving and entertaining guests, while the business of everyday life went on elsewhere. That at Bispham in 1678 contained merely three tables, a chest, a clock, a grate and four coats of arms. Fairhurst Hall, Wrightington in 1619 had a long boarded table and forms, a square table, three chairs and four stools. Sefton Hall, Skelmersdale in 1646 had similarly a long table and forms, a little folding table, chairs, stools and cushions. At Crooke Hall, Shevington (98), a table measuring 18ft x 3ft with a 1630s date inscribed upon it is also recorded.

Somewhat anachronistically, the screens passage plan appears to have been retained as the means of entering the hall from the exterior. A partition by the entrance at Gidlow Hall, Aspull (7) of 1574 suggests one existed formerly and the configuration of the trio of Birchley (12) Winstanley (124) and Bispham (13) halls leads one to suspect the porch led to a screens passage in each case. As we have already seen, Harrock (134) had three service doors at the lower end of the hall, implying a passage formerly existed (figure 21). Why this arrangement was perpetuated probably has just as much to do with the screens passage being regarded – like the lateral hearth – as a status symbol as its practical role as a division of the main household from the inferior service end.

But as a counterpoint, vast progress was being made in other areas of the houses through a proliferation of rooms for the private use of the family. These were sited upon not only the ground floor but also the first which – extending the tradition of the medieval solar – came to hold the principal private rooms and established first-floor living as a hallmark of progressive gentry lifestyle in the C17.

On the ground floor, the principal private room was the parlour, usually sited in the upper wing and frequently heated. Sizeable houses had more than one. In 1653 Parbold Hall (88) had no less than four: a 'greater' and a 'lesser' with a further one on the N side and an 'out' parlour in the old building to the W. The first two would appear to be the rooms in the present E wing. Bispham Hall (13) in 1678 had a 'great parlour' and a 'little parlour', the former probably the room to the rear of the wing illuminated by a superb bay window. Crawshaw Hall, Adlington (3) had an 'outer parlour' and a 'little parlour' in 1626; Ashurst Hall, Dalton (34) a parlour and little parlour in 1618.[63] Although only the 'new parlour' is referred to at Harrock in 1629, the name itself implies there was another, older one. In smaller houses a single parlour was the norm, as was the case at Sephton Hall, Skelmersdale (101) in 1646; and Langtree Hall, Langtree (59) in 1653.[64] Parlours were usually sited within the upper crosswing but an exception occurs at Bradley Hall, Langtree (57), where it occurs as a short projection forward of the upper end of the hall. A similar arrangement may have been the 'parlour at the upper end of the hall' at Worthington Hall, Worthington (128) in 1613.

At the beginning of the C17 the parlour had not yet assumed the role of sitting room with which it is associated today. Inventories of the time reveal it was put to several uses, but generally it functioned as a principal bedroom and remained as such throughout most of the century. Frequently too it had a dual role. The 'new parlour' at Parbold Hall in 1623 contained not only a feather bed and blankets etc, but also was used for storage, housing six stones of wool and ten of feathers! Both parlours at Crawshaw (3) functioned as bedrooms; but the little parlour also stored beef and bacon worth £3, and the outer parlour spinning wheels and feathers suggesting it – and possibly that at Parbold – had a role to play in textile production. Elsewhere, the room had already taken on a more refined role either as a dining room or a sitting room. At Fairhurst Hall, Wrightington (133) the parlour contained in 1619 not beds but a long table and forms, several other tables, stools and 22 cushions, suggesting it was used for dining. The Nelsons were a relatively 'new' gentry family so perhaps they were eager to show their sophistication by abandoning the parlour's traditional role for something more progressive. At Harrock, a square table, cupboard and iron grate in the 'new parlour' in 1629 implies its use for either sitting or eating. Later, in 1678, the well-furnished 'great parlour' at Bispham Hall (13) with its three tables, three carpets, 13 chairs, a child's chair, grate and coat of arms was clearly the sitting room as a specific dining room was recorded also. However the 'little parlour' was still a bedroom with its contents including a bedstead and a 'bed with furniture.' (ie, fittings).

But the most important floor in these buildings was the first – or chamber –- floor. The end of the open hall and the ability to construct multi-storeyed buildings had given an increased significance to their height – and as we have seen Birchley Hall (12) and its imitators made a great play of it. Consequently gentry families developed a taste for first-floor lifestyle which implied politeness and superiority. Furthermore, hospitality was an important element of gentry life and consequently their houses were equipped with a high number of private bedrooms and other apartments. Those of the major gentry were noted for their abundance of bedrooms: 24 were recorded in Rufford Old Hall in 1620, 28 at Lytham Hall in 1634.[67]

The quota belonging to middle and minor gentry families was more modest, but still considerable. Seven chambers used as bedrooms were recorded at Parbold Hall (88) in 1623, six at Fairhurst (133) in 1619 and five at Worthington (128) in 1613. The chamber floor was accessed from below via a main staircase normally sited at the upper end of the hall, which in many cases led to a first-floor gallery offering ease of access to all the rooms but also ensuring privacy for those within them. Such a gallery existed at Bispham Hall (13) and Billinge Hall, Billinge (11) and is referred to at Parbold and Langtree halls in 1653;[68] its existence at Standish Hall (102) is implied by the extensive 20-light mullioned windows running the entire length of the hall range at first-floor level (plate 29).

Frequently these chambers take their names from the room below – eg, parlour chamber, buttery chamber – but occasionally they are given names which indicate use by a specific member of the family. 'My Uncle Nelson his chamber' at Fairhurst Hall (133) in 1619 shows this was the private room of the late Richard Nelson, in whose inventory it is recorded. Similarly, 'Madam Bispham's chamber' is referred to at Bispham Hall in 1678; there was also a 'batchellors chamber', not in use as a bedroom, but implying accomodation for unmarried male guests. At Parbold (88) in 1653 there is reference to the 'Duke Chamber'[69] but this may be a corruption of the 'dark chamber' mentioned 30 years earlier in the inventory of Thomas Lathom. Sometimes the names give an indication of decoration – Bispham had a 'green chamber' and a 'little green chamber' in 1678. Whether this refers to furnishings or wall painting is unclear, but a 'painted chamber' is referred to at Bogburn Hall, Coppull (29) in 1621.

Chambers with uses other than private bedrooms are also found. During the C17 it became a refined gentry practise to dine at first-floor level. Therefore in 1623 we find a 'dining chamber' at Parbold Hall (88) containing a little table with carpet ('carpet' being a table covering at the time), two chairs, 12 stools and 12 cushions. In the 1653 survey of the hall, the dining room is located over the 'greater and lesser parlours' which indicates it was sited on the first floor of the upper (present E) wing. In the same year a dining room was recorded on the floor above the hall at Langtree Hall (59) and its presence here in one of the smaller manorial houses suggests first-floor dining must have been accepted practice among all levels of the gentry by this time.[70] At Bispham in 1678 the location of its dining room – with three tables and carpets, 18 chairs, a looking glass, eight pictures a grate and tongs – is not specified but its mention after the 'great staircase' tends to confirm it was on the first floor. The extent of the furnishings suggests the Bisphams were used to entertaining large numbers of guests.

Another private room whose location is generally unspecified, but one which might be assumed to be among the first floor apartments is the study. They are infrequent, recorded at Langtree in 1653, Harrock in 1629 and Bispham in 1678. The whereabouts of that at Langtree is precisely known, for 'a chamber over the parlour with a study in it' was itemised by the Parliamentary surveyors, showing it to be in the upper end of the building. The contents of the study at Bispham were a table, a carpet, a 'nest of boards', a desk, chair and 'books given as legacies to ye heire.'

At the other end of the scale were chambers with more mundane uses. Chambers for servants are sometimes recorded although these are unlikely to have been upon the same floor as the principal bedrooms and it is probable some servants slept in outbuildings.[71] At Parbold in 1623 (88) the 'servant chamber' is listed between the inner lower chamber and the buttery which implies it was part of the old (pre-1600 rebuilding) service wing which stood at the west end. It contained three pairs of bedsteads, two coverlets, one feather bed and one bolster, valued 13s. 4d. The smaller halls of Crawshaw and Sephton also had servants' chambers, the former with just one bed in 1623 and the latter with two pairs of bedstocks and one chaff bed in 1646. Again their position in the inventory suggests locations at the lower end of the buildings. Few gentry houses – unlike those of the yeomanry – used chambers for storage of food and husbandry equipment however, as these items were kept in outbuildings which, as we have seen, once existed. Where this does occur is at the lower end of the scale. At Sephton Hall in 1646, the parlour chamber doubled as a bedroom and for storage of barley and winnowed oats. Flaxen yarn and canvas yarn along with three cheeses were kept in the buttery chamber. Flax along with sacks, windowsheets and saddles were also stored in the dayhouse (dairy) chamber at Crawshaw Hall (3) in 1626, but this may of course have been an outbuilding. However the attics of some larger houses may have served as storage rooms. At Fairhurst Hall (134) in 1619, the 'higher height' (room in the attic) the contents were of notable variety: husbandry equipment, cooper timber, eight apple trees, two pack saddles; also a pair of bedstocks and a featherbed and bolster suggesting it may have housed servants as well as the odds and ends of everyday existence.

Similarly inferior in status were the service rooms at the lower end of the buildings. However their functions were still vital and several gentry houses appear to have been well-provided with them. All had a kitchen, which was usually heated and therefore relieved the hall fireplace of the burden (and social stigma) of cooking. At Bispham (13) and Fairhurst (133), the kitchens are denoted internally by wide stone hearths and externally by stacks of massive proportions. Another room invariably found is the buttery, for storage of drink. In gentry inventories it is usually listed along with other service rooms indicating it was positioned at the lower end of the houses; a distinction from yeoman homes where it was usually sited at the upper end close to the parlour (for closer supervision of its contents). Other rooms appear occasionally. 'Brewhouse' occurs at Harrock (134), Parbold (88), Fairhurst (133) and Crawshaw (13). Dairy or 'deyhouse' is mentioned at Fairhurst, Crawshaw and Parbold. Larders are found at Fairhurst and Worthington (128).

Not all of these rooms may have been present in the main building. Because of the attendant fire risk, kitchens in some medieval gentry houses are known to have been sited outside the main structure. This practice may have persisted into the C17, but it is known that at Martholme, Great Harwood, Sir Thomas Hesketh incorporated a formerly external timber-framed kitchen into the main building when in was remodelled in stone in 1561 and the trend for incorporation may have followed from there. Because of their nature, these structures may have frequently needed renewing and therefore, the service wings at Parbold (88) and Harrock (134) may not been incorporated into the rebuilt main structures because they may hve been relatively recent in date. However the fact that these wings were exempt from improvement not only indicates they were considered as inferior but also that they were in effect still being regarded as separate entities – a view which may have resulted from a physical detachment that previously existed. Possibly though, it was merely a case of the money not being able to stretch to rebuilding the service end. But where the desire for symmetrical facades was matched by the ability to pay for it, the result was that the service wing became an integral part of the buildings such as Birchley (12), Bispham (13) and Winstanley (124).

Pl. 38
Behind the tall façade of Bispham Hall, a well-furnished first floor dining room catered for entertaining on a large scale, with 18 chairs within it in 1678.

EPILOGUE: DECLINE OF THE GENTRY

To summarise, the half-century from 1570 to 1620 witnessed the building of substantial homes by the middle and minor gentry families throughout the area. Some took the form of all-new homogeneous structures while others were partially rebuilt and retained some part, usually the service wing, of the preceding building. All however are distinguished by having halls that were no longer open to the roof and emphasis on ample provision of chambers, parlours and other rooms for the private use of the family. The more progressive were built in stone while others retained timber-frame and the first impressions of the Renaissance are shown in the adoption of symmetrical facades from the 1590s onward.

Spectacular, innovative and aspirational as these homes were, they reflected a glory that was relatively short lived. Within this fluid society, families came and went and by the middle of the C18 many of the gentry who had built these fine houses had

Pl. 39
Chisnall Hall symbolises the decline of the gentry: an extensive stone manor house of c.1600 drastically cut down in size c.1800.

gone. The survival of the gentry depended upon two things: a male heir to succeed and intermarriage with other families to provide additional capital. When this did not happen, it signalled the end. Thus, the families of Worthington of Crawshaw, Anderton of Birchley, Bispham of Bispham and Chisnall of Chisnall all died out in the late C17 or C18 through lack of sons to continue the line.

The decline of others was hastened by their religious and political leanings. Most of the old established Lancashire gentry supported the Roman Catholic faith and were financially penalised for it. Convicted recusants were, for example, forced to pay double in the subsidy of 1628 and among those thus affected were the Andertons, Bisphams, Worthingtons of Worthington, Langtrees and Rigbys of Harrock. During the Civil War, the majority aligned with the king and consequently suffered under the retribution exacted by the Commonwealth authorities. They found themselves facing charges of treason, recusancy or deliquency and the confiscation of some or all of their estates. Some immediately lost all, or were dealt a blow from which they were never recovered. In 1652 the estates of Thomas Langtree were confiscated for recusancy and sold off – subsequently the family vanished from record.[72] Similarly those of Richard Lathom of Parbold, accused of treason, were ordered to be sold in the same year.[73] The family hung on, but under pressure of debts sold Parbold around 1680. Eleven years later another recusant family, the Billinges of Billinge Hall (11) disposed of their part of the manor of Billinge, having had the whole of their estates sequestered in 1652.[74]

Thus, the triumph of the provincial gentry was quickly eclipsed by their decline. Into their places in the C17 and C18 came families of differing origins and outlook. Many looked unkindly on the residences built by their predecessors and desired something more refined. Consequently some were lost, but others endured. Yet the vision shared by the Tudor gentry still lived on in another context: in the new generation of houses built by the yeomanry in imitation of an ideal symbolised by the homes of their superiors.

NOTES

1. J P Earwaker (ed) 'A list of the Freeholders in Lancashire in the year 1600'. RS, vol. 12, 1885.
2. J Gillow (ed) 'Lord Burghley's Map of Lancashire, 1590'. Catholic Record Society
3. Nigel Morgan, 'Enumerating the Gentry of Early-Modern Lancashire', unpublished TS, University of Central Lancashire, 1997, which cites: John Harland (ed) 'General Levy of Arms, Armour and Houses in Lancashire, 1574' in 'The Lancashire Lieutenancy under the Tudors and Stuarts', Chetham Society (OS, vol 49) 1849; 1588 Direction of the Earl of Derby that cost of a demilance should be shared (LCRO DDF 2440 f 118); William Farington's Book of the Lancashire Lay Subsidy 1593 (LCRO DDF 2430); 'List of Demilances 1632', Sir Gilbert Houghton's Lieutenancy Book (LCRO DDN/1/64)
4. VCH IV, p85
5. VCH IV, p97
6. VCH VI, p225
7. Joyce Bankes and Eric Kerridge (eds) 'The Early Records of the Bankes Family at Winstanley', Chetham Society 1973, p5.
8. VCH VI, p174. The Hospitallers lands in Harrock Hill, Parbold and Wrightington were sold by the crown in 1546.
9. VCH VI, p174
10. Private survey for Mr W Ainscough by Nigel Morgan and Garry Miller, 1990
11. J P Earwaker, "List of Freeholders in Lancashire in 1600", RS vol 12, 1885
12. VCH IV, p225-226
13. VCH IV, p81
14. Visitation of Lancashire by Sir William Dugdale, CS vol 65, p200-201
15. VCH VI, p175
16. 'Visitation...' CS vol 65, p216
17. Lancashire County Council Sites and Monuments Record, Lathom House 758/759
18. William Farington's Book of the Lancashire lay Subsidy, 1593 LCRO DDF 2430.
19. J Paul Rylands (ed) Lancashire Inquisitions, Stuart Period, part 1, RS (1880) p185-190
20. VCH IV, p195
21. Rylands, 'Inquisitions', part 3 (1890) p404-406
22. Rylands, 'Inquisitions', part 2, (1887) p97-99
23. Rylands, 'Inquisitions' part 1, (1880) p73
24. G J Piccope (ed) 'Lancashire and Cheshire Wills and Inventories', Chetham Society vol 51 (1860), p109
25. Rylands, 'Inquisitions' part 3 (1890) p 405
26. Rylands, 'Inquisitions', part 1, (1880) p74
27. VCH VI, p 173-174
28. Cruck barns of six bays are found at Duxbury Hall, Chorley, Rivington Hall, Rivington, Catforth Hall, Woodplumpton near Preston, and Hacking Hall, Billington.
29. Private report for Mr W Ainscough by Nigel Morgan and Garry Miller, 1990; dendrochronology by Pat Legatt.
30. Department of Culture, Media and Sport, list of buildings of special architectural or historic interest, Wigan MBC, Aspull parish.
31. PRO SP23/58
32. LCRO WCW 1619
33. LCRO WCW 1617; printed in Bankes and Kerridge 1973, p43-46.
34. LCRO WCW 1623
35. LCRO WCW 1629

36. LCRO WCW 1626
37. LCRO WCW 1613
38. Bankes and Kerridge, 1973, p7
39. LCRO WCW 1646
40. John Langton, 'Geographical Change and Industrial Revolution, Coalmining in South West Lancashire 1590-1799' (1979), p35-36
41. Langton, p46
42. Langton, p50
43. John Chandler, 'John Leyland's Itinery: Travels in Tudor England' (1993) p269
44. Bankes and Kerridge, 1993, P3
45. J J Bagley, 'The Will, Inventory and Accounts of Robert Walthew of Pemberton', RS vol 109 (1965), p117.
46. Sarah Pearson, 'Rural Houses of the Lancashire Pennines' RCHM 1985 p34-36.
47. LCRO WCW 1620
48. LCRO WCW 1633
49. LCRO WCW 1678
50. Nikolaus Pevsner, 'The Buildings of England', North Lancashire, 1969, p239-245.
51. Pevsner, North Lancashire, 1969, p128-129.
52. Pearson 'Rural Houses...' 1985 chapter 2, p38-57.
53. Department of Culture, Media and Sport, listed buildings West Lancashire district, Aughton parish.
54. Surveyed by Garry Miller, December 1987.
55. Surveyed by Garry Miller,
56. 'Visitation of Lancashire by Richard St George, 1613', CS, p50.
57. VCH IV, p121
58. Pevsner, North Lancashire, 1969, p148.
59. Donald Anderson 'Life and Times of Haigh Hall', 1991, p108/110.
60. The service end itself was C19, reconstructed c1980.
61. PRO SP23/58.
62. Pevsner, North Lancashire, 1969, p61.
63. English Heritage Register of Buildings at Risk 1998, Greater Manchester, Tameside District, p35.
64. PRO SP 23/58.
65. Inventory of William Ashurst, LCRO WCW 1618.
66. Parliamentary survey of Langtree estates; Porteus, History of Standish, 1927, p148-149.
67. O Ashmore, 'Household Inventories of the Lancashire Gentry, 1550-1700' Transactions of the Historical Society of Lancashire and Cheshire vol 110, p61. Quoted in Pearson, 1985, p52.
68. Parliamentary survey of Langtree estates; quoted in Porteus, 1927, p148-9.
69. PRO SP 23/58.
70. Porteus, 1927, p148-9.
71. Pearson 1985, p55 for instances of servants' chambers in gentry outbuildings in the Burnley area.
72. VCH IV, p198.
73. VCH VI, p179-180.
74. VCH IV, p86.

CHAPTER IV

Houses of the Yeomanry 1600–1720

By 1600 the ability to build substantial houses was no longer a gentry prerogative. From this time on, fine houses – modelled on those of their peers – were being built by the wealthiest members of the yeomanry. Thus began what became a mainstream force in rural society: reshaping the appearance of the countryside, and the lifestyle of its inhabitants.

The yeoman rebuilding stands without parallels as the most powerful statement of the new and prosperous post-feudal society. It is the first 'building boom' to have left tangible evidence – the earliest surviving homes built by ordinary men. It was not something to be embarked upon lightly. Yet, hundreds of yeoman families in the Douglas Valley – along with their counterparts throughout England – felt the compulsion to go through this expensive and disruptive process.

At yeoman level the rebuilding was a more complex and drawn-out phenomenon than that experienced by the gentry. Among the less-affluent, limited resources meant considerable number of houses experienced a rebuilding that was staggered over a number of generations. A revealing contemporary picture of the complexities involved is given in the autobiography of schoolmaster Adam Martindale (1623-1686) whose father was a yeoman farmer at Moss Bank near St Helens, just outside our area. He wrote: *'The particular place of my birth was at the High Heyes, by Mossbanke, in that prettie neat habitation called then the new house (in opposition to the old one then standing), which father first built and annexed to his new barn, from which in time, when the whole tenement was his owne, he removed to the old house, pulling down the inner walls, floores and chimnies, of the new one, and laying it to the barne to furnishe him with more storage for his corne. And in the process of time he, together with my brother Thomas, pulled downe the old house ..... And built that strong and large stone house that now stands in its place.'* [1]

What comes across foremost in this is the determination for constant improvement which is only assuaged when the goal of the 'strong and large stone house' is finally achieved – the implication being that both the 'old' and 'new' predecessors were timber-framed, possibly of cruck construction. The result was that Martindale's father was engaged in three separate acts of rebuilding – which have parallels elsewhere in the staggered improvement of other homes, as we shall see. Another implication is that the provision of a new house did not necessarily mean the destruction of the old – here, as possibly elsewhere, both dwellings continued side-by-side for a time at least. Eventually the 'new' house was demoted to a barn and again this may have been a common practice. Elsewhere the reference to the 'old house' in inventories such as William Darbyshire of Crow Nest Farm, Billinge (14; LCRO WCW 1641) and Roger Rigby, possibly of Rigby House, Adlington (4; LCRO WCW 1676) suggests the earlier house was allowed to remain. Physical evidence of this appear to survive at North Tunley, Wrightington (137). The stable wing of the barn has heavy crucks with chamfered blades which may too have had a domestic origin, as the predecessor of the fine brick house built c1620. Possibly other examples occur but, as North Tunley shows, the extent of the alterations makes precise analysis difficult.

The cumulative effect of all this upheaval was far beyond that of merely increased domestic comfort: it was the beginning of a transition to a modern way of life. During the C17 homes of essentially medieval plan were gradually replaced by ones radically redesigned to cater for a more progressive, restructured household. The rebuilding therefore was the conduit through which the yeomen finally emerged into the modern world and shook off the medieval legacy of their ancestors.

THE YEOMEN: EMERGENCE AND HIERARCHY

By the end of the C16, the yeomen had arisen from medieval obscurity to become one of the most dynamic strata in the new capitalist society that evolved out of the decline of feudalism. Beneath the gentry they were its most important group: but although more numerous than their peers they still represented a small and privileged niche. In Upholland for example, out of 109 persons listed by occupation in the 1653 survey, just 15 (13.7%) were named as 'yeoman'. The largest group were 'husbandmen', 47 in all (43.1%).[2] A further three are named as 'gentlemen' but in reality these were most likely wealthy yeomen of the highest order.

In the Douglas Valley area, more than 100 houses of non-gentry status have survived or have been recorded. However, their distribution (maps 8 and 9) is uneven, even allowing for destruction in modern times of early buildings in the built-up area around Wigan (such as Walthew House, (90), at Pemberton and The Meadows, (123). This suggests a variance in the numbers of yeomen between the townships. An explanation may be found in the landowning hierarchy. It has been suggested that

Pl. 40
Urban growth in the Wigan area resulted in several early buildings being demolished, such as The Meadows, Wigan, dated 1689.
(Wigan Heritage Service)

feudal society broke down at varying rates in the five hundreds of Lancashire, accounting for why some have apparently more yeomen than others.[3] Some of the townships with the fewest yeoman houses are those dominated by a single manorial family – in particular, Standish, Haigh, Parbold, Worthington, Winstanley and Langtree. The freeholders list of 1600 (map 7) shows that other than the lords, relatively few freeholders existed. In Standish, Worthington and Langtree there were none at all. Therefore this suggests a society still feudal in nature in these townships, with a predominant lord at the apex controlling a wide base of dependent tenants with few or no freemen to form an intermediate level: and consequently, few houses of any substance other than the manor house.

However those townships which display comparatively large numbers of surviving yeoman houses display a differing landholding pattern. Maps 8 (p98) and 9 (p103) show a concentration of non-gentry houses in the townships of Upholland, Dalton and Wrightington. In the case of Wrightington, the manor had from an early date been divided into four parts, some of which were changing hands in the C16, under a number of smaller lords. Possibly a more open society had evolved as a result, allowing the rise of minor landowners who developed into the yeomanry. Dalton too had been similarly divided, only coming into the hands of a sole controlling family, the Ashursts, around 1600. The case of Upholland however is different: this manor had been held by the Earls of Derby since 1489 as a reward for Thomas Stanley's

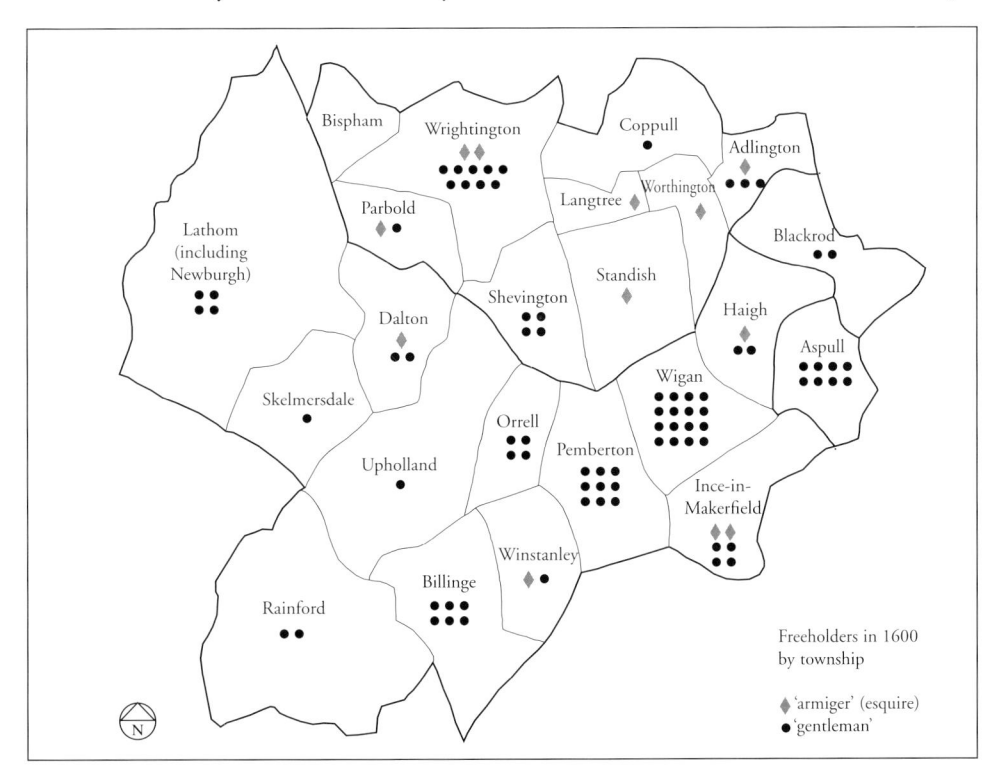

Map 7
Freeholders in 1600.

Township	House	Family	Status	Tenure	1593 Lay Subsidy G=goods L=lands	Date of House	Building Material	No. of hearths 1664	Remarks
Billinge	Crow's Nest	Darbyshire	yeoman	leasehold	–	1635	stone	4	Range and upper wing; stair turret; demolished 1960s-70s
Dalton	Holland's House	Holland	yeoman	freehold	G£5.00	c1605	timber-frame	4	Range and parlour wing; stair tower; clad in stone c1700
Rainford	Guild Hall	Naylor	yeoman	freehold	G£3.00	1629	brick	3	Range and parlour wing; porch and additions 1688
Shevington	Club House Farm	Prescott	yeoman	?	G£9.00	c1600-1625	timber-frame	3	Range and parlour wing; clad in stone 1663 (?)
Standish	Giant's Hall	Lathom	yeoman	copyhold	–	c1600-1625	timber-frame	1	Range and parlour wing; clad in stone 1675
Upholland	Halliwell's Farm	Brownlow	yeoman/gent	freehold	–	c1649?	stone	6	Parlour wing added to ? timber-framed range; porch added 1671; rebuilt C18
Upholland	Johnson's Farm	Naylor	yeoman	copyhold	–	1647	stone	4	Parlour wing added to open hall, ceiled C16-C17, rebuilt later C17
Wrightington	North Tunley	Rigby	yeoman	freehold	–	c1620	brick	3	Range and parlour wing; later outshut
Wrightington	South Tunley	Wilson	yeoman/gent	freehold	L£1.00	1622	timber-frame	4	Range, parlour and service wings; latter clad in brick 1667
Upholland	Dean House	Naylor	yeoman	copyhold	-	pre-1650	stone	5	? Range added to pre-existing wing

Table 5
Analysis of documented early yeoman houses, 1600-1650.

support of Henry VII at Bosworth. The fact that this family were non-resident probably encouraged the growth of smaller landowners. In the early C17 this was a thriving community with 14 freeholders, 37 copyholders and 72 tenants-at-will (leaseholders) recorded in 1605[4]: in the early 1630s a notably high number of leases were granted by the Stanleys, possibly to boost their income in times of need.[5] These circumstances probably accounted for the 'great number of freeholders and considerable yeomen' that the area was renowned for in the 1640s.[6]

The houses of the yeomanry present clear evidence of the prosperity enjoyed by this class in the C17 and early C18. Examined individually, they suggest a considerable variation in wealth between the various strata which must have influenced the ability to rebuild. By the end of the C16 the wealth of certain sections of the yeomanry was already apparent. Evidence comes in the Lay Subsidy of 1593, in which the wealthiest members of each township were taxed on either their lands or their goods, whichever was of greatest value.[7] As we have seen in Chapter III, the gentry were generally assessed on lands, and in the area as a whole 44 people were taxed in this way. But a total of 32 were assessed on goods and it is these non-landed families who can be seen as the wealthiest of the emergent yeoman and those most likely to be the first to rebuild. Several can in fact be identified with surviving early houses, as table 5 shows. Some enjoyed wealth on a similar scale as members of the minor gentry (table 5). When one considers the lowest assessment was £1, the amounts paid by the Hollands of Dalton (£5), the Naylors of Rainford (£5) and the Prescotts of Shevington (£9) puts into context a prosperity that eventually expressed itself in buildings of high quality.

It is these more prosperous families which were the first to rebuild, with others following suit later. Analysis of the earliest documented yeoman homes (table 5) shows the largest group of owners were freeholders. Within the yeoman hierarchy the freeholders represented the elite, but numerically were few. In the 1600 list, 90 freeholders were recorded in the area, of which 27 were gentry of middle or minor status. The remaining 63 can be interpreted as belonging to the upper yeomanry. However the list may not have been complete: some may have slipped through the net. None of the house-building yeoman families in table 5 are recorded in the 1600 list and, as we have seen already, Upholland – where just one freeholder is named in 1600 – had 14 five years later.

Although the freeholders emerge at the forefront of the rebuilding, it was not their exclusive right. Early homes were also being built by families whose tenure was copyhold or leasehold. Copyholders were particularly well-placed as they enjoyed virtually the same benefits as freeholders: security of tenure, the right to inherit and ancient rents made purely nominal by inflation. The appearance of early houses such as Giants Hall, Standish (102) and Dean House Farm, Upholland (111) along with improvements to Johnson's Farm, Upholland (117) is testimony to their position at the vanguard of the movement. Leaseholders, who may have made up the majority of the less-affluent yeomen, were by comparison at a disadvantage, but this did not preclude them from rebuilding. Although the terms were discretionary, the policy that existed among the lords was generally one of 'fair play' with the idea that reasonable terms would allow the tenant to improve their lands. Once the comparatively steep entry fine was overcome, the granting of leases on a term of lives granted a period of security in which investment in new homes could be made. Crow Nest Farm, Billinge (14) and probably Balcony Farm, Upholland (107) show wealthy leaseholders were able to do this at an early date. Later in the C17 the appearance of many smaller leasehold houses such as Lower Tower Hill, Upholland (119) of 1684 and Jump's Farm, Lathom (65) of 1690 demonstrates that the rebuilding was not beyond men of quite modest standing.

AGRICULTURE AND OTHER INCOME

Whatever their tenure, most yeomen were principally farmers. Agriculture was the foundation of their wealth and even those who described themselves as 'gentlemen' were accustomed to rolling up their sleeves and performing manual labour as a matter of course. Probate records show their wealth lay principally in cattle and to a lesser degree in crops. These are frequently the most valuable items listed, but the amounts show considerable variation among the yeoman hierarchy. Some wealthy freeholders kept herds larger than those of the minor gentry. This suggests cattle being reared not only for subsistence but commercial reasons as well. Richard Holland of Holland's

Pl. 41
Balcony Farm, Upholland, of around 1600, was built in an area of the township that was predominantly leasehold and shows that those who held lands in this way could afford to rebuild at an early date.

House, Dalton (43) had 29 cattle valued at £47 16s 0d in 1668,[8] William Naylor of Guild Hall, Rainford (91) 28, worth £57 13s, in 1628[9] and Robert Walthew of Walthew House, Pemberton (90) had 30, worth £80, in 1676.[10] At the other end of the scale, smaller herds were probably for the household only, such as the seven cattle worth £18 owned by Robert Stannanought of Stannanought, Dalton (47) in 1729[11] and the eleven worth £13, that belonged to Robert Holland, possibly of Lower House, Dalton (44) in 1681.[12]

A similar variation occurs in the amount of crops. Generally the inventories list principally oats and barley although wheat is occasionally mentioned. Richard Holland of Holland's House owned oats and barley worth £21 3s 0d and wheat £14 and William Naylor of Guild Hall barley, oats and peas worth £34, amounts which suggest they were being grown for a wider market. By comparison, subsistence use only is suggested by the £4 of wheat and £3 10s 0d of corn and hay owned by Robert Holland and the £2 6s 0d of corn which was Thomas Ayscough's of Jump's Farm, Lathom (65) in 1672.[13]

The presence of sizeable barns is a physical indication of farming on a large and possibly commercial scale. Like the houses, these were initially timber-framed but subsequently of stone or brick. One of the earliest and most extensive is that at North Tunley (137) Wrightington, a farmstead occupied by the Rigby family in the C17. It consists of a five-bay barn of cruck and post-and-truss construction and a stable which began life as a physically separate two-bay cruck building (which, as we have noted on page 88, may once have been domestic). North Tunley was one of the farms which collaborated in a medieval arable enclosure upon Harrock Hill (see Chapter I, p23) which was clearly the foundation of some prosperity for the Rigbys as theirs is one of the finest yeoman barns in Lancashire. These substantial barns combined several functions of the farmstead under a single roof. Such a 'combination' barn exists at Club House Farm, Shevington (97), built in stone in 1660. The inventory of its builder, yeoman Seth Prescott, records barn, shippon, stable and smithy, all of which were probably sited within. But even more modest yeomen equipped themselves with reasonable barns. At Lower Tower Hill, Upholland (119) the Hooten family built a combination barn which, although using a cruck framework, had used stone walls and incorporated a stable and shippon. That built by the Darbyshire family at Smith's Farm, Dalton (46) in 1689 was decidedly superior to the house.

Smith's is one example of how certain yeoman gave priority to investment in their barns before their homes.[14] Some were among the more wealthy. At Club House Farm, Shevington, the barn was built in stone in 1660 some three years before the house – a post-and-truss structure of the early C17 – was clad in the same material. Similarly at Halliwell's Farm, Upholland (115) the stone barn of 1663 pre-dates by eight years an improvement of the house in 1671. In both these cases, superior domestic accommodation was already being provided as the houses had already experienced some rebuilding. But elsewhere, yeomen living in far poorer dwellings still chose to invest first in their barns rather than their homes. At Dalton both the Scotts of Belle Vue Farm (37) and the Stannanoughts of Stannanought (47) were taxed on single-hearth – ie, probably cruck-framed – structures in 1664. The Scotts built stone barns in 1680 before erecting a fine new house three years later. At Stannanought, the time-lapse is more pronounced. The barn is dated 1690; the house – less ostentatious than Belle Vue and noticeably conservative – 1714, and occurring at the tail-end of the rebuilding. Therefore, the family would have endured relatively primitive conditions for a long period and lay in the shadow of their neighbours' achievements. Possibly these yeomen put their barns first because they hoped that investment in their business would eventually finance an improvement in living standards. As we can see however, this result was more quickly achieved in some cases than others.

Pl. 42
Club House Farm, Shevington, originally an early C17 timber-framed building, was clad in stone in c1663, some three years after the Prescott family constructed a large stone barn on the farmstead. Pictured c.1900.
(Miss Hilton)

Agriculture was not the only means by which yeomen acquired or consolidated wealth. Some, probably the more wealthy, pursued the financial dealings practised by the gentry, with loans or investments. These men would have acted as informal bankers, lending money at interest to their neighbours, perhaps to finance a major investment such as acquisition of land, or rebuilding a house. But the minor amounts also revealed in probate inventories indicates money also being borrowed for less substantial purposes. For those who had the means to practise it, the rewards from money lending could be great. The chief exponent was Robert Walthew of Walthew House, Pemberton (90) whose great-grandfather was a blacksmith: initially an agriculturalist, money-lending became his principal business and brought an income which put him on the same standing as the area's gentry. On his death in 1676 Walthew had no less than £2,750 out on loan to 120 clients, the amounts ranging from mere shillings to £164.[15] This was four times greater than the total value of the goods recorded in his inventory (£591 18s 3d). With so many people beholden to him, Walthew must have exerted great influence in the locality. His activities not only financed a substantial house but also the fledgling grammar school in Upholland. The rise of Walthew parallels, on a lower social plane, that of James Bankes and Sir Gilbert Gerard who demonstrated great proficiency in their exploitation of the new capitalist economy as a means to unprecedented power and wealth.

In comparison, the financial dealings of other yeomen are decidedly modest. William Naylor of Guild Hall, Rainford (91) had £74 in specialities in 1628, 16% of his inventory total of £464 18s 0d. John Naylor of Johnson's Farm, Upholland (117) was owed £20 in 1675, 19% of the total value of his inventory of £101 00s 6d.[16] Yet although the amounts were relatively small, in some cases their cumulative totals represented a considerable proportion of their wealth. At his death in 1621, the yeoman Peter Fisher of Shevington, freeholder and father of Henry who went on to build Douglas Bank Farm, Upholland (14) had 43% (£46 18s 0d) of his inventory total of £105 18s 0d accounted for by money owed by seven individuals.[17]

Walthew was also among those who speculated in real estate. The buying, selling or sub-letting of land offered another means by which wealthy yeomen might boost their position. Copyhold land in particular offered scope for considerable profit due to the ridiculously-low annual rents. Robert Walthew used land deals to finance his money lending, drawing at least £100 per year from lands he held in Pemberton, Orrell and Upholland.[18] Walthew was among those who had profited from the downfall of others in the post-Civil War retribution exacted by the Commonwealth authorities. Between 1653 and 1655 he acquired the copyhold estate in Upholland that formerly belonged to royalist William Prescott, swamped with debt as a result of financing insurrections against the Commonwealth including the failed rebellion of 1651 which led to the execution of James, Earl of Derby. Most of the land in turn was sold on in 1667 to four yeomen including Lawrence Halliwell of Halliwell's Farm (115) and John Naylor of Johnson's Farm (117) who clearly also practised this sideline.[19] The ruination of the recusant Langtree family, lords of that manor, also proved advantageous to the opportunistic. In 1644 part of Thomas Langtree's estate was sequestered for recusancy and let out to farm; the 1653 survey of the manor found Langtree Hall was let to Roger Haydock, yeoman, of Bogburn Hall, Coppull (29) at a rent of £56 10s but was said to be worth almost double.[20] In 1663, Haydock – a member of the Quaker freeholding family who appear to have declined from minor gentry to yeoman status by this time – rebuilt their hall at Bogburn and the Langtree transaction may directly or indirectly have helped to finance this improvement.

In other cases, yeomen were primarily industrialists, with income from trades surpassing what could be obtained from the land. Occupations such as tanning were highly profitable for some as indicated by the inventory of William Darbyshire of Crow Nest Farm, Billinge (14; LCRO WCW 1719) where the most valuable items were not livestock or crops but 184 hides at £120 6s 10d. Another branch of this family were also involved in textiles (see below, page 94). The prosperity of the Walthew family of Walthew House, Pemberton (90) although later consolidated by Robert's financial dealings, was founded upon an ancestor who had been a blacksmith. Others such as Richard Prescott of Coppull (probably Holt Farm, 33) spread their net far and wide over several business interests. The rebuilding itself was a potential source of profit for Prescott for he ran an extensive brickmaking operation with 'forrtie thousande of Bricks' along with ten thousand more 'in the Brick Kyll' (kiln) recorded in his will and inventory (LCRO WCW 1631). Among Prescott's other interests was coal. The fact that three carts are recorded in his inventory, along with coal and cannel worth 25s 8d, makes commercial mining seem highly likely. for Coal provided attractive prospects not only the gentry, for as we have already seen, the terms of copyhold in Upholland and possibly other manors allowed yeomen to sell off coal and other materials found on their lands. This would have been extremely advantageous in areas where the seams lay close to the surface. Consequently, the presence of 'coal carts' in probate inventories of men of varying status indicates they may have been directly involved in mining, either alone or in partnership with others: these range from wealthy freeholders and copyholders such as Richard Holland of Holland's House, Dalton (43) in 1668 and John Naylor of Johnson's Farm, Upholland (117) in 1675 to modest leaseholders such as William Ayscough of Jump's Farm in Lathom (65) in 1708. Other yeomen appear to have benefited indirectly from the extensive operations of gentry families who realised the potential of coal. In the will of William Darbyshire of Smith's Farm, Dalton (46) dated 1715, he states he is 'entitled to a certain part of the profits of coals yet remaining ungotten within the lands I lately exchanged with Sir William Gerard of Garswood.'[21] Out of this he expected to pay his four younger children the considerable sum of £20 apiece. This suggests Darbyshire, who held copyhold and leasehold estates not only in Dalton but elsewhere including Bickerstaffe and Ashton (presumably Ashton-in-Makerfield, where the coals most likely were) had profited from coal already mined and this may

Pl. 43 (above left) An arrangement over profits from coal mining may have financed the rebuilding of Smith's Farm, Dalton, home of the Darbyshire yeoman family.

Fig. 22 (above) Smith's Farm: plan.

have financed the staggered rebuilding of the house which took place from the late C17 to the early C18. It is unlikely he was alone in transactions such as this and similar arrangements with coal-masters may have contributed to the affluence of many other yeomen.

Another embryonic Lancashire industry – textiles – also engaged the attention of the yeomanry. For some it was a sideline, for others the principal occupation. Where the latter was the case, an idea of the prosperity that resulted can be gained from Darbyshire House, Billinge (15), built by linen webster Thomas Darbyshire (d.1718). This prodigious building (plate 56) was the first in which all aspects of classical plan and decoration were correctly combined. Unfortunately no inventory survives to indicate the extent of Darbyshire's business, which was probably located on the extensive attic floor. But elsewhere inventories give an indication of other families' level of involvement. Where households had one spinning wheel, this suggests their use was purely domestic, but larger numbers may indicate a degree of commercial activity. Judging by the Darbyshire House example, it may be no coincidence that these multiple-wheel houses are among some of the finest. Both Richard Naylor of Dean House, Upholland (111) in 1647[22] and Henry Fisher of Douglas Bank Farm, also Upholland (114) in 1692[23] had three spinning wheels. At the latter house, they were stored in the chamber over the kitchen, which was inaccessible from the rest of the chamber floor. The isolation of this room suggests people other than Fisher's family may have been employed to do the work.

An unspecified number of spinning wheels were also owned by Oliver Halliwell of Copyhold Farm, Wrightington (131) in 1668[24] and John Naylor, of Johnson's Farm, Upholland (117) in 1675. This was another of Richard Prescott of Coppull's activities, for substantial amounts of the raw material of the industry appear in his inventory: five stones of flax worth 12s and 6d along with yarn worth 40s 8d and cloth 30s. The finished products are represented by 40 pairs of sheets valued at a total of £35 9s 8d. Similarly, Richard Naylor of Dean House had considerable quantities of white and grey yarn, worth 33s 4d, kersey wool worth 30s, white cloth worth 30s also and linen worth 12d. Although no spinning wheels are recorded in his inventory (which is incomplete) Roger Rigby of Adlington in 1676 owned 29 pounds of flax worth £1 and wool valued at 14s.[25] Indisputable evidence that a family was heavily involved in textiles occurs when rooms set aside for this specific purpose are found. This was the case at the house of Robert Billinge (possibly Billinge Hall, 11) where his inventory (LCRO WCW 1729) records the presence of a 'shop' containing a pair of looms. Although textiles formed a lesser part of the local economy than in other areas of Lancashire, for example around Burnley, they nevertheless made some financial contribution to the construction of fine houses.

YEOMAN HOUSES PRIOR TO THE REBUILDING

The rebuilding has left us with the earliest surviving homes of families beneath the level of the gentry, many of whom had probably never before been able to build on a substantial basis. However evidence exists that some of the more prosperous yeomanry occupied superior homes prior to the C17. As we have seen in Chapter II, open halls of non-gentry status existed from possibly the early C16 at Dam House, Langtree (58) and Holt Farm, Coppull (33; plate 19). A further open hall at Johnson's Farm, Upholland (117) was occupied by the yeoman Naylor family in the early C17, this one possibly being of aisled form and therefore earlier and more prestigious. More fragmentary evidence of a substantial predecessor to Prior Wood Hall, Dalton (45; plate 60) comes in the form of moulded re-used timbers of the C15 or early C16.

But in contrast the majority of the yeomanry are likely to have occupied structures that were distinctly more down to earth. This is strongly supported by the 23 non-gentry houses that contain either full crucks or some re-used element of them. The dominance of these structures is further indicated by the hearth tax returns which show a majority of single-hearth structures in most townships (see map 4). Furthermore it shows a number of families who later went on to build sizeable houses occupied single-hearth homes prior to that time. The Scotts of Belle Vue Farm, (37; plate 49), the Stannanoughts of Stannanought Farm (47) both in Dalton, the Hootens of Lower Tower Hill in Upholland (119; plate 50) and the Ayscoughs of Jump's Farm in Lathom (65) were all taxed on one hearth only in 1664. The quality of these houses would have showed great variation. The best are probably represented by those at Worthington Manor House (126) and Black Lawyers, also Worthington (125; plate 12) which as Chapter II has suggested, may have been late medieval homes of wealthy tenants who were forerunners of the yeomanry. The other extremity is at Lower House, Dalton (44; plate 15) where the trusses are far poorer and probably date from the declining years of this method of building.

When the yeomanry came to rebuild, it began with the wealthiest and percolated downwards through the various strata of its hierarchy. Before new houses were constructed, initial improvements were probably made in the late C16 - early C17 by inserting floors in open halls, as happened in houses of the gentry. This is suggested by the ceiling inserted in the hall at Johnson's Farm, Upholland (117) and that in the cruck-framed housebody of Harsnips, Dalton (42). From around 1600 however the first new homes of the yeomanry appear and thus began a cycle of activity which continued until around 1720. However a closer examination reveals two distinct periods: an initial phase from 1600 to 1650 which involved only the most wealthy, and a more widespread rebuilding from 1650 through to 1720 which represented the movement at its height.

THE YEOMAN REBUILDING: PHASE 1, 1600-1650

Relatively few could afford to rebuild before 1650: map 8 shows just 28 houses belonging to this period. Where documentary evidence exists, many are shown to be the homes of freeholders (table 5) showing this privileged section of the yeomanry were first to afford this considerable expense. But several homes belonging to copyholders are found also, indicating they were not far behind, if at all.

The rebuilding closely copied the precedents set by the gentry. It took two forms: construction of 'new' houses and improvement of older ones by the addition of wings. Map 8 shows that the former are slightly more numerous – nine compared to eight – if one excludes the houses whose original form is uncertain, although these make up the largest group. The 'new' houses are all large, substantial structures which clearly denote they belong to men of substance. The fact that some of these men bordered upon gentry status is proclaimed by the way in which the houses emulate those of their superiors. Consequently, Balcony Farm, Upholland (107; plate 41) of around 1600, Holland's House, Dalton (43) possibly of c1605, North Tunley, Wrightington

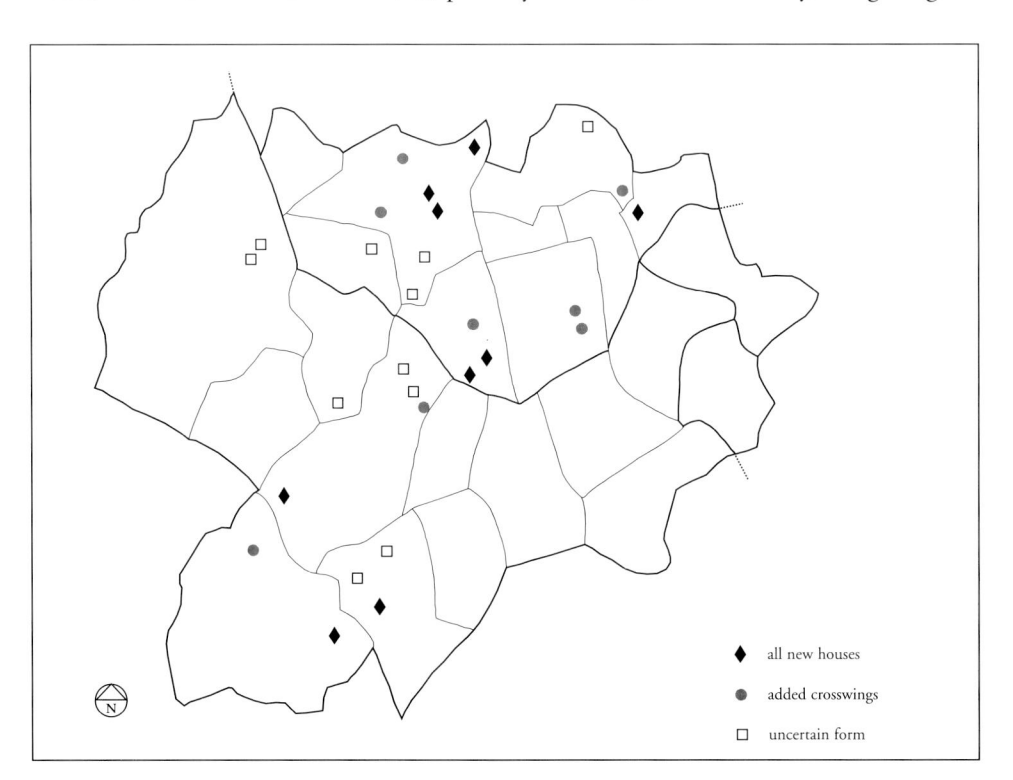

Map 8
Pre-1650 houses of the yeaomanry.

(137; plate 11) possibly of c1620 and Guild Hall, Rainford (91; plate 44) of 1629 are all manor houses in miniature.

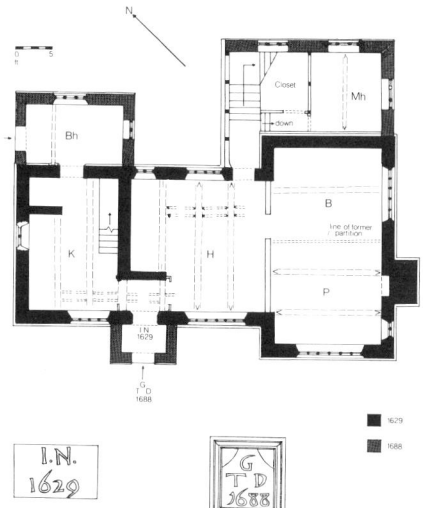

Fig. 22 (above) Guild Hall plan.

Pl. 44 (above left) A manor house in miniature: Guild Hall, Rainford, was built by the freeholding Naylor family in 1629 and extended in 1688.

The similarity extended within to the rooms and their functions. All these houses are based around the medieval plan of a hall with upper and lower ends, resulting in a three-unit layout which became standard for houses of the major yeomanry in the period before 1650. Although the functions were similar, the yeoman referred to the hall as the 'housebody' or 'firehouse', the latter deriving from its medieval origins as the only heated room. A crucial physical difference though was that the majority of yeoman houses did not have a screens passage or a lateral chimney stack on the rear wall of the housebody. This was because, as noted already, the yeoman hearth had a dual function – heating and cooking. The yeoman housebody was a more workaday room than the gentry hall which was a reception room only, a heated kitchen elsewhere performing the menial function of cooking. Yeoman hearths are consequently found not on the rear wall of the housebody but on the main axis against the entrance. The hearth and its massive stack occupied the space where the screens passage would formerly have been sited. Inside the front door there was a small lobby formed by the side wall (spere) of the fireplace. This arrangement is termed a 'lobby entry' or 'baffle entry' plan.

However two of the earliest and largest yeoman houses do not conform to this. Both Balcony Farm, Upholland (107) and Great Houghwood, Billinge (18) have housebodies with lateral stacks and therefore probably also had through-passages. We

99

Pl. 45
A number of early yeoman houses were rebuilt only partially by adding new cross wings to earlier, presumably open, halls. This example is at Sanderson House, Wrightington.

can infer two things from this. Firstly that their builders were wealthy, aspired to gentry status and used this plan to further their claim. Secondly, that they also had heated kitchens in which to cook. However the latter is impossible to physically confirm as the service end at Great Houghwood has been demolished and that at Balcony is a C18 replacement of something earlier, possibly pre-rebuilding. Both these buildings are unusual also in respect of this service provision. Although gentry houses such as Birchley Hall, Billinge (12) and Winstanley Hall, (124) had service wings with heated kitchens, the yeomen had no need of them when cooking took place in the housebody. As a result, yeoman kitchens (used for preparing food and storage) are therefore usually an unheated single-bay continuation of the main range and rather than a lower wing although examples of these do occur occasionally (below, page 104).

In contrast, the yeomanry placed great emphasis on their parlours. Frequently therefore we find them sited within prominent crosswings. The fact that some were heated is also underlined by the use of an external stack, often of massive proportions, for all to see and presumably envy. The parlour usually shares the crosswing with a buttery, used for storage of drink. This is another significant departure from the gentry precedent, as there the buttery was located in the service wing. Among the yeomanry however, limited space and a desire to keep its contents under supervision explains its elevation to the superior end of the building.

These early yeoman houses also borrowed the more fanciful elements introduced by the gentry in an attempt to win prestige. Typical of this are porches and stair towers. Porches played a major part in emphasising the height and power of facades such as Birchley and the desire for a similar effect at yeoman level is seen at North Tunley (137). Stair towers too played a similarly emphatic role and are also displayed by North Tunley, Holland House (43) at Dalton, Balcony Farm (107) at Upholland, and Rigby House Farm(4) at Adlington.

Clearly improvements on this scale were an expensive business. Table 5 (page 90) shows that many of the documented early houses were the homes of freeholders: testimony to their prosperity of this group as they clearly had the necessary substantial funds at their disposal. But where funds were more limited then the rebuilding was restricted accordingly and therefore a number of houses show evidence of partial improvement. This usually takes the form of the addition of a crosswing at the upper end, copying gentry practice as illustrated by Kirklees Hall at Aspull (9). Nevertheless, some of these are important houses. The most notable is Johnson's Farm, Upholland (117) home of the Naylor family whose stone wing of 1647 was added to an open hall of possible aisled form and of C16 date at least. This must therefore once have been one of the most prestigious buildings in a township with no resident lord. At Holt

Farm, Coppull (33) another open hall of post-and-truss form was upgraded by the addition of a fine timber-framed wing of early C17 date. At Bannister Farm, Wrightington (129) a new stone wing was added to a cruck hall possibly once of sub-manorial rank, and further north in that township Sanderson House (138) has a wing and stair turret appended to a now-vanished hall range probably of post-and-truss construction. Smaller added wings occur at Upper Standish Wood Fold, Standish (104) and Maggot's Nook, Rainford (93). As always there are exceptions to the rule, and a reversal of this pattern occurs at Dean House, Upholland (111) where a new pre-1650 range appears to have been added to a now-vanished wing.

An important aspect of this first phase of the yeoman rebuilding is the decline and abandonment of timber-frame and its replacement by stone and brick. Some of the earliest houses – and some of the finest – were of post-and-truss construction. Holland's House, Dalton (43) of c1605, and Giant's Hall (102) and Upper Wood Fold (104) at Standish, fall into this category. But at the same time, others were appearing in stone. They include Balcony Farm at Upholland (107) and Great Houghwood at Billinge (18), both of which set a precedent at yeoman level that others would follow. Certainly post-and-truss construction continued during the first quarter of the C17. The latest dated timber-framed house is South Tunley, Wrightington of 1622 (139; plate 22), which suggests this method of construction ceased not long after this time. From this decade on we see the emergence of brick, which in areas where stone was scarce became the natural successor to timber. Possibly the earliest brick-built yeoman's house is North Tunley, Wrightington (137; plate 11) which may be of around 1620. A more definite use occurs in 1629, the date of Guild Hall, Rainford (91; plate 44) which also incorporates fragments of an earlier timber-

Pl. 46
Giant's Hall, Standish is a post-and-truss yeoman house of the early C17 clad in stone in 1675; thus it is one of a number of homes to experience staggered rebuilding.

framed building. Brick was relatively untried in the area at that time, having been little used by the gentry, so a certain amount of novelty and prestige must have been attached to its use.

Thereafter, the 1630s probably saw the gradual decline of rebuilding activity as political unrest erupted into the Civil War which during the next decade caused extensive disruption in south west Lancashire. Amid the hostilities, Lathom House (66) was beseiged and destroyed in 1644-45 and the Earl of Derby executed at Bolton in 1651. As the diarist Adam Martindale, resident in Upholland in the 1640s, put it: *'The great trade that my father and two of my bretheren had long driven was quite dead. For who would build or repair a house when he could not sleep a night in it with quiet or safety.'* [26] But despite a petition protesting at the extreme poverty of the Wigan area in 1649[27] some yeomen were evidently sufficiently unaffected to be able to afford to rebuild. The 1647 datestone at Johnson's Farm, Upholland (117) bears witness to this as does a datestone of 1649 discovered at Halliwell's Farm (115) in the same township. In nearby Pemberton wealthy Robert Walthew was said to have built the now-demolished Walthew House (90) around 1650.[28] From this time on, the pace of rebuilding quickens notably suggesting that the war was not an insurmountable handicap to the yeomanry's desires to rebuild. Furthermore, the war may have been of direct benefit to some yeomanry as some may have chosen to purchase their estates during the Commonwealth sell-off of Derby properties following the Earl's execution. A number of houses with 1650s datestones in Upholland, a manor owned by the Stanleys, may be the result of this occurence.

THE YEOMAN REBUILDING: PHASE TWO, 1650-1720

After 1650 the rebuilding ceased to be the prerogative of the wealthiest freeholders and copyholders. From this time on smaller houses began to appear which suggests those of more modest status were able to follow suit. The result was a building boom which lasted, with varying intensity, through to the second decade of the C18. Although not a strictly scientific analysis, the datestones that survive from this time illustrate the growing momentum with its peaks in the 1670s and 1680s and from 1700-1720 (table 6).

The dramatic results of this activity can be seen in map 9, which shows a substantial increase on those built from 1600-1650 (map 8). The geographical distribution is much wider, but with the emphasis on the western townships. Fewer remain in the east around Wigan where C19 and C20 urban growth is likely to have eradicated many earlier buildings. But the highest concentrations occur in the township of Dalton and Upholland, where few freeholders were recorded in 1600 and consequently few pre-

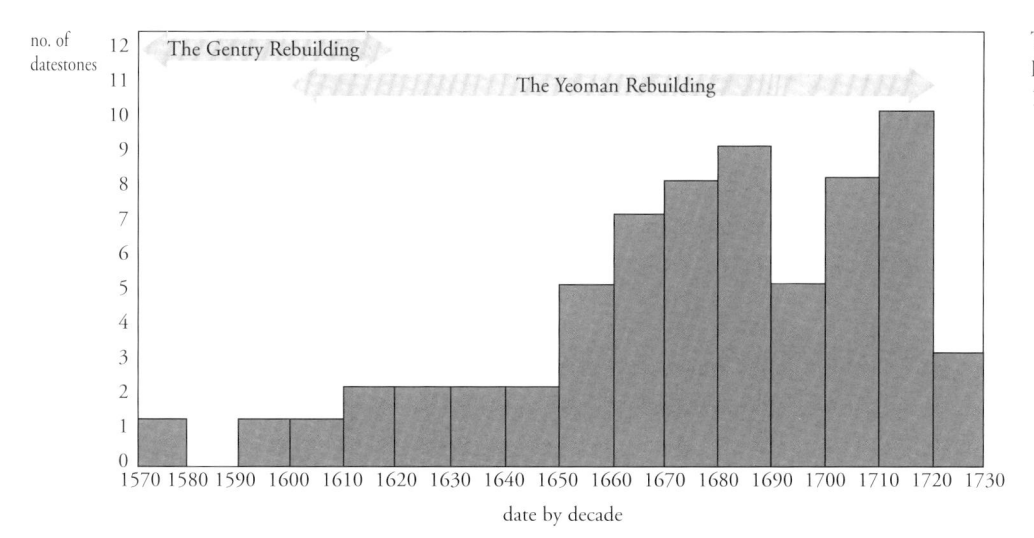

Table 6
Frequency of datestones, 1570-1730.

1650 houses exist. But the proliferation of post-1650 homes indicates these townships were dominated by a thriving yeomanry based largely upon copyholders and leaseholders of middling and minor status who were now in a position to rebuild.

As a result, the second phase of rebuilding is considerably more complicated than the first, although it continued the basic trends established earlier. Analysis of map 9 shows the majority of homes (about 52%) were those rebuilt in their entirety. A smaller number (about 19%) were partially rebuilt with the addition of crosswings. But another

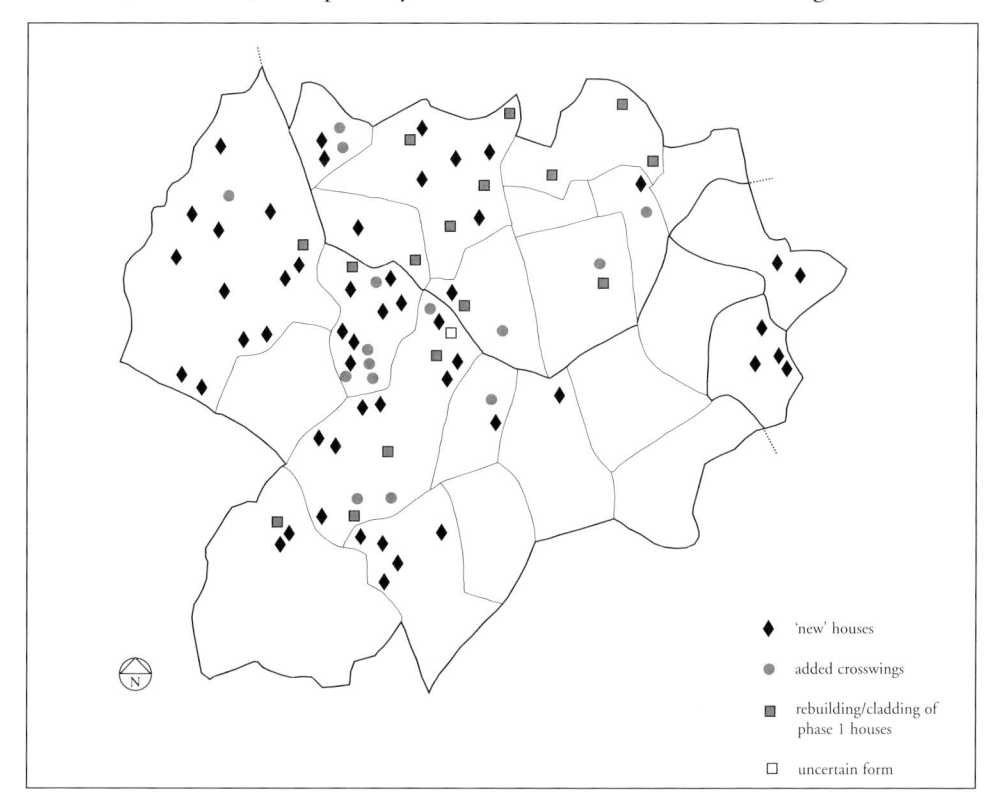

Map 9
Yeoman houses 1650-1720.

103

significant category emerges: the 20% which involve cladding of earlier (phase one) houses built initially in timber-frame. These statistics indicate the majority of these lesser yeomen found the resources to rebuild their houses in one go. But equally significant is the fact that others found sufficient money within the space of a generation or so to effectively rebuild twice. It all points to the widespread availability of the considerable capital required to finance these far-reaching domestic improvements.

Among the all-new houses, we initially see the continuation of the substantial three-unit crosswing type established prior to the Civil War by the freeholders as the pattern for the homes of successful yeomen. Overall though they are few in number compared to the profusion of minor dwellings which appeared. This suggests that most of the wealthy yeomanry had already rebuilt prior to 1650. Superior homes that do occur may consequently be a result of rebuilding postponed due to the Civil War, or where owners had profited from the sale of confiscated Royalist lands. Undoubtedly the finest of these large houses is that of Henry Fisher at Upholland of 1656 (114; plate 47). Douglas Bank Farm is a physical rendition of the aspirations and achievements of the flourishing yeomanry, rivalling – if not surpassing – some of the homes of the minor gentry. The scale of Douglas Bank is indicated by the fact it has both both upper and lower wings, something which, as we have noted, is rare at yeoman level. The other symbols of gentrification are there also, in the form of a porch, coupled to the lower wing, and a stair tower. Four hearths were recorded in 1664, denoting a high standard of comfort as well as the ability to pay for it. A close rival to Douglas Bank is Copyhold Farm, Wrightington of 1659 (131; plate 48) built by schoolmaster Oliver Halliwell. A six-hearth structure initially, this however has no service wing but instead an outshut to the rear of the kitchen. Considerable time then elapses before

Pl. 47 (below right) Douglas Bank Farm, Upholland, a miniature version of a gentry house. Built by Henry Fisher and his wife Margaret in 1656, symbolises the aspirations of the yeoman rebuilding.

Fig. 23
Douglas Bank Farm: plan.

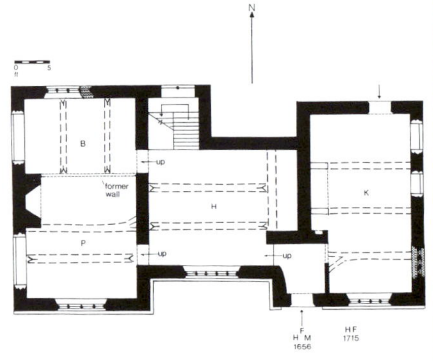

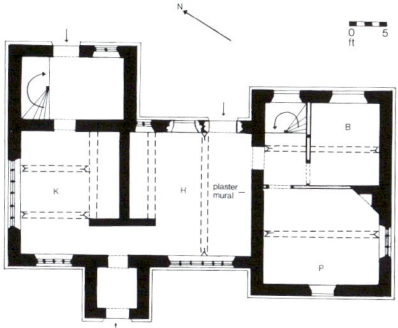

Fig. 24 (above)
Copyhold: plan.

Pl. 48 (above left)
Six hearths at Copyhold Farm, Wrightington, indicate a high standard of comfort within. An extensive plaster mural in the housebody (plates 121,122) also indicates the affluent lifestyle of schoolmaster Oliver Halliwell.

the appearance of other houses of similar scale, two impressive and almost identical buildings both in Dalton. Probably the earliest is Prior's Wood Hall, (45) c1680 (the datestone is illegible), possibly replacing a substantial timber-framed building, as some re-used moulded timber suggests. It probably inspired the building in 1683 of the now-ruinous Belle Vue Farm (37; plate 49) previously called Scott's Fold after the yeoman family of that name. The building it replaced however was certainly not as substantial as the Priors Wood predecessor, probably being cruck-framed to judge from of the single hearth recorded in 1664 and a roof truss containing re-used cruck blades (plate 81).

To progress to this extent, the Scotts must have been one of Dalton's rising families. But viewed against the background of the many smaller and inferior houses already appearing, their house – the last dated example of the substantial three-unit crosswing type — seems awkwardly belated, indicating a family crossing the rebuilding threshold many paces behind their social equals. These smaller houses began to appear in some numbers in the 1660s and make up the bulk of the rebuilding activity from then onwards. A minority are still of three-unit form, but with the notable exception of the crosswing. The result was a building of simple rectangular shape such as Lower Wrennall of 1673 (136) and Cowling's Farm of 1677 (132) both at Wrightington, and the extremely late example of Bentham's Farm at Dalton (38) of 1718. Possibly the now-derelict Lyme Tree House at Billinge (20) was of this type also. Without the benefit of the parlour wing, the accommodation at the upper end is considerably more economical. At Lower Wrennall this bay is

Pl. 49
Belle Vue Farm, Dalton, was a belated three-unit crosswing house dated 1683. This view is of c1900; now it is in ruins. (Author's collection)

Pl. 50
Lower Tower Hill, Upholland, a 1684 rebuilding of a cruck-framed house, is typical of the homes of the minor yeomanry appearing later in the C17.

subdivided to create a small parlour and buttery. Although scarce in the Douglas Valley, houses of this form are more widespread upon the Lancashire coastal plain – where the hall-and-crosswings type is scarce – and can be interpreted as a direct translation into stone or brick of the basic plan inherited from three-unit houses of cruck construction (see Chapter II, pages 42-43).

The commonest type of small yeoman's house consisted of two units only. They dispensed with the service bay – unneccesary as cooking took place in the housebody – and comprised only the latter and an upper end, subdivided into parlour and buttery. In these houses the firehood was sited at the end gable and the entrance opened against the spere to create an end-baffle-entry. Two of the earliest examples were Carr Lane Farm, Upholland (110) of 1660, and Butterfly Hall, Aspull (5) of the same year (both now demolished). But even among these diminutive houses parlour wings were greatly aspired to, showing the significance attatched to them even among yeomen of modest means. Wings occur at both Carr Lane and Butterfly Hall, Charity Farm, Wrightington (130); and, at Lathom, Jump's Farm, (65) of 1690 and Taylor's Farm (70), although in the last two examples, kitchens were added later.

Others made a pretence of having a parlour wing where in fact there was none. Both Heyes Farm, Upholland (116) and Cicely's Cottage, Dalton (39) are rectangular structures where the roof over the parlour end is treated in the manner of a gable at right angles to the rest. Elsewhere, other attempts were made to embellish relatively modest structures. Porches were used at Butterfly Hall and also at Webster's Farm (73) of 1682 and Aspinwall's Farm (61) both at Lathom. Again these illustrate that even in the late C17 the influence of the gentry houses of a century earlier was still being felt.

Where resources were more limited, partial improvement took the form of the addition of a parlour wing. During this phase of the rebuilding the practice is more widespread, with 13 surviving examples recorded, four of which form a cluster at Elmer's Green at Dalton (map 9). Of the 13, five are wings added to cruck-framed halls: Harsnips (42) and Lower House (44; plate 15) in Dalton, Manor House (126) at Worthington, Bounty Farm (109) and Lower Tower Hill of 1684 (119; plate 50) at Upholland. Re-used cruck blades within the added wing at Smith's Farm, Dalton (46; plate 43) also suggest its original range was cruck-framed. Although there are wealthier precedents, the strong inference therefore is that this method of improvement was practised by less affluent yeomen. The fact that many of these houses were cruck-framed and that the wings themselves are sometimes quite minimalistic in nature tends to confirm this. The cluster at Elmer's Green suggests this area must have been only of marginal prosperity at this time.

The dates on many of these wings show they were built during the 1670s and 80s during the busiest decades of the yeoman rebuilding. The earliest dated example is

Manor House, Worthington, 1671; the latest certain example Lower Tower Hill, Upholland, 1684.[29] The eclectic combination that resulted in many cases verged on the bizarre – as shown by the reconstruction based on Smith's Farm, Dalton (figure 25). It is no surprise therefore to find the main ranges were subsequently rebuilt. This took the form of either a straightforward cladding as at Manor House or Lower Tower Hill, or a radical reconstruction. But the latter created the problem of how to visually integrate the wing into the new building. Generally, this was ignored. The result, because of changing architectural styles during the time that had elapsed, is usually incongruence to a shocking degree. This is typified by the example of Eccles House, Bispham (25), where a new, classically-influenced range of c1710-1720 sits most awkwardly alongside a late C17 crosswing. Others made a little more effort. At Yew Tree House, Dalton (51, plate 51) the wing of 1679 was balanced with one built at the opposite end of the new 1710 range in attempt to court the new fashion for symmetry. This house exemplifies what was probably the case elsewhere, in that the rebuilding was something undertaken when a new generation succeeded. At Yew Tree, the wing of 1679 was built by John Crane, yeoman, at the upper end of what was probably a cruck-framed range. He died in 1709, and the datestone of 1710 upon the rebuilt range shows his son Thomas wasted little time in upgrading the accommodation.

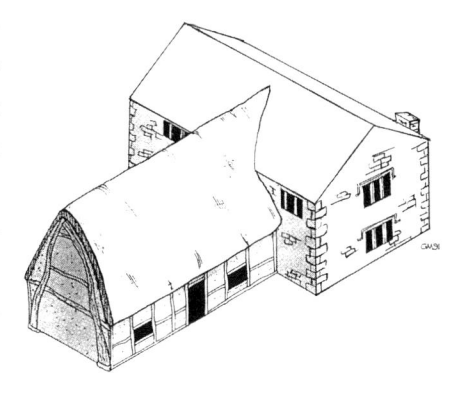

Fig. 25
Cruck-framed range and added stone wing: reconstruction shows how Smith's Farm, Dalton was 'improved'.

A final aspect of this phase of rebuilding affected houses originally built in timber-frame in the early C17. By the last quarter of that century attitudes towards this material had clearly changed and the prevalance of stone and brick had made it appear antiquated. Cladding therefore modernised structures which in themselves met all the other requirements of C17 yeoman life. Thus affected were Giants Hall, Standish (102; plate 46) cased in stone in 1675; Willow Barn, Wrightington (144; plate 52) cased in brick c1660-1670; Draper's Farm, Parbold, clad in stone, late C17; and Knight's Hall, Upholland (118) rebuilt in 1716. There were exceptions though, and

Pl. 51
Yew Tree House, Dalton, was rebuilt twice, in 1679 (the right wing) and 1710: in the latter, the attempt was made to balance the structure into a symmetrical composition.

Fig. 26
Yew Tree House: plan.

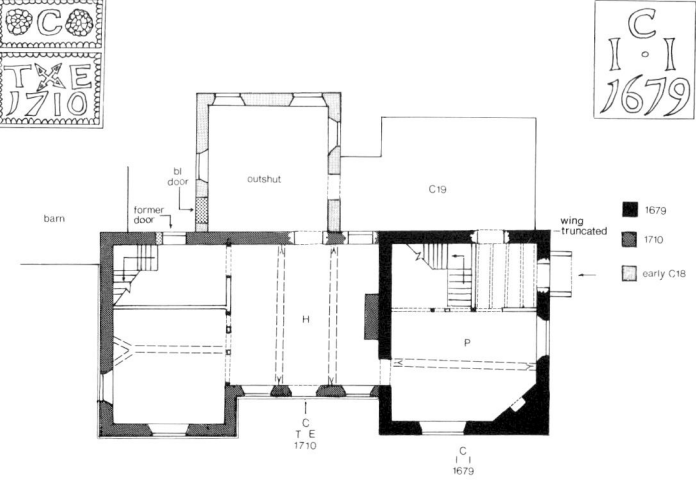

107

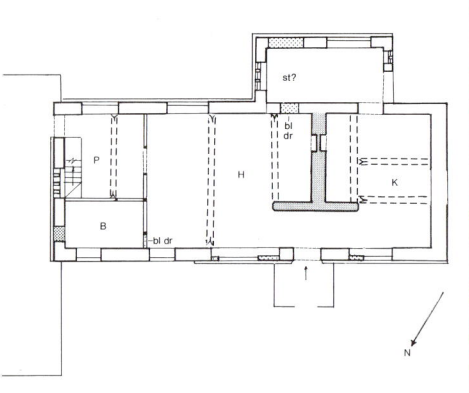

Fig. 27
Willow Barn: plan.

Pl. 52
Willow Barn, Wrightington, is an early C17 timber-framed house clad in brick, probably c.1660-1670

some rather odd. Variations in the stonework shows that at Holland House, Dalton (43) the parlour wing may have remained timber-framed when the rest was clad c1700. At South Tunley, Wrightington (139) the service wing only was clad in 1667, the rest retaining its timber-frame until the 1950s. And Spring Bank, Wrightington (141) remains as a curious, partly-stone-clad fragment of a once larger house of post-and-truss construction (plate 23).

THE DEVELOPMENT OF PLANS: 1660 – 1720

During this second phase of the rebuilding a radically new approach was introduced to the way houses were planned. From the 1660s, evidence emerges that families who were more culturally aware took a fresh look at this matter, in the light of changing lifestyles and architectural trends. The result was the slow replacement of the traditional hall-and-crosswings plan by something more modern, compact and convenient.

Far-reaching innovations in art and architecture had come to Britain in the C16 as the influence of the Renaissance spread from the Continent. Lancashire, as a remote northern county, was largely ignorant of these developments until the C17. In architectural terms, the Renaissance drew its inspiration from the classical designs of ancient Greece and Rome and this slowly began to replace the Gothic style which had proliferated since the C13 and was now completely stale. Purely classical buildings were fundamentally different from anything that had gone before. They were planned to a rigid series of conventions which placed supreme importance on the attainment of correct aesthetic appearance. In Gothic buildings, form was secondary to function, resulting in houses somewhat haphazardly designed around various groupings of the hall and its associated elements which were essentially left up to the builder. In classical buildings, all these components had to conform to an aesthetic which stressed that form took precedence over function. But within there were major changes too. Lifestyles had progressed beyond that based upon the hall and now required a plan that was more convenient and ordered, allowed ease of access to all rooms, and – importantly – created strict internal segregation between the territories of master and servant.

First and foremost classical building required a façade that was symmetrical. Rambling multi-gabled exteriors were ousted by ones composed of a simple, flat-fronted block in which the doorway was central and balanced by equal numbers of windows on either side. Behind this, the rooms were taken out of their old positions and drastically re-marshalled into new ones. Houses up to now had always been linear in plan, with rooms ranged either side of the central halls. Instead, builders began to experiment with utilising depth, resulting in homes which were planned with rooms at the front and the back. The result was the double-depth or double-pile plan in which the principal rooms – housebody and parlour – were positioned at the front with service rooms, typically buttery and kitchen, relegated to the rear. This plan stemmed from – and encouraged – the trend for increasing segregation within the household and clear distinction between what was the domain of the master and that of the servant. The placing of the service rooms out of sight to the rear physically reflects the progression away from the concept that the medieval hall was the confluence of the various elements. In classically-influenced houses, the housebody – as it was still termed – was strictly private space.

As we have seen already, the notion of symmetry was accepted by the late C16 gentry as it is evident in the facades of halls such as Birchley (12) and Bispham (13) at Billinge and at Winstanley (124). However it was little more than a token gesture to classicism as these were still essentially medieval in layout with central halls flanked by gabled wings. The classical revolution in house design approached maturity in the later phases of the yeoman rebuilding. As this progressed, its principles became more widely understood and more widely diffused among rural societies. The result was that by the early C18 double-depth houses of almost purely classical form – with classically-inspired detailing of doors and windows also – were appearing in the Douglas Valley. But the transition from hall-houses to these aspirational forms was a slow and complex one. Conservative yeomen clung to established practises and their imitation of the gentry homes meant Gothic principles were perpetuated long into the C17 and even the following century. Probably this was because the hall-house had been established by the gentry as an icon symbolising wealth and position. However a number of more enlightened yeomen, probably the more wealthy, began the breakaway to classicism in the 1660s.

Pl. 53
Bogburn Hall, Coppull, set the pace in the movement towards classicism. It is a 1663 remodelling of an early timber-framed gentry house into one of Lancashire's earliest centralised plans behind a symmetrical façade.

Fig. 28
Bogburn Hall: plan.

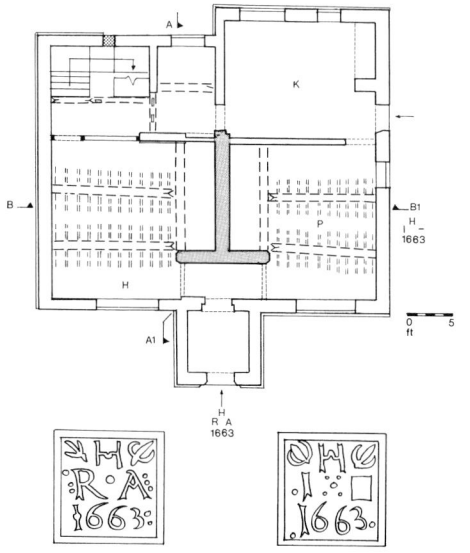

The first signs of this progression are a small but significant number of houses whose plans depart from the traditional linear form and instead are what could be termed 'centralised'. Typically, this is a more compact layout in which the principal rooms – housebody and parlour – are placed to the front in a two-unit range, with a wing to the rear containing service rooms. Thus classicism is recognised by a plan partly aspiring to double-depth and allowing a symmetrical façade, while tradition also is acknowledged by the retention of the wing element. The earliest of these is early for Lancashire as a whole. In 1663, Bogburn Hall, Coppull (29; plate 53) a timber-framed building of possibly early C16 date was substantially remodelled when clad in brick by its owners the Haydock family. The result is a symmetrical two-unit front with central baffle entry, a wing containing the kitchen to the rear of the second bay and an outshut containing stair to the rear of the first, thus producing an extremely advanced layout which is one of the pioneers of centralised planning in Lancashire. Bogburn was followed elsewhere in the county by New Hall, Clayton-le-Dale of 1665[30] and Stainscomb, Goldshaw Booth, near Burnley of c1670,[31] but early examples are relatively few indicating that the Haydocks must have been considerably more aware of these developments than the majority of their contemporaries. This is reinforced by the fact that it is not until almost two decades later that the next surviving centralised plan is encountered. Scythe Stone Delph Farm, Rainford (94; plate 54) is smaller than Bogburn but takes another step towards classical form by abandoning the baffle entrance in favour of hearths at gable ends of the main range. Again, as at Bogburn, the kitchen is contained in a wing to the rear, which incorporated an outshut containing a further service room. It clearly made an impression for in 1703 the nearby Hydes Brow Farm, originally a cruck-framed structure, was adapted to follow this plan. A new two-unit front was built at right angles to the cruck range, which was demoted to a service wing at the rear. Toogood Hall, Wrightington (143) of 1708 shows evidence of similar adaptation to a pre-existing timber-framed building. Both this and Hydes Brow however clung on to the central baffle entry despite the lead Scythe Stone had taken. Centralised houses were still being built by around 1720 as the Lathom examples of Needless Inn (68) and Watkinson's Farm (72) show, but by this time end stacks had replaced the baffle entry – yet in both cases the stacks still projected in the manner of a hundred years before.

Yet, both these houses were glaringly obsolete from the moment they were built. From around 1700 the first houses to use a double-depth plan in conjunction with a symmetrical façade begin to appear. This layout had been pioneered in 1686 by the now-demolished Dower House at Ince (53), a prodigy handicapped by an oddly-asymmetrical façade. The first dated example of a correct classical combination is the Colliers Arms, Aspull (6) of 1700, followed by Green Barn Farm, Blackrod (27), Fir

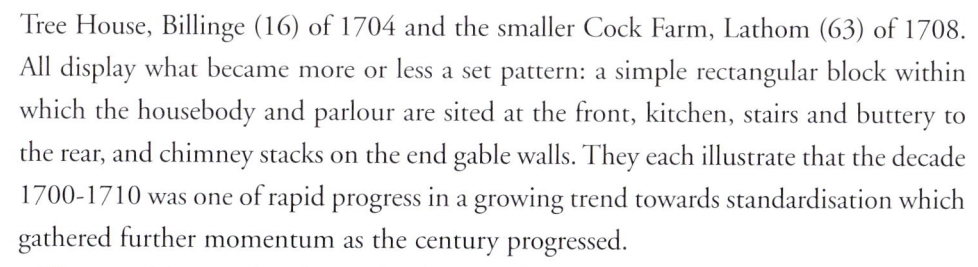

Tree House, Billinge (16) of 1704 and the smaller Cock Farm, Lathom (63) of 1708. All display what became more or less a set pattern: a simple rectangular block within which the housebody and parlour are sited at the front, kitchen, stairs and buttery to the rear, and chimney stacks on the end gable walls. They each illustrate that the decade 1700-1710 was one of rapid progress in a growing trend towards standardisation which gathered further momentum as the century progressed.

The transition to double-depth plans was however not always straightforward. In certain cases, double-depth form was not achieved without a considerable degree of compromise. Surprisingly some of the most prestigious houses had difficulty with this concept. Between 1700 and 1710 were built two superior yeoman houses: Stone Hall, Dalton (48) and Lowe's, Newburgh (78). Both were of double depth plan: but achieved it by breaking the rules. Both have fine, symmetrical façades, but behind them the discipline breaks down alarmingly. The principal rooms are in fact sited in a two-unit main range from which twin gabled wings project at right angles to the rear, containing the service rooms. The stacks are sited not at the end gables but inside, at the point where the range and wings meet. The degree of idiosyncracy is increased further at Stone Hall because the stair is sited – almost incredibly – in a narrow outshut placed between the wings. At Lowes it is more conventionally housed within one of the wings but the manner in which these form coupled gables at the rear is greatly at odds with the composure of the façade.

These unconventional arrangements probably result in part from problems builders faced with roofing houses which were more than one room in depth. Up to now they had dealt only with houses of single-depth form, where load-bearing masonry walls

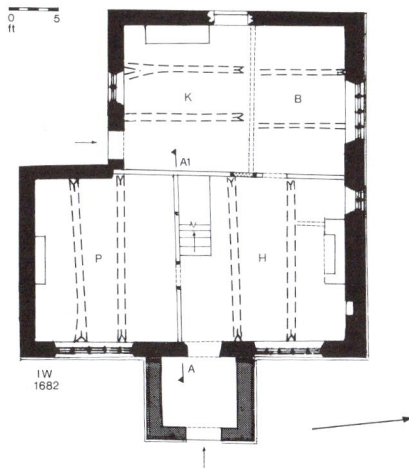

Pl. 54 (above left) Scythe Stone Delph Farm, Rainford, displays an innovative centralised plan with a symmetrical façade and gable-end stacks.

Fig. 29 (above) Scythe Stone Delph Farm: plan.

Pl. 55
Stone Hall, Dalton, combines an early classical façade with an unconventional double-depth plan.

Pl. 56
Textiles financed the building of Darbyshire House, Billinge, in 1716 to almost perfect classical standards. Pictured in 1987, before restoration.

supported the purlins at the external gables and internally they were carried by timber roof trusses. But double-depth houses brought a complication as the distance between the front and rear walls was usually too great for trusses to span comfortably. This was the case at Lowe's and Stone Hall, both large and deep structures, the former 36 feet from front to rear. Both circumvented the problem by the front range-rear wings plan, within which the roof construction was of hybrid form, using both trusses and load-bearing walls. Quite curiously in each case the trusses are of upper cruck form. Stone Hall uses one over the front range between masonry walls while Lowe's has two, coupled internally at the junction of its range and the rear wings. These improvisations achieved a double-depth plan and maintained classical dignity on the façade but not at the rear. This, in the strictest classical terms, was not acceptable.

The solution to these problems came through the abandonment of roof trusses and the use of load-bearing walls carried up to the roof. This occurs early in the brick service wing at South Tunley, Wrightington (139) probably of 1667. The first dated house built exclusively this way is Webster's Farm, Lathom (73), which despite its modest nature is thus extremely advanced for the date of 1682. The idea of 'purlin roofs' was slow to catch on though and a certain amount of hesitance is detected in early double-depth houses. Therefore Green Barn Farm, Blackrod (27) of 1704 follows the example of Stone Hall and uses a spindly truss (but not of upper cruck form) to uncomfortably span the 28 feet between its front and rear walls, despite a central masonry crosswall. Poor quality purlins probably required its presence as a safeguard. However at Fir Tree House, Billinge (16) of the same date, total reliance is placed on a central structural crosswall instead. More caution is shown though at Cock Farm, Lathom (63) of 1708 where the front purlins are carried on masonry yet the rear ones rest on timber half-trusses which were set upon timber-framed walls on either side of the stair. This same arrangement occurs at Darbyshire House (15) of 1716 and Greenslate Farm (19) of c1720, both at Billinge.

In the early C18, visual signs of the transition to classicism occurs with the use of details and ornament inspired by this style. Horizontal mullioned and mullioned-and-transomed windows were replaced by ones which were vertical, and classical decoration was applied to doorways. Both Lowes and Stone Hall were pioneers of this form of embellishment. Their windows are vertical ones of the 'cross' type with one mullion and one transom only, a form associated with the early stages of classicism. Stone Hall also has a fine doorway with scrolly pediment, although its handling is unfamiliar and quite rustic (plate 92). Elsewhere confusion reigned. Both Colliers Arms and Green Barn retained mullioned windows, but Fir Tree House had cross windows originally. Their builders didn't follow the Stone Hall fashion for a pedimented doorcase, preferring plain surrounds instead. Finally a degree of concord occurs at Darbyshire House, Billinge, of 1716 (15) which with its pedimented doorcase and cross windows seems to bond all the classical principles and symbolises, virtually at the end of the rebuilding, that the transition to this style was complete.

Yet amid the rapid progress of the early 1700s, there were as many stragglers as there were innovators. The three-unit, parlour-wing plan retained considerable support. Its use at Lys Cottage, Newburgh (79) of 1691 was already conservative considering the advances made by centralised houses by that time, but to find it at Higher Highfield, Aspull (8) and the demolished Dial House, Upholland, (112) makes one wonder what the builders had in mind. Others showed a degree of compromise. Newgate Farm, Upholland (122) is a remodelling of 1707 of an earlier building but combined a retrograde asymmetrical front with an attempt at a double-depth plan. A similar, earlier layout appears to have occurred at The Meadows, Wigan (123) of 1689 and now demolished. Newgate still however featured a crosswing, something which by then had been relegated to the rear by those a little more conscious of progress: such as Bispham Hall (24; plate 57) of c1700 and Stannanought, Dalton (47) of 1714. But although Bispham – admittedly a superior building – had achieved façade symmetry despite its plan, the builders of Stannanought made little attempt with the wing – despite its position to the rear – unbalancing the disposition of windows on its façade. Yet, even more astonishing, is Barker's Farm, Dalton (35; plate 58) of 1742 and of

Pl. 57
Bispham Hall, Bispham, shows similarity of detail to Stone Hall and is a classical interpretation of the traditional 3-unit linear plan.

Fig. 30
Bispham Hall: plan

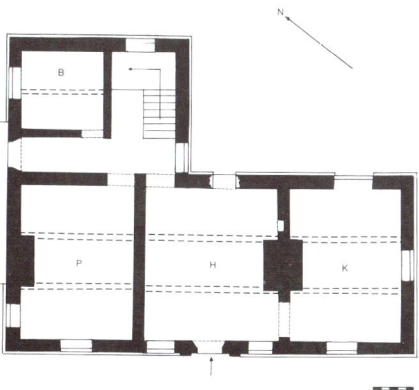

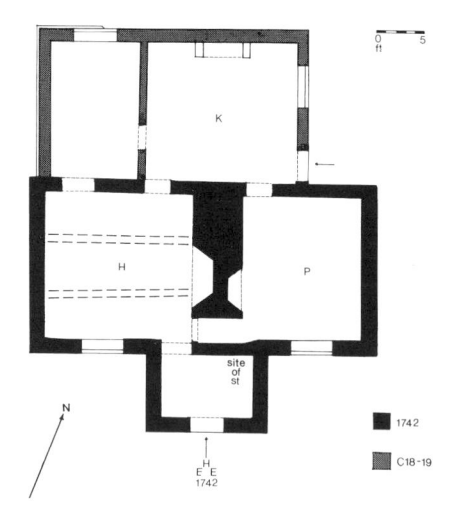

Fig. 31
Barker's Farm: plan

Pl. 58
Barker's Farm, Dalton, is a belated, centralised house dated 1742, but in all probability older.

centralised – not double-depth – plan with two-unit front and rear wing: the type pioneered by Bogburn Hall (29) more than 80 years earlier. In this case one wonders whether the datestone represents a remodelling of an earlier house: or else its builders, the Hatton family, had merely let the architectural revolution pass them by.

ROOMS IN THE YEOMAN'S HOUSE

Throughout much of the C17 the yeomanry pursued a lifestyle that was fundamentally medieval. This reflected in the layout and use of rooms, which were focused around the centrally-positioned housebody with its upper and lower ends. The adoption of classical plans during the late C17 and early C18 forced this arrangement to change as rooms were moved from their traditional positions into new ones and houses took on a layout more recognizably modern. Some rooms changed both in location and in their function.

Throughout the survival of the medieval hall-house plan and its derivatives, the housebody retained its traditional, predominant position as the focus of the household and the convergence of its respective elements. The name sometimes applied to this room in probate inventories – 'firehouse' – has in itself medieval overtones originating from the time when this was the only heated room in the dwelling.[32] This tradition meant the housebody was always the largest room, although the dimensions varied with the size of the building and ultimately the status of the occupants. In one of the largest yeoman houses, Holland's House at Dalton (43; plate 59) the housebody measures some 378 square feet. Lower down on the social scale, the housebody at Harsnips, Dalton (42) in a former cruck-built dwelling is little more than half the size, measuring 208 square feet. The presence of tables, forms, stools etc in probate inventories shows its general use as a dining room, sitting room or both, especially in these houses – and this was the majority in the C17 – where the parlour served as a bedroom.

The evolution of classical plans meant the housebody's central position and focal role diminished. Instead it shared a new location at the front alongside the parlour, although as before the main entrance still led directly into the housebody. Yet although the strict segregation within had relegated service rooms to a decidedly inferior position at the rear of these buildings, the lack of a heated kitchen within smaller houses meant cooking would have continued in the housebody regardless of the momentous changes in plan. This would have been the case at Kathry, Newburgh (77) of c1700, Fir Tree House (16), Billinge of 1704 and Greenhill Farm, Newburgh (75; plate 74) of 1748. Consequently, a medieval tradition lived on here behind the veneer of a fine C18 classical exterior. Only in the largest houses such as Lowe's, Newburgh (78) and Stone Hall, Dalton (48) were the kitchens heated. Although its predominant role was challenged by the rise of the parlour, the housebody still remained the largest room. At Fir Tree House it comprised 289 square feet compared to 156 in the parlour and at Greenhill 196 compared to 121 (figure 36).

Of all rooms, the parlour underwent the greatest change during the duration of the rebuilding. Throughout most of the C17 it was mostly used as a bedroom. This continued into the early C18, for beds could be found in the parlours at Jump's Farm, Lathom (65) in 1708 and Yew Tree House, Dalton (51), in 1709.[33] However during the course of the C17 it began to evolve as a sitting room, as had occurred earlier in the houses of the gentry. At Copyhold Farm, Wrightington (131) the presence of a long table and stools in the parlour in 1668 indicates it was used as a sitting/dining

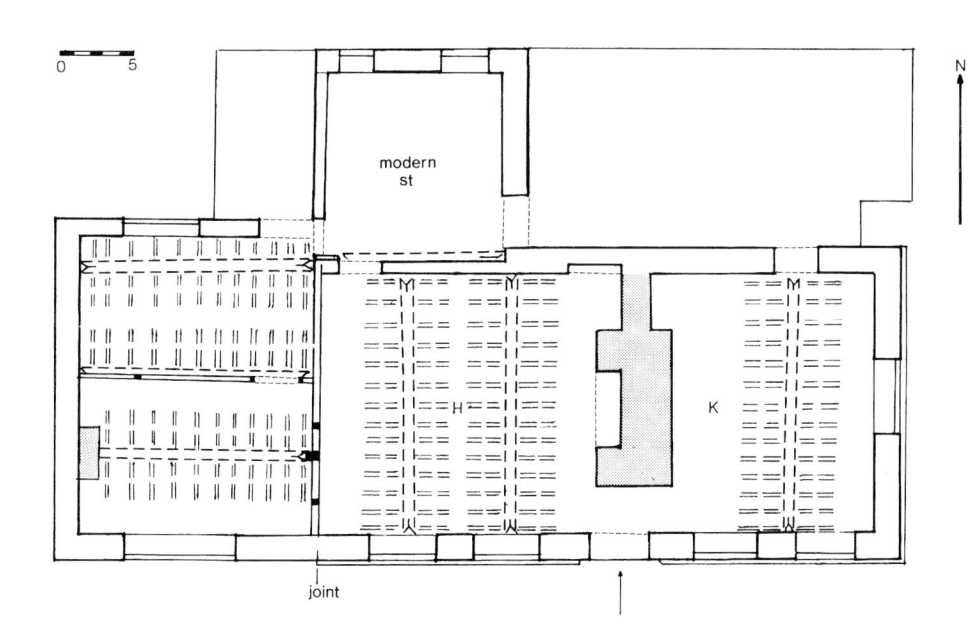

Fig. 32 Holland's House plan.

Pl. 59.
Holland's House, originally timber-framed, has one of the largest yeoman housebodies.

room by Oliver Halliwell, who as a schoolmaster would have been more culturally aware of lifestyle trends. The parlour at Guild Hall, Rainford (91), was in use as a sitting room by Thomas Gill, gentleman, in 1708.[34] By 1729 a yeoman of more modest means, Robert Stannanought of Stannanought, Dalton (47), put his parlour to the same use also.[35] Unlike the gentry, most yeomen had one parlour only. However in the large early houses of wealthy freeholders, two parlours are sometimes found. This was the case at Holland's House, Dalton (43) in 1668, where Richard Holland had a 'little parlour' and a 'great parlour'. The smaller room was in use as a bedroom while the larger was a sitting room with a table and forms, but also stored items including three cheeses, seven barrels, a little firkin and three 'combes'. At Halliwell's Farm, Upholland (115) in 1683, an 'old parlour' is specified, implying a 'new' one existed as well.[36]

After the housebody, parlours were usually the next room to be heated where this was within the means of the householder. Early houses such as Guild Hall, Rainford (91) of 1629, Upper Wood Fold, Standish (104) and Sanderson House, Wrightington (138) had large external stacks appended to the parlours and these became symbolic of the owner's affluence. External stacks of this type were still being built in 1683 at Belle Vue Farm, Dalton (37), but by that time they were somewhat outdated. More modest houses heated their parlours using a 'cross corner' fireplace which made little show externally, being constructed in the inner angle of the room as the name implies and could be inserted with relative ease into a room that had previously been unheated. These occur in the wings added to Yew Tree House, Dalton (51) in 1679 and nearby Smith's Farm (46) and in the larger, single-build structures of Copyhold Farm, Wrightington (131) in 1659 and Prior's Wood Hall, Dalton (45) of c1680. Not all houses had heated parlours though. This was the case not only at smaller, two-unit houses such as Webster's, Lathom (73) of 1682 and Kathry, Newburgh (77) of c1700 but more surprisingly at substantial houses such as North Tunley, Wrightington (137) of c1620 and Newgate Farm, Upholland (122) of 1707.

An indicator of the importance placed upon the parlour in certain households is the fact that it was given a separate entrance. This avoided the need to cross the housebody to access it and thus considerably increased its sense of isolation from the rest of the house. Such doorways occur at Maggot's Nook, Rainford (93,) in the added parlour wing of the early C17, Mill Bridge Farm, Worthington (127) of 1694 (unusually, one of twin doorways within the single-storey porch) and Kathry, Newburgh (77) of c1700. A similar intention can be seen also at Bispham Hall, Bispham (24), again of c1700, where instead of leading directly into the parlour, an external door opens into a passage at the upper end from which this room, along with stairs and buttery, can be reached (figure 30).

Although all yeoman houses had a housebody and parlour, the provision of service rooms varied considerably. Kitchens certainly were viewed as dispensable in the smaller two-unit homes, although in two examples, Jump's Farm (65) and Taylor's Farm (70) at Lathom, kitchen bays were added at a later date. Where they did occur they were not always heated and even some of the larger yeoman houses did not have this luxury. This was the case at Guild Hall, Rainford (91) of 1629 and Prior's Wood Hall, Dalton (45) of c1680, which both follow the hall-and-crosswing plan. In these houses, the kitchen would really have functioned as what we would now term a utility room, involving food preparation and storage. However a few households saw a heated kitchen as a necessity. The will of Richard Prescott, probably of Holt Farm, Coppull, (33; LCRO WCW 1631) refers to a hearth in the kitchen, and so does that if Henry Fisher of Douglas Bank Farm, Upholland (114) in 1692. Willow Barn, Wrightington (144) of the early C17 has a large firehood in the kitchen, at the expense of a small, unheated parlour. This was achieved by back-to-back firehoods serving this room and the housebody. A similar arrangement occurs nearby at Copyhold Farm, Wrightington (131). As one would expect, larger houses such as Lowe's, Newburgh (78) and Stone Hall, Dalton (48) of c1700-1710 have heated kitchens, using masonry hearths which by this time had superseded firehoods.

By contrast one room invariably found, even in the smallest houses, is the buttery, used for storage of drink. Unlike gentry houses however, this room was normally located at the upper end, close to the parlour, presumably for close supervision of its contents. These needed to be kept cool, so the buttery was generally sited away from the sun. Although a small room, it therefore clearly exerted an influence during the planning stage of the building. In south-facing crosswing houses it is located to the rear and accessed via the stair lobby, as at Copyhold (131); where the house faces north, such as Belle Vue Farm (137) and Stannanought, Dalton (47) the buttery is placed at the front of the wing. In two-unit houses such as Webster's, Lathom (73) of 1682 and Cicely's Cottage, Dalton (39) of the late C17, the buttery is sited next to the parlour as the smaller element of a subdivided upper bay. This also occurs in three unit houses lacking a crosswing, such as Gathurst Hall, Shevington (100), Willow Barn (144) and Lower Wrennall, Wrightington (136) of 1673. In the double-pile plan the buttery moved to the rear as one of the service rooms grouped around the stair lobby, but retained its association with the parlour by being positioned at that end, as at Fir Tree House, Billinge (16) of 1704, Darbyshire House, Billinge (15) of 1716 and Greenhill Farm, Newburgh (75) of 1748.

Occasionally other service rooms are mentioned in inventories relating to larger yeoman houses, although these may well have been placed in outbuildings rather than the main structure. 'Milkhouse' (dairy) is referred to at Holland's House, Dalton (43)

Pl. 60
Gathurst Hall, Shevington, an early C17 timber-framed house lacking a crosswing.

in 1667, Copyhold in 1668, and Club House Farm, Shevington (97) in 1679.[37] 'Brewhouse' is listed also at Holland's House and Copyhold at the same time. At Copyhold, either of these rooms may have been sited in the outshut to the rear of the kitchen. At Holland's, the mention of the brewhouse between the 'great parlour' and the kitchen implies it was an integral part of the house and not an outbuilding.

Chambers (ie, rooms on upper floors) were an important element of yeoman houses too. For many, they were an innovation. To those who inhabited cruck-framed structures previously – such as the Ayscoughs of Jump's Farm, Lathom (65), the Scotts of Belle Vue Farm, Dalton (37) and the Stannanoughts of Stannanought (47) in the same township – they represented a tremendous advance in their lifestyle. The chamber floors of yeoman's houses never achieved the distinction they held in those of the gentry however. They were notably more down to earth and the limited space placed restrictions upon their use. A major problem was privacy. As we have seen, gentry chambers were accessed via the gallery which extended from the stairhead and thus each room was isolated from the next. Yeomen's houses lacked this refinement and consequently a situation was created where certain chambers could be reached only by passing through others. This placed restrictions on how the rooms were used. The most important chambers became the ones that were most private. Generally these were the ones over the parlour. This was because the stairs were usually sited at the upper end of the building before the advent of centralised plans and the parlour chamber could consequently be entered directly from the landing. Its high status is reflected in the fact that it frequently contained the most expensive beds. This was the case at Copyhold (131) in 1668 – where the parlour was used, somewhat prodigiously, as a sitting room – and at Jump's Farm, Lathom (65), in 1708 where the parlour was still being slept in. Furthermore, at the house of Richard Prescott of Dalton in 1680 (probably Priors Wood Hall, 45) it is termed the 'best room'. Yet at the home of Richard Naylor of Upholland in 1647, Dean House Farm (111) the best beds were in the 'high chamber' over the housebody, which suggests it must have been reached directly from the stair and relatively isolated from the other chambers.

At an early date some yeomen made attempts to increase the extent of privacy on the chamber floor. At North Tunley, Wrightington (137), of c1620, the stair rises to a small lobby from which the chambers over the housebody, parlour and buttery lead off. Certain other households recognised a need for clear segregation between the elements within. Here two staircases were provided, one for the family and the other for servants. This occurs at Guild Hall, Rainford (91) of 1629 and at Copyhold, Wrightington (137) of 1659. At the latter, two spiral staircases were employed – the main one accessing the housebody, parlour and buttery chambers from a lobby and a further one in the outshut at the service end serving the chamber over the kitchen.

Pl. 61
Windows and clay floors within the attics at Prior's Wood Hall, Dalton, possibly c.1680, may indicate their inhabitation by servants.

But it was not until the development of centralised and double-depth plans that the privacy problem was more widely eliminated. At Bogburn Hall, Coppull (29) rebuilt in 1663, the stair, placed in an outshut to the rear, rises to a landing which connects all the chambers. A similar strategy occurs at Scythe Stone Delph Farm, Rainford (94) of 1682 where the stair, placed in front of the entrance, also opens onto a landing from which the chambers are reached. This solution became standard with the adoption of the double-depth plan in which the stair was placed in its own lobby to the rear and could easily be accessed from all rooms on all floors.

With space at a premium, the upper floors of yeoman houses, unlike those of the gentry, were not exclusively used for sleeping. Most chambers doubled as storage rooms as well as bedrooms although the parlour chamber, being the most prestigious, may frequently have escaped this compromise to its status. Where it did not, as at Widdow's Farm, Dalton (50) in 1704, it contained not only beds but cheese, oatmeal, yarn and cloth.[38] Where these chambers had the advantage of being sited near a fire or firehood, the drier atmosphere made them particularly suitable for storing produce and perishable items. This was probably the case at the house of Roger Rigby of Adlington (probably Rigby House Farm, 4) where his 'cheese chamber' in 1676 contained (not surprisingly) 41 cheeses valued at £2.13s.4d together with beds, flax and wool. In addition to beds and household implements, the kitchen chamber at Douglas Bank Farm, Upholland (114) in 1692 also housed three spinning wheels which may indicate the room was the site of commercial textile production by the Fisher family. Spinning wheels and linens in the housebody chamber at Copyhold Farm, Wrightington (131) in 1668 may indicate a similar operation.

Limited space also meant that attics also played an important role, as they offered valuable accomodation for the clutter of household, farm and business – and also their more lowly human elements. Seth Prescott of Club House Farm, Shevington (97) had a 'cheese loft' containing apples, among other things, in 1679. At Darbyshire House, Billinge of 1716 (15) windowless rooms in the attic space at the rear were probably used for textile storage by Thomas Darbyshire, linen webster. Elsewhere, windows and clay floors (as at Priors Wood Hall, Dalton, 45) suggest some attic rooms may have been used for grain storage (the clay was supposed to be mouse-proof) or possibly for living-in servants. Among the goods of Richard Naylor of Dean House, Upholland (111) in 1647 was a bed 'which the servant man lyes in' but its location is unclear. Elsewhere, servants occupied outbuildings as suggested by the loft over the stable, reached by external steps, within the barn of 1689 at Smith's Farm, Dalton (46).

CONCLUSION

The many surviving buildings are primary evidence that the yeomanry of the Douglas Valley, as in other parts of Lancashire, were engaged in widespread rebuilding activity from around 1600 to 1720.

Hitherto it appears the majority of yeomen occupied cruck-framed structures though evidence exists that some inhabited open halls of post-and-truss construction. The strong timber-framing tradition meant that during the early stages of the rebuilding, many houses continued to be of post-and-truss type. By around 1630 however, these had probably been superseded by stone and brick. The new houses built by the yeomanry show wide variation in size, status and date. The earliest, and among the most substantial, were built by wealthiest freeholders and copyholders in the period 1600-1650. Following this, a second period of rebuilding from 1650-1720 was far more intensive and created smaller homes of less affluent yeomen, some of which experienced a staggered rebuilding over a period of generations. During this latter stage, changing lifestyles and architectural concepts meant traditional linear plans based on the medieval hall-house began to be replaced by ones of centralised form. In turn these too evolved into classically-inspired double-depth layouts which ultimately became a standard pattern. With these came classical forms of decoration and all elements eventually combined to produce homes of truly classical discipline by the time this phase of the rebuilding was exhausted in about the second decade of the C18.

Through these achievements, the yeomen played a key role in the social development of Lancashire in the C17 and C18. Their houses remain as monuments to their progress. But the yeomanry, as a class, did not enjoy a matching longevity. Their decline was alarmingly rapid. Even by the 1790s it was evident as industry replaced agriculture as the backbone of the Lancashire economy.

Pl. 62
The yeomen dwindled in number as the county became more industrialised in the C18. This gravestone at Ormskirk Parish Church records the passing of the Culshaw family of Greenhill Farm, Newburgh.

John Holt, writing in 1795, commented: 'The yeomanry, formerly numerous and respectable, have greatly diminished of late. Not only the yeomanry, but almost all the farmers, who have raised fortunes by agriculture, place their children in the manufacturing line.'[39] Eclipsed in this way, the yeomanry were among the first casualties of the Industrial Revolution. Next would be much of the land they once farmed as the growing manufacturing towns spread steadily across the landscape in the dark and relentless progress of urban expansion.

NOTES

1. 'Life of Adam Martindale', ed Rev Richard Parkinson, CS vol 4 (OS) (1845) p1-2.
2. 1653 Commonwealth Survey (LCRO).
3. Nigel Morgan, 'Ennumeration of 'The Gentry' in Lancashire, c1550-1640, PhD thesis p43-44.
4. The 1600 Freeholders list recorded just one; but 16 are recorded in the 1653 Commonwealth survey.
5. 1653 Commonwealth survey: 15 leases were granted in 1631 and 19 in 1633, all for three lives; the average number granted in the 14 other years recorded is 2.8.
6. 'Life of Adam Martindale,' p34.
7. LCRO DDF/2430.
8. LCRO WCW 1668.
9. LCRO WCW 1628.
10. J J Baggley, 'The Will, Inventory and Accounts of Robert Walthew of Pemberton', RS vol 109 (1965).
11 LCRO WCW 1729.
12. LCRO WCW 1681.
13. LCRO WCW 1672.
14. This was briefly touched upon by W F Price in 'Notes on Some of the Places, Traditions and Folklore of the Douglas Valley', Historic Society of Lancashire and Cheshire, (1899) p213.
15. J J Baggley 'Robert Walthew', p52.
16. LRO WCW 1675.
17. LRO WCW 1622.
18. J J Baggley, 'Robert Walthew', p53.
19. J J Baggley, 'Robert Walthew', p53-54.
20. Rev T C Porteus, 'History of Standish' (1927) p149.
21. LRO WCW 1718.
22. LRO WCW 1647.
23. LRO WCW 1692.
24. LRO WCW 1668.
25. LRO WCW 1676.
26. 'Life of Adam Martindale', p31.
27. F Walker, 'Historical Geography of South West Lancashire', CS vol 103 (NS) p107.
28. J J Baggley 'Robert Walthew' p52.
29. Possibly the cottage south of Birch Green Farm, Skelmersdale, a single-bay structure dated 1694, was a crosswing added to a subsequently-demolished range. (Skelmersdale Development Corporation report, 1965).

30. Surveyed by Garry Miller, April 1987.
31. Surveyed by Garry Miller, January 1988; Sarah Pearson, 'Rural Houses of the Lancashire Pennines', RCHM (1985) p72-73, 149.
32. Examples in recorded buildings include: Richard Prescott of Dalton (probably Prior's Wood Hall, 45) LCRO WCW 1680; William Jackson of Widdow's Farm, Dalton (50) LRO WCW 1704.
33. Will of John Crane, LCRO WCW 1709.
34. Will of Thomas Gill, LCRO WCW 1708.
35. Will of Robert Stannanought, LCRO WCW 1729.
36. LCRO DDAl 102.
37. Will of Seth Prescott, LCRO WCW 1679.
38. Will of William Jackson, LCRO WCW 1704.
39. Holt 'General View of the Agriculture of the County of Lancashire' (1795) p13.

CHAPTER V

The Zenith of Classicism 1720-1770

The middle decades of the C18 saw the construction of some of the finest houses in the Douglas Valley. In numerical terms, they were few: but in terms of quality they excelled.

These houses developed and perfected the classical style which had shown an increasing influence from 1700 onwards. Houses of both gentry and yeomanry subsequently evolved into the epitome of this new discipline. All were built according to strict architectural codes which at the same time were generating similar houses in other parts of the country. In this way the classical homes of the C18 became regional elements – differentiated only by local materials – in what was an emerging national pattern of building. This trend was set, once again, by the gentry – but not the 'old' gentry of provincial stock who had rebuilt a century earlier. At the vanguard of this evolution was a new type of gentleman – cultured and of cosmopolitan outlook, who moved in influential circles and rubbed shoulders with princes and nobility. During the C18 several manors changed hands and their new owners, wealthy businessmen and government officials, set about rebuilding their houses to suit their more refined standards.

GENTRY HOUSES: A NEW REBUILDING

In the early C18, gentry families began again to improve their homes. Unlike before, this was not an economy-driven phenomenon but instead an upgrading of houses which had become quickly out of date in what was an era of enlightenment. We have already established that the gentry were sufficiently well-placed to remodel their houses every few generations: and life had moved on considerably since the buildings created to suit the post-medieval needs of the late C16. Then, houses such as Birchley Hall (12) at Billinge and Winstanley Hall (124) were icons of the residences aspired to by the progressive, successful gentry. But although they have acknowledged the first stirrings of classicism in their adoption of symmetry, they remained nevertheless medieval in concept, and built using few rules and therefore with tremendous potential for idiosyncracy.

In the new era of the early C18, such nonconformity was out of the question. The accelerating classical movement had produced templates for what was strictly acceptable in gentry and lesser houses in this new age, and these left less room for undisciplined flashes of the imagination. From 1700 on, classical country houses designed to strict conventions began to appear across Lancashire: landmarks include the west front of Croxteth Hall, Liverpool, of 1702,[1] the west front of Knowsley Hall, Knowsley, from 1720 onwards,[2] and the west range of Townley Hall, Burnley, of 1725[3] and at a later date the new front at Lytham Hall, 1757-1764.[4] They set a code which made those who failed to follow it quickly look absurd: such as the Manor House at Crawford, Upholland (120) whose wealthy yeoman builders grafted a full-height gabled porch (plate 99) onto its double-pile block and thus in their ignorance effectively set the building back more than 20 years.

To build homes in the correct manner, the nation's gentry began to turn to the rapidly rising profession of architects who were spreading the gospel to landowners of varying status. It was to one of their ranks that MP Sir Thomas Bootle turned when he acquired the manor of Lathom in 1724. Sir Thomas, whose family held land in Melling, near Liverpool, and the Inner Temple, London, was a prominent figure whose public offices included baron of the Exchequer of Chester and Chancellor to Frederick, Prince of Wales. He therefore moved in a world acquainted with the latest architectural styles. That world was then being stirred by the vision of Robert Boyle, Lord Burlington, a passionate follower of the Italian architect Andrea Palladio (1508-1580). Under his influence and patronage, a number of fine country houses were being built in emulation of Palladio's simple but elegant classical style. In 1715 Burlington had invited to England a Venetian architect, Giacomo Leoni, to assist with the production of an English edition of Palladio's works. It was to Leoni that Sir Thomas Bootle turned to design a mansion inspired by the fashionable houses appearing elsewhere under Burlington's guidance. The result was without parallel in Lancashire at that time. Lathom House (12; plate 63,64) was the first of seven superlative houses Leoni built in this country. Three were in Lancashire: Lathom, built c1725-1730, Bold Hall, south of St Helens, completed c1732,[5] and Alkrington Hall, Middleton of 1735-1736.[6] Of these, Lathom was was the masterpiece.

The mansion consisted of a stiffly-formal, rectangular main block measuring 156 feet by 75 feet and connected by more relaxed curving Ionic collonades to twin flanking service wings. This was an enlarged form of the rural 'villas' which Palladio had been building in northern Italy in the later C16. Seen from the entrance front, the latter drew the eye to the main block and emphasised its might (plate 64): it consisted of two-and-a-half storeys with a double flight of steps to the main entrance within a higher, slightly projecting centre crowned by a pediment. No less than 14 massive chimney stacks towered above an exterior which in its detailing also revealed the hierarchy present within.

The age which created these mansions had defined new territories for master and servant. The idea of both circulating on the same floor level – as expressed in the old

Pls. 63 & 64
Lathom House was the area's most monumental expression of classicism. The two main façades were treated slightly differently as these views of the north front (left) and the south (below) indicate.
The latter shows the mansion in its heyday, with its massive service wings and surrounded by a five-acre deer park.
(Twycross 'Mansions of England & Wales', Vol. 3, 1846)

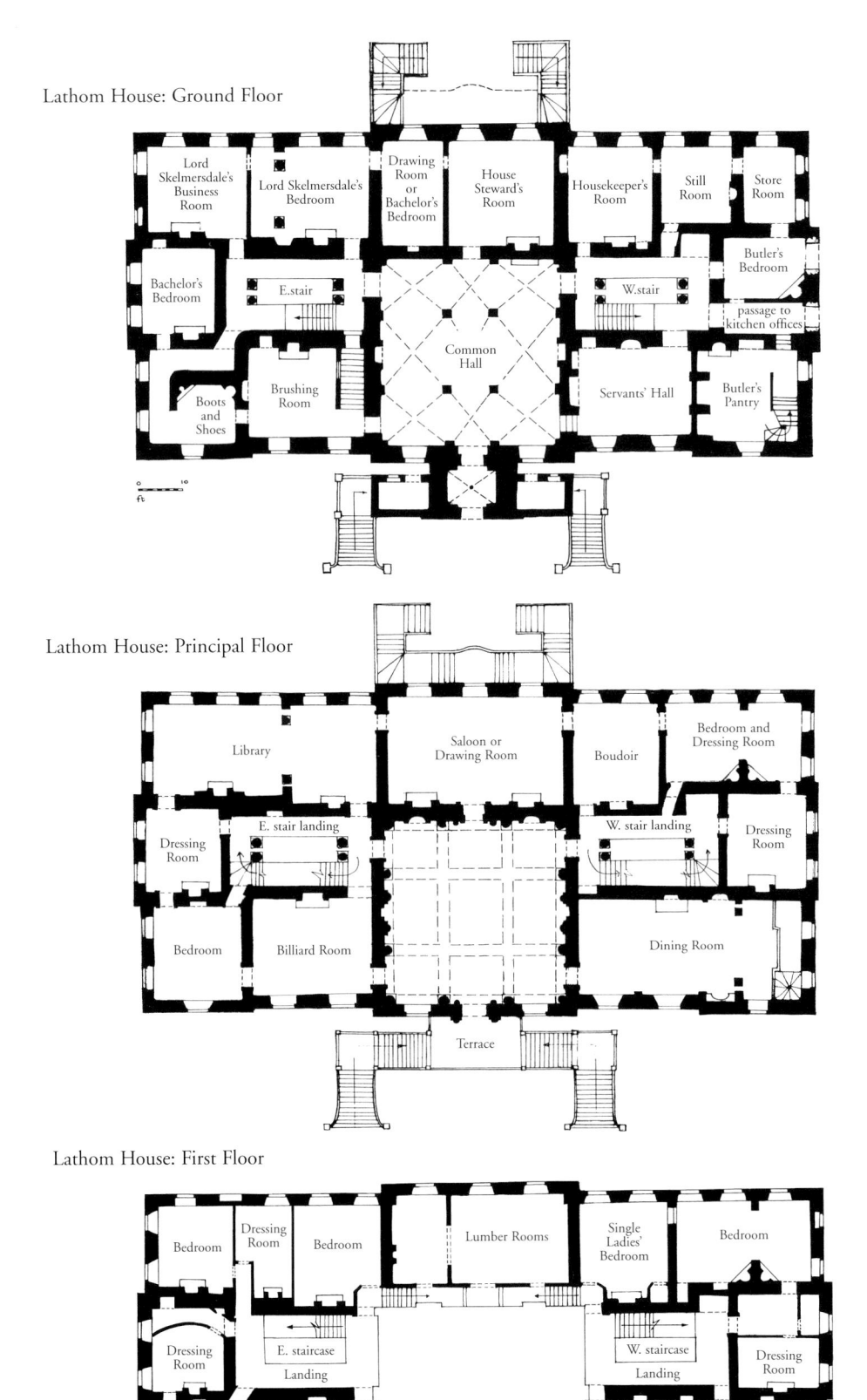

Lathom House: Ground Floor

Lathom House: Principal Floor

Lathom House: First Floor

Fig. 33
Lathom House: plans
showing room functions
c.1870.
(copied from LCRO DDHi)

hall-and-crosswings plan – was replaced by one which symbolised the vertical structure of society itself. Accordingly, the service rooms are sited on the ground floor at Lathom – figuratively providing 'support' for the private rooms and apartments ranged overhead. The distinction of function was expressed in the masonry itself – the ground floor was built of rusticated stone with the rest of the house in smooth ashlar. Plans of Lathom from c1870[7] show a large 'common hall' occupying the centre with other rooms including a housekeeper's room, servants' hall, butler's pantry, house steward's room and one for boots and shoes grouped around. Further services were provided in the wings, with the east containing brewhouse, agent's room, store room, smoking room and store room. The west wing, which survives, held the stables with workshops for carpenters and plumbers, storage for hay and straw and living rooms and bedrooms for the keeper.

Back in the main building, the role of the first floor as the *'piano nobile'* (Italian for great or noble floor) – holding the principal rooms – was emphasised externally by balustraded steps up to the entrance and a series of pediments above the windows. Its arrangement and use of rooms reflects the early C18 desire for a lifestyle more sophisticated than that centred around the hall and its environs. Country houses of this period invented new rooms for new forms of social intercourse. For large gatherings and balls there was the saloon: in some ways the successor of the hall but unlike it, a room where servants and lower ranks were out-of-bounds. For dinner parties there was the dining room, and afterwards the drawing room to which the ladies could retire for polite conversation. The men, or both sexes for that matter, may play cards in a games room and alternative after-dinner entertainment might have been found in the music room.

Lathom was a product of this polite world and its reflection is visible in its plan. Entrance from the steps was directly into the 'grand hall', 40 feet square and towering 38 feet high[8] through two storeys, which occupied most of the pedimented central section of the building. To its rear was the saloon, and on either side twin staircases, along with the dining room, a library and private apartments. The second floor principally contained bedrooms – two of which in c1870 were for the use of 'single ladies' among the guests being entertained – along with dressing rooms and a lumber room above the saloon. The attics above the central section contained a further three single ladies' rooms and six 'ladies' maids rooms' presumably for the servants accompanying guests. This was polite living on a superlative scale: cosmopolitan Home-Counties society transplanted to a relatively remote corner of the provincial North.

The splendour of Lathom makes it all the more outrageous that it has been demolished. Lancashire has not been kind to Leoni's legacy: Bold Hall met the same

Pls. 65 & 66
Relics of Lathom's glory: the sole surviving gatepier (above) and the cupola above the west wing (below).

fate too. At Lathom the main block was pulled down in 1929 and the eastern service wing around 1960: acts of destruction which defy understanding and say little for the cultural progress between these generations. Just the west wing remains[9], still powerful in its functionality: when one considers this was merely the stables, it becomes clear how monumental the main structure must have been.

Lathom set the pattern for all future gentry houses and in the decades that followed came several imitators. None were on the same scale, but all made equal statements of (or at least, attempts at) grandeur and dignity. Lathom clearly served as the model in the remodelling of Parbold Hall (88) in the 1740s, although its architect is unknown. Possibly Leoni had a hand in it somewhere. Parbold differed from Lathom in that it was a transformation of something already there. It was an attempt at ennobling what was crude and provincial with a cloak of aristocracy: but it failed to completely gloss over the origins. Parbold's owner was again a man of national affairs: Thomas Crisp (1690-1758), Sherriff of Lancashire 1715-1716 and MP for Ilchester in 1727. His merchant father John had acquired the manor of Parbold c1680 but appears to have lived there in the 1660s[10]. Around 1700 he had undertaken improvements to the upper (east) wing of the house built by the Lathoms c1600. These were retained during the 1740s transformation, and as a result a degree of discord exists between the two elements. Overall, Parbold is much more compact and intimate than Lathom and unlike its predecessor, a difference in character exists between the two main fronts. The entrance front, facing north (plate 67) clearly shows some awkwardness resulting from the attempt to unify both the old and new phases. It consists of a slightly-projecting pedimented centre with doorway and large Venetian window above, and three-bay elements on either side. The centre and the portion to its right (the west wing) are all new work, two storeys in fine smooth ashlar. The east wing however is the core of the upper end of the original house and had two-and-a-half storeys, rubble masonry and mullioned windows to the cellar. The strong impression the entrance front initially makes cannot conceal these inherent flaws for long. However the south front, to the garden (plate 68), is a more unified, straightforward and successful composition, two-and-a-half storeys throughout with a recessed centre between slightly projecting wings. Its commanding position overlooking the valley gives an almost palatial air, which is clearly what Crisp intended.

Inside, Parbold's layout is a hybrid of C17 and C18 requirements resulting from the shaky marriage of the old upper wing and the new work. The former contains what were originally two parlours plus the stair but during the 1740s remodelling these rooms were demoted to a service role instead. The new work is more enlightened, the north front leading to a central entrance hall with a dining room beyond (the present garden hall) and possibly a saloon and other private apartments in the west wing.

Pl. 67
The attempts to elevate Parbold into a post-Lathom Palladian country house never completely concealed its rustic origins. This is particularly apparent in the north front, where the new work of the 1740s is at odds with the earlier remains to the left of the entrance.

By this time other gentry houses were being similarly reconditioned. The southeast front of Haigh Hall (52) was rebuilt in brick by Sir Roger Bradshaigh, 3rd Baronet and MP for Wigan from 1695 until his death in 1747.[11] A drawing of 1826[12] shows a seven bay front with recessed centre and projecting wings with ornate pedimented doorway. In 1748, Wrightington Hall (145), seat of the Dicconson family who had acquired the manor by marriage in the C17, was also upgraded. Like Parbold, this incorporated earlier work,[13] originally timber-framed and possibly of early C17 date but rebuilt in stone c1700 and fitted with supposedly 'the first sash windows in Lancashire and north of the Trent.'[14] Some of this predecessor was incorporated into the 1748 work, which is of stone with slightly projecting wings. In the same year a new main wing was added to Standish Hall (103) at right angles to the hall range of 1574, three-storeyed, brick, and with a pedimented doorway.[15] The style was distinctly minimalistic – compared to Lathom and Parbold – and has the aura of the fashionable town houses that would appear later in that century (plate 69). Some time later, in 1770, Adlington Hall (1) was transformed from a timber-framed structure to what appears almost as a miniature version of Lathom Hall but in brick. Its builder

Pl. 68
The south front of Parbold, overlooking the Douglas Valley, presents however a more balanced and almost palatial picture in a relatively small building.

Pl. 69 (below right)
Classicism expressed in brick at Standish Hall's main wing of 1748. The style is very minimalistic in comparison to Lathom and Parbold.
(Miss Hilton)

Pl. 70 (below)
Coming almost half a century after Lathom, its influence can still be detected in the simple but powerful lines of Adlington Hall of 1770.
(M D Smith)

was Sir Richard Clayton, 1st Baronet, whose family had acquired the manor before 1700.[16] The hall had a seven-bay front with pedimented centre supported on pilasters within which was a first-floor balcony and rusticated entrance (plate 70).

By the late C18, most of the gentry families had updated their residences to suit more modern tastes and in doing so they invested the locality with some of its finest buildings. The glory however was not a lasting one. Standish Hall followed the fate of Lathom and was finally demolished in the 1970s; Adlington had already been bulldozed some 20 years earlier. The enlightenment that spawned these houses is something modern times have failed to inherit.

HOUSES OF THE YEOMANRY

The intensity of the yeoman rebuilding was such that few houses appear after 1720, suggesting those who could afford to had rebuilt by this time. The ones that do appear are isolated occurences, the products of individual circumstances rather than a regional cycle as before.

Apart from renegades such as Barker's Farm, Dalton (35; see above, p113-114) houses built after 1720 show the yeomanry had more or less been fully converted to classicism by this time. Its universal acceptance is indicated by the appearance of double-depth homes of varying size relative to the status of their occupants.

The most spectacular houses of this period are a trio built more or less contemporaneously for members of the upper yeomanry. These took the double-depth plan pioneered by houses such as Green Barn Farm, Blackrod (27) and Darbyshire House, Billinge (15) a stage further by extending it to three units instead of the normal two, and two-and-a-half storeys in height throughout. Consequently these structures take on massive proportions. The trio are Manor House, Crawford, Upholland (120) of 1718, Woodcock House, Newburgh (83) of 1719 and Finch House, Shevington (99)[17] of 1724 and now demolished. Each embraced classical principles to a greater or lesser extent. All had symmetrical facades, but as we have noted already that at Manor House was compromised by an outdated central porch and Finch House was similarly penalised by a three-gable façade with recessed centre between slightly projecting wings. Woodcock (originally, Newburgh House) is more enlightened in adopting a flat front although it too retains three gables (plate 71). Manor House is let down further by using (almost unbelievably at this date) mullioned-and-transomed windows. Woodcock has cross windows throughout, typical of the date, but sashes had by this

Pl. 71
Classical dignity (despite the gables) in a wealthy yeoman house: Woodcock House, Newburgh.

Fig. 34
Woodcock House: plan.

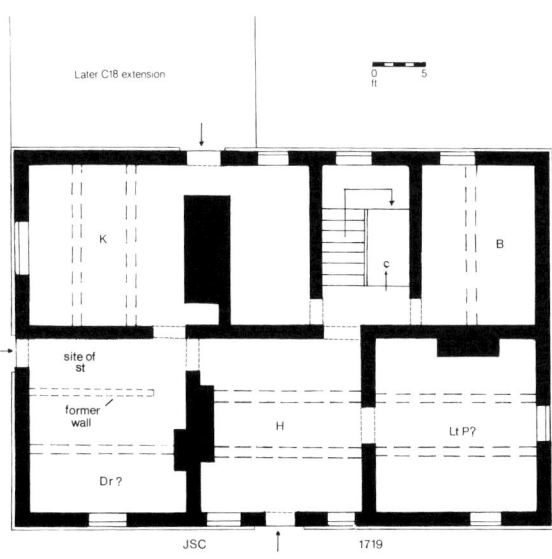

131

time already been pioneered by the gentry at Parbold (88) and Wrightington (145) halls and possibly, at yeoman level, by Knight's Hall at Upholland three years earlier (118). A photograph of c1900[17] shows Finch House with sashed windows on the principal floors and cross-windows within the attics, but as the house is long gone it is not possible to comment on their authenticity.

Evidence shows that in one of these houses at least, attempts were made at a more refined lifestyle emulating that of the gentry with rooms for a variety of uses and greater segregation of the elements of the household. Woodcock Hall was built by wealthy James Spencer and his wife Catherine. Its plan (figure 34) shows six rooms on each floor, with the usual double-depth distinction between principal rooms at the front and service rooms at the rear. In addition to the main stair there was formerly a smaller stair adjacent to the kitchen which would have been used by servants. This was a household therefore clearly segregated by rank. Spencer's inventory (LCRO WCW 1723) described him as 'gentleman' and indicates, as does the building, a lifestyle which pursued this aspirations.

Within the hall (housebody) are recorded among other items an oval table, stools, and a 'pair of virginals' (a keyboard instrument), indicating a room for assemblies and entertaining similar to that which evolved as the saloon in the residences of the gentry. For meals there were two dining rooms probably on the first floor – the 'great dining room' obviously catered for larger gatherings as it contained a 'great oval table', two smaller tables and eight chairs. The other dining room was more informal, with a

Fig. 35
Manor House: plan.

Pl. 72
The Manor House at Crawford, Upholland, effectively ruined a progresive double-depth plan by using Gothic detail. The gatepiers, ex-situ, must have been a subsequent flash of inspiration. Pictured in 1988 before restoration.

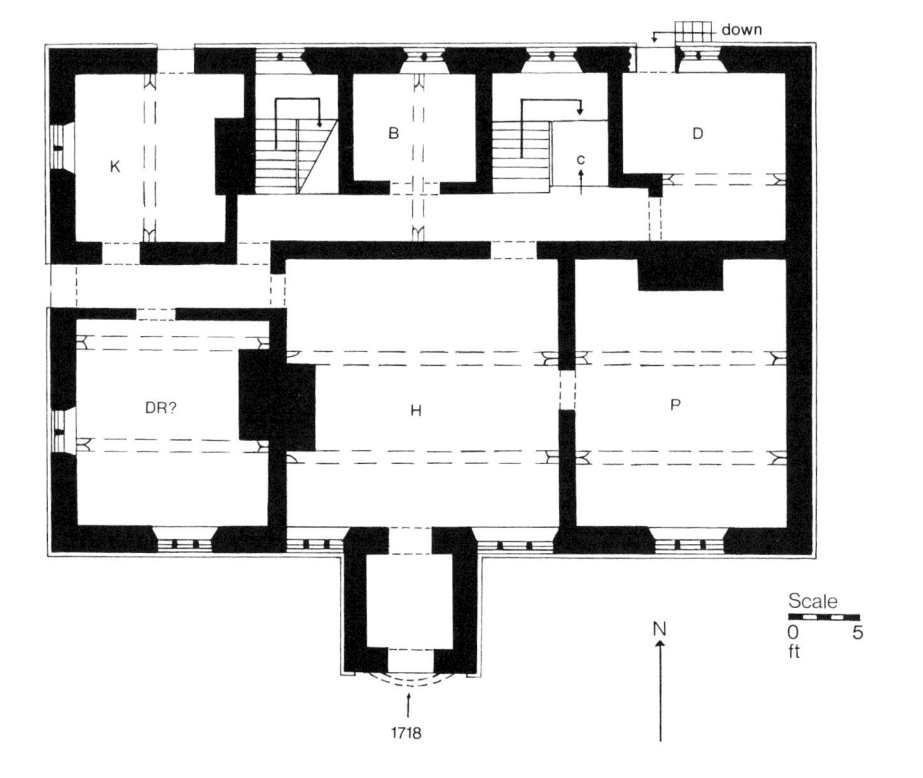

table and two forms. Other rooms given specific uses were the 'nursery', which contained several beds, and the 'children's room' which contained chairs, stools, a cupboard and stored among other things two spinning wheels. The principal bedrooms were the 'white room' and 'red chamber', but – a surprising concession to long-standing yeoman tradition – the 'little parlour' contained several beds also. Listed too was a 'serving men's chamber' which would have been within the attic space – a reversal of the gentry hierarchy displayed by Lathom Hall which now placed servants on the ground floor.

A household run along similar lines is suggested by the plan of Manor House (figure 35) whose builders were probably the Pennington family of wealthy leaseholders. It is fractionally greater in length than Woodcock but of similar depth: yet what is notable is that its principal rooms occupy a much greater proportion of the building. At 360 square feet the entrance hall is particularly large in comparison to Woodcock's of 240 square feet. This suggests an even stronger hierarchical separation between master and servant, again reinforced by the presence of two stairs and a staggered passageway running the length of the building unmistakeably dividing its social elements.

In the confines of smaller homes, lesser yeomen were unable to practise this degree of segregation and within them the hierarchical divisions become blurred. For example, as we have noted already, houses lacking a heated kitchen would have used the housebody for cooking and in the double-depth plan this severely compromised the notion of a front/rear social division. To their occupiers these gentry-led distinctions would have been impracticable social niceties. A number of compact houses appearing after 1720 show the double-depth plan was aspired to even at a modest level, as illustrated by Holmes House, Blackrod (28; plate 73) of 1721, Millets, Upholland (121) possibly of 1725, Maddocks, Billinge (22) of c1720-1725 and at a later date Greenhill Farm, Newburgh (75; plate 75) of 1748.

Similar houses also appeared in less conventional circumstances. Several buildings which underwent a staggered rebuilding – with wings added to pre-existing, timber-framed ranges – subsequently had those ranges rebuilt to classical form. This happened at Ambrose Cottage, Upholland (106; plate 74) of c1720-30 and Lyme Vale Farm, Billinge (21) of 1733. The results of this uncomfortable union are unavoidably discordant. Nowhere is this more so than at Lyme Vale, where the new, double-depth, two-and-a-half storey work towers above the diminutive remnant of the earlier wing. Another bizarre marriage, under different circumstances, occurs at Great Houghwood, Billinge (18) where an addition in classical style (but not double-depth) of c1750-1770 is grafted on as a continuation of the upper wing of the existing house of c1600.

The adoption of the double-depth plan meant houses became increasingly

Pl. 73
Holmes House, Blackrod, combined an innovative double-depth plan with a more traditional end-baffle-entry, which indicates confusion over the two styles was still occurring in the 1720s.

Pl. 74
Ambrose Cottage typifies the strained union that occurred when a classically-inspired range was grafted on to an earlier wing.
Pictured in 1981, before restoration.

Pl. 75
Greenhill Farm, Newburgh, symbolises the perfection of classicism in a small yeoman house. Even in this form, however, the housebody remained the largest room and would still have been used for cooking.

Fig. 36
Greenhill Farm: plan.

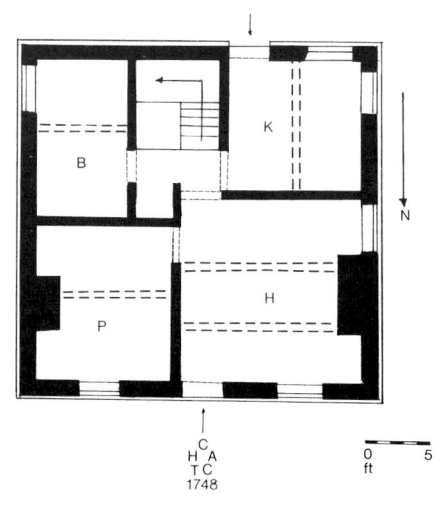

stereotyped. But the earliest show that the concept of façade symmetery was not always fully grasped. Both Holmes House and Maddocks failed to achieve this because they did not have central doorways, choosing instead to retain the end-baffle-entry which was characteristic of the two-unit houses of the late C17 (see above page 106). More progressive contemporaries must have quickly made them seem archaic.

A major factor in the standardisation process was the adoption of sash windows. Both Maddocks and Holmes House show mullioned windows were still a requirement for some in the 1720s. Others such as Ambrose Cottage had moved on to cross windows by the same time and remarkably, Lyme Vale Farm, Billinge (21) still

Pl. 76
The classical standardisation of Moorcroft House, Newburgh, is reinforced by the use of sash windows. The cellar window at the rear is, however, mullioned.

had wooden mullioned-and-transomed windows in 1733. However by the 1740s, Moorcroft House (80; plate 76) and Greenhill Farm, of 1741 and 1748 respectively and both at Newburgh, display sash windows which were now classical convention. A touch of the vernacular is still to be found in the canopy at Greenhill though, whereas at a later date the pedimented doorcases at Otterheads, Lathom (69) and the cottage at Great Houghwood, Billinge (18) are of a style that can be found throughout the region – and further afield – in town as well as rural houses. A house such as Otterheads (plate 77) probably of c1770, could be transplanted to anywhere within Lancashire and not look unduly out of context: by his time the double-pile, sash window convention was virtually universal.

Pl. 77
Otterheads, Lathom, of c1750-1770 is classicism standardised to such an extent that it would blend in with the scenery virtually anywhere in the country.

CONCLUSION

As the C18 progressed, the classical style introduced at its beginning was pursued and ultimately perfected in houses of both the gentry and the yeomanry. From the 1720s on a further gentry rebuilding occurred. The driving force were not families of ancient, provincial stock but wealthy, educated men of national prominence who pursued a more cultured lifestyle than their predecessors. The ultimate symbol of this was Lathom House, built 1725-30. Behind a monumental Palladian exterior it contained two floors of rooms to accommodate an expansive gentry lifestyle which must have been renowned not just in the locality but much wider afield. Several imitators, notably the halls of Parbold and Adlington, followed.

Meanwhile, much in the shadow of these goliaths, the yeomanry more modestly pursued a classical ideal. Several built large, three-unit double-pile houses in which a polite lifestyle, with strong segregation, was pursued. Smaller homes however made little progress in this direction as the absence of a heated kitchen continued the tradition of cooking in the housebody. In aesthetic terms yeoman houses adopted what were essentially classical templates which make them almost indistinguishable from their contemporaries elsewhere in the county and beyond. By 1770, as Lancashire was just beginning to experience the Industrial Revolution, its centuries-old traditions of vernacular building had been submerged beneath the powerful mainstream force of polite standardisation.

NOTES

1. Pevsner, South Lancashire (1969) p216-217; Fleetwood-Hesketh (1958) p48-49.
2. Pevsner, South Lancashire, p132-134; Fleetwood-Hesketh p48-49.
3. Pevsner, North Lancashire, p82-83.
4. Pevsner, North Lancashire, p174
5. Pevsner, South Lancashire, p387.
6. Pevsner, South Lancashire, p350-351.
7. LCRO DDHi
8. J Aitkin, 'Description of the Country from Thirty to Forty Miles Around Manchester' (1795) p316.
9. Restoration work, as part of a new development on the site, began in 1999.
10. Kuerden wrote of him in 1666 as 'Mr Crispe a great userer of London'. Quoted in John Martin Robinson. 'A Guide to the Country Houses of the North West' (1991) p225.
11. Donald Anderson, 'Life and Times of Haigh Hall' (1991) p108.
12. LCRO DP 291
13. VCH VI, p172-173.
14. Aitkin, (1795) p293.
15. VCH IV, p196.
16. VCH VI, p218.
17. Illustration in VCH VI

CHAPTER VI

The Fabric of Traditional Buildings

Until the appearance of the first stone gentry houses in the closing decades of the C16, rural dwellers were used to a countryside dominated for centuries by buildings of timber construction. Those new gentry homes would at first have been regarded as a novelty. But as the C17 advanced, the yeoman rebuilding affirmed that stone — and subsequently, brick — represented the future and thus timber began its long decline into obscurity. But for a time in the late C16-early C17 a polycultural approach to materials existed, with the more forward-thinking gentry and yeomanry experimenting with stone and brick and the more conservative retaining timber frame. Each type of fabric had its own peculiar character that often extended beyond simply the appearance of the building to influence the lifestyle practised within.

TIMBER-FRAMED BUILDINGS: CRUCK CONSTRUCTION

To recap what Chapter II has shown: crucks were in widespread use in the Douglas Valley from the medieval period until the C17. They were used by all levels of society and the surviving examples reflect this, falling into two categories. The first comprises those erected by the gentry in the medieval period, considerably superior and distinguished by the fine quality of their timber and construction. The second are later examples of inferior quality and status, found within houses of the yeomanry and dating probably from the C16 or even the early C17. The first group represents the tradition at its height, the second in its decline.

Cruck construction was certainly current elsewhere in the North West of England by the early C14. Three examples in the Tameside area east of Manchester have been dendrochronologically dated to have been felled between c1242-1320.[1] Nationally, a survey in 1981 recorded 3,054 surviving of which 153 were tree-ring dated over a period covering 1210-1690[2]; and 95% of these originated from 1270-1650 showing the decline of the tradition in the mid-C17. More examples come to light all the time:

Pl. 78
Detail of cruck blade at Manor House, Worthington, with moulding at its base. This was probably the central truss in the hall of a wealthy tenant and may be late C15 in date.

Pl. 79
Carved roundel on the yoke of former central truss at Kirklees Hall, Aspull.

in that 1981 survey, none of the 19 domestic examples of full crucks recorded in this book were recorded (map 4).[3]

The massive crucks that housed the sub-manorial gentry provide a yardstick against which the later and poorer examples can be judged. Those at Peel Hall, Ince (56; figure 1) are some of the finest early crucks in Lancashire and are possibly of C14 date. Similar trusses at nearby Kirklees Hall at Aspull (9) may be C15. The height and width of these trusses reflect their status, and probably also their early date, as older trusses have been shown to be larger and squarer than more youthful counterparts.[4] Peel's central truss is 21 ft 6 inches high and 17 feet wide, with the remaining intact truss at Kirklees measuring 22 feet by 19 feet. The dimensions of the blades themselves are similar too, typically 20 inches by 10inches at Peel and 17 inches by 7 inches at Kirklees.

Of the two, the timbers at Peel are more visible and less altered and therefore are an excellent illustration of the techniques involved. Here and at Kirklees, the blades were originally set some two feet above ground level upon a stone plinth. At the apex, the blades meet above a yoke, a similar detail found also at Kirklees and at Black Lawyers, Worthington (125; plate 12). The central truss of the former hall at Peel (figure 1) has a cranked collar set at mid-height and arch-braced to the blades to produce a very distinctive form which denotes this truss as the most important one within the building. A similar arched signature was given to the solitary truss surviving at Manor House, Worthington (126; figure 3) which again must have been the centrepiece of the former hall; one may have been present also upon the cruck at Bannister Farm, Wrightington (129). Outside the area, at Tameside a cruck at Taunton Hall, Ashton-under-Lyne is of similar style and its felling has been dendro-dated to c1315-20.[5] At Peel the central truss shows the superior treatment frequently given to the side which faced the high table or dais end. This side has been embellished with a run-out chamfer and the blades are more smoothly finished. Further special treatment of the dais side is seen at Kirklees where the blades have a hollow chamfer.

The external walls of cruck buildings were virtually free-standing and non-loadbearing and secured to the trusses by mean of a spur, a short horizontal timber projecting from the blades to the wallposts. These survive at Peel and also at Manor House. The spurs also carried the wallplate, a horizontal timber running the length of the structure into which the feet of the rafters were secured. Again at Peel, the wallplates survive with peg holes showing the position of the former wallposts. Tenoned into the wallposts at intervals were horizontal rails and together they formed the outer walls —the resulting pattern being termed 'square framing' — and the spaces between the timber infilled with wattle-and-daub.

The inadequacies of the cruck tradition were revealed with the advent of post and truss construction in the C14 and C15 which allowed the construction of storeyed wings. Subsequently, its demise was assured when single-storeyed halls became obsolete in the mid C16. Thereafter many cruck halls were upgraded by the insertion of a ceiling to create a room above. However, this still involved some difficulty: due to the steepness of the roof pitch, headroom was always distinctly lacking on the newly-created upper floor. As both Peel and Manor House illustrate, one method around this was to raise the height of the roof. This was done by removing the purlins from their original housings upon the blades and setting them upon outriders, which were new timbers inserted between the blades and spurs to reduce the pitch of the roof, raise the eaves and thus create marginally more headroom (figure 1). A useful upper storey could then be achieved, but this was only possible if the cruck itself was of sufficient height. At Peel and Manor House this was not a problem. But in the poorer crucks found in yeoman houses a more drastic solution was sometimes necessary. Both Harsnips at Dalton (42) and Higher Barn, Wrightington (135) are houses where the owners took radical action by removing the upper portion of the cruck completely and instead creating a full-height room above by using load-bearing walls supporting principal-rafter roof trusses. The remains of the cruck then functioned only to support the ceiling. To do this however required considerable effort and expenditure and the advantages in poorer buildings may have been minimal: despite the use of outriders the room above the housebody at Lower Tower Hill, Upholland (119) remains merely a loft. At Lower House, Dalton (44) the occupier never even went to the trouble of ceiling the housebody, the room remaining open to the roof even after cladding in the C17-18.

The crucks found in houses such as these are much poorer than the benchmark examples of Peel and Kirklees. Of the 15 full crucks belonging to yeoman houses (see map 4) a considerable variation in quality occurs but all are distinctly inferior to the gentry examples, in both height and width of the structure and the dimensions of the timbers themselves. At Lower Tower Hill the height of the sole remaining truss is 16 feet 6 inches compared to the 21 feet 6 inches at Peel; the lower portion of the blades have been removed but their span could have been no more than 14 feet wide. At Lower House the blades of both trusses are notably irregular (figure 5) and in places are just 7 inches in width.

These and the other surviving 'yeoman' crucks belong to modest buildings and the impression therefore comes through that those who could afford to rid themselves of crucks did so during the rebuilding. It would appear that in some early cases crucks were replaced first by superior post-and-truss houses, as the cruck blades reused within roof trusses at Willow Barn (144) at Wrightington and Giants Hall, Standish (102; figure 6) both of the early C17, indicate. Thereafter the use of load-bearing walls of stone and brick generated the widespread appearance of storeyed houses which made the cruck tradition well and truly obsolete. Yet, its final vestige, the upper cruck, (essentially a principal rafter truss with curved principals) saw limited use through the late C17 and into the early C18, as their surprising use at the fine classical houses of Stone Hall, Dalton (48) and Lowe's, Newburgh (78) demonstrates (figure 9). But it must never be forgotten that although the method of construction probably ceased to be current by the middle of the C17, cruck buildings were still a dominant feature of the landscape into the C19 as the accounts of contemporary writers such as Hewitson (above, page 39) and present-day statistical analysis of surviving buildings (table 1, page 32) both indicate.

TIMBER-FRAMING: POST AND TRUSS

Post and truss construction was introduced to Lancashire in the C14, when Baguley Hall, south Manchester, pioneered the technique which became standard for all homes at major gentry level in the following century.[6] The fine halls of Smithills, Ordsall and Rufford all bear testimony to this, and by the early C16 the middle and minor gentry of the Douglas Valley had followed suit as Bradley Hall, Langtree (57) and Crawshaw Hall, Adlington (3) and possibly Bogburn Hall, Coppull (29) indicate.

Later, the halls of Standish (103; plate 29) and Worthington (128, plate 85) show post-and-truss was still being adhered to during the C16 gentry rebuilding despite the appearance of fine stone houses elsewhere. The pioneers of the yeoman rebuilding used the technique too, as South Tunley (139; plate 22) Wrightington and Giants Hall, Standish (102) illustrate; the latter and Willow Barn, Wrightington (144) demonstrating also that these buildings appear to have been a direct replacement for cruck-framed predecessors. However, Spring Bank, Wrightington (141; plate 23) was built with a ground floor of stone and an upper storey which was timber-framed, indicating that transition to more permanent materials was slowly occurring.

Some 44 buildings containing or formerly containing post-and-truss construction survive in the area. Their distribution is fairly widespread, but with a greater concentration on the Parbold-Harrock-Coppull landmass north of the river (see map 5, page 38). This may reflect either conservatism or inaccessibility of stone, as several of these buildings, such as Willow Barn (144) Bogburn Hall (29) and Coppull Old Hall, Coppull (32) were rebuilt in brick at a subsequent date. As this was a more sophisticated, potentially decorative — and expensive — method than cruck construction, post-and-truss was likely to be within the reach of the wealthier section of society, and of the 44 recorded examples (map 5), 22 (50%) are identified with families that were of middle or minor gentry status. The occurence of these houses

Pl. 80
Joints in timber-framed construction are frequently indicated by carpenters' marks, which were used to aid asembly and can take the form of symbols, or Roman or Arabic numerals. These fine examples are in the parlour wing of Holland's House, Dalton, possibly c1605.

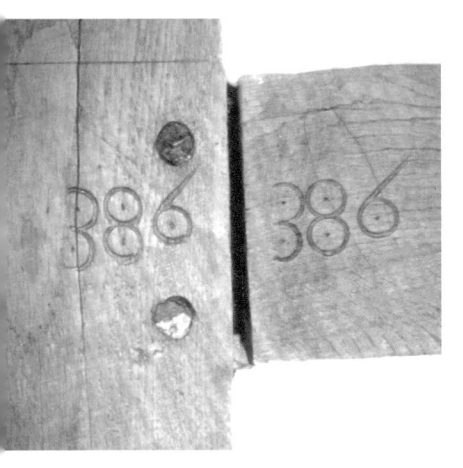

Pl. 81
Principal rafter trusses continued to be used for some time before the practice of load-bearing walls was sufficiently developed. These examples were exposed during the decay of Belle Vue Farm, Dalton of 1683, with that above the parlour wing (right of photo) containing re-used cruck blades as principals.

Pl. 82
Fine herringbone kingpost truss, braced to wallposts below, at Rose Cottage, Newburgh, indicating that this was once a fine timber-framed building of the early C17.

throughout the area is another indication of its prosperity in the C16-17.

They also represent the time when the carpentry tradition was at its height, as the halls of Bradley (57), Bogburn (29) and Crawshaw (3), are composed of fine timbers which demonstrate the status of their occupants not only through their heavy dimensions but also by the overall height of the structures. At Bradley the former open hall stands at more than 27 feet in height. Compare this with the 21 feet 6 inches of the crucks at Peel Hall, Ince (56) – the best of this type – and at once the superiority of post-and-truss houses becomes clear.

Post-and-truss construction also offered considerable opportunities for display and decoration. This usually expressed itself upon the roof trusses, where they were open to view, and the wallposts supporting them. The most usual form of truss was the principal rafter type with struts in the angles which were either straight or curved. This appears early at Bogburn (figure 10) and Crawshaw, both probably of late C15-early C16 date and the smaller C16 yeoman open halls of Dam House, Langtree (58; figure 17) and Holt Farm, Coppull (33; figure 15) and subsequently in the early C17 yeoman houses such as Upper Standish Wood Fold (104).

Occasionally more decorative trusses replace this basic form. The most superior was the kingpost truss, which makes an appearance in the C15 service wing added to Peel Hall at Ince (57, figure 1). But unlike the robust, high-status kingpost trusses found elsewhere in open halls such as Alston Old Hall, Longridge, Lancashire, probably of the mid C15 and examples of the C15-C16 in West Yorkshire[7], that at Peel verges on the bizarre, as it is forked at the base and forms an inverted Y-shape. This form of truss also appears in more conventional — but highly decorative — configuration in the early C17 where it enjoyed some popularity as a means of embellishing external gables

141

Pl. 83
Detail of the fine kingpost truss at Ackhurst Hall, Orrell, possibly c1618. Its use in the attic above the parlour wing suggests it may have embellished a chapel used by the Catholic Leigh family.

Fig. 37
Superior arch-braced truss of probably C15 date at Gidlow Hall, Aspull, indicating an important building existed here at that time.
Subsequently re-used in attic of stair tower during 1574 rebuilding.
(Based partly on drawing by GMAU.)

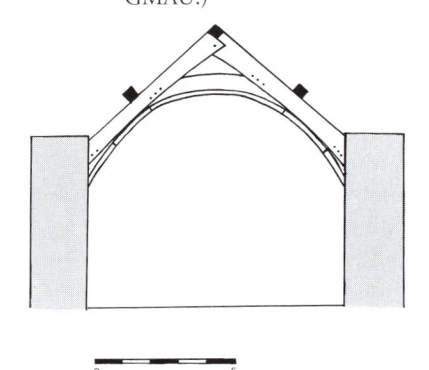

by using several pairs of struts in a 'herringbone' effect. This occurs at Rose Cottage, Newburgh (81; plate 82) and was present at Crooke Hall (98) Shevington of 1608 and the upper wing of South Tunley (139) at Wrightington of 1622, both now demolished. Elsewhere this form served a different purpose: Ackhurst Hall, Orrell (84) used a decorative turned kingpost within its attic, again in the early C17, possibly to accentuate a room used as a secret chapel by the Catholic Leigh family (plate 83).

Another decorative variation was a truss which was arched-braced to a collar, a translation of the technique used to elaborate the central crucks at Peel and Manor House, Worthington (126). Two C15 examples of this type survive, but neither in their entirety. The most complete is at Gidlow Hall, Aspull (7; figure 37) reused within the stair turret of 1574; the other is partially exposed in the service wing at Bradley Hall, Standish (57). Their use alongside more conventional principal rafter trusses in both houses suggests they belonged to and embellished superior rooms, possibly the solar.

The wallposts supporting the roof trusses were also given a limited adornment. The head of the post, where it is jointed to the tiebeam, was normally of greater width than the lower portion and was either flared (a gradual taper) as at Peel or Bradley or jowled (with a pronounced step) as at Bogburn or Knights Hall, Upholland (118). An exceptional treatment occurs in the early C17 reconstruction of the wing at Bradley, where the wallposts end in distinctive carved capitals (plate 84) Here, the posts themselves are given a quarter-round moulding matching the beams, in sharp contrast to the plain chamfer and stop of the C15 wallposts of the hall range. A similar quarter-round treatment is found on the wallposts at Knight's Hall. For stability, and decorative effect, wallposts are generally secured to the tiebeam of the truss with braces which are usually curved; those at Peel's service wing (figure 1) rise from mid-height on the posts but more normally the braces are set closer to the tiebeam.

Externally, highly decorative treatment was possible where this lay within the means of the owner. The square panels of the outer walls, formed by the intersection of posts and rails, were embellished with a variety of decorative shapes. This trend began and flourished with the major gentry halls of the C15 such as Smithills, Ordsall and Rufford and continued in the C16, evidently also as a prerogative of the gentry. The demolished Standish, Crooke and Wrightington halls all displayed decorative framing, and some presently remains at Worthington Hall (128) Worthington, dated 1577 (plate 85). Standish had by far the best display, with tiers of quatrefoil panels on the ground floor of the hall range and large cusped saltires above in a striking demonstration equalling that of any of the C15 examples quoted above (plate 29). Worthington originally had a more extensive decoration than now remains, using saltires along with crosses and ogee bracing, but although the effect is more varied than

Standish it is somewhat less impressive. By 1608 the decoration had become more minimalistic as Crooke demonstrated, where the decorative panels had largely given way to herringbone bracing but with some saltires on the porch and crosses upon the dormer above the hall.

It is probable of course that other timber-framed gentry halls, such as Bradley (57) at Langtree were similarly decorated, but all evidence of this has been taken away by subsequent cladding. Similarly no trace survives within the early yeoman houses. The only one to retain its timber-framing until the 1950s was South Tunley at Wrightington, but its exterior used simple square-framing without decorative panels. The absence of this form of decoration in a substantial house such as South Tunley, at the forefront of the yeoman rebuilding, suggests it was not widely practised in this class – if at all – and was restricted mainly to gentry use.

As Chapter II shows, post-and-truss construction ceased in the early C17, but long after, its influence continued into the generation of stone and brick houses which succeeded it. Throughout the rest of the C17, and in some cases into the C18, triangulated roof trusses – mainly of principal rafter form – continued to be used, set no longer upon wallposts but walls of stone or brick. It was not until the later C17 that sufficient confidence was placed in the load-bearing ability of these materials to support the roof directly without the need for trusses. Furthermore, timber-framed walls of square framing continued to be used for internal walls throughout the same timespan. The timber legacy can in both these respects be detected even in so

Pl. 84
Wallposts in the service wing of Bradley Hall, Langtree were given unusual carved capitals which denote this must have been a superb timber-framed building of c1600.

Pl. 85
Gentry exuberance: remains of decorative square framing of 1577 at Worthington Hall, Worthington.

advanced a house as Darbyshire Farm, Billinge (15) as late as 1716, where the staircase is flanked by full-height timber-framed walls supporting half-trusses carrying the purlins at the rear.

STONE

Stone symbolised the spirit of the rebuilding. It expressed, in a landscape dominated by wooden houses, a sense of wealth, status and permanence. Hitherto reserved mainly for churches and castles, stone became – through its use in the gentry homes of the late C16 – associated with high social standing and thus subsequently evolved as a key element in the gentrification process.

All the aspirations connected with stone can be seen in the buildings which pioneered its use. The earliest dated stone house is 1574, Gidlow Hall at Aspull (7; plates 7 & 31): a surviving fragment of a substantial house which resulted from a far-sighted decision by a minor gentry family to select stone rather than timber-frame. By comparison, the Standish family, one of the area's most prominent landowners, were at about the same time still using timber for their hall, which makes Thomas Gidlow's choice of stone all the most significant. Therefore, Gidlow was a man who clearly realised – well ahead of his wealthier but clearly more conservative contemporaries – that the desired image of gentility could be furthered by a substantial residence using the most prestigious building material.

Others saw the advantages of stone not just in building terms. Its use was encouraged by the rising 'new gentry' who hurried the rebuilding along in the closing years of the C16. To them, a substantial stone manor house was compensation for – and a distraction from – the lack of an ancient lineage. Hardly surprising then that self-made men such as James Bankes used stone for Winstanley Hall (124) and the Andertons, newcomers to their manor, for Birchley Hall, Billinge (12) in the 1590s. The sight of innovative houses such as these subsequently pressured the established gentry to follow suit, with the Bisphams building Bispham Hall, Billinge (13) and the Rigbys Harrock (134) both c1600. As we have seen, the earliest phase of the yeoman rebuilding still saw investment in timber-framed homes, but they too saw the advantages of the new material in both structural and social terms. The earliest stone house of the yeomanry is probably Balcony Farm, Upholland (107; plate 41) of c1600. The acceleration of the rebuilding after 1660 saw the use of stone become widespread, both for new building and the cladding – 'modernisation' – of older timber-framed ones.

The fabric of these buildings is mainly sandstone, the rock which sculpts both the Ashurst-Billinge and Parbold-Harrock-Coppull landmasses that define the Douglas

Valley. Mostly it is the Carboniferous type, buff in colour, but variations occur in particular localities. The pioneering Gidlow Hall (7) at Aspull, would have been even more striking to its contemporaries because of its use of sandstone which is bright yellow-orange in colour. A similar stone is used for decorative effect across the valley at Halliwell's Farm, Upholland (115) where it is used on the porch of 1671 (plate 9). One drawback of this material is that it is quite friable and in both cases weather erosion has taken its toll of detailing. Another variation in colour is presented by the Triassic outcrops which occur to the north of Harrock Hill. Their warm red-brown hue, found at Lower Wrennall (136) of 1673 and Sanderson House (138; plate 45) of C17-18 date, give a distinctive appearance not found anywhere else in the area. Another variety found in this northern area is the Millstone Grit, a harsh, coarse sandstone which, hewn into massive blocks, provides quoins and plinths for early timber-framed buildings such as Bogburn Hall (29) and Holt Farm (33) both at Coppull.

With the exception of the gritstones, sandstone is easily workable and lends itself to intricately-sculpted details, such as the moulded responds which were a feature of several porch doorways in the C17. For walling, they were generally hewn into 'rubble' stone which were roughly squared blocks laid in courses between 18 inches and two feet thick. However stone walls of exceptional thickness – three feet and more – are found at Crawshaw Hall, Adlington (3) and Knight's House, Upholland (118) in both cases associated with the cladding of timber-framed buildings. At Crawshaw, unusually for a gentry building, the stone is of a type termed 'random rubble', which is laid not in courses but in an irregular pattern. This and the thickness of the walls suggests an unfamiliarity with the handling of this new material.

On the Ashurst-Billinge ridge, outcrops of more fissile sandstone, which splits into thin slabs rather than the more usual blocks, lends a distinctive appearance to local buildings around Dalton and Upholland. Poorer structures such as the C17 wing of Bounty Farm, Upholland (109) and Cicely's Cottage, Dalton (39) are composed entirely of these striated stones, while more substantial houses such as Belle Vue Farm, Dalton (37) made use of higher-quality squared blocks on the façade and relegated the thin slabs to the rear. These fissile stones are unsuitable for detailing, giving a somewhat spartan appearance to the buildings they produce: doorways are plain and hoodmoulds merely a series of thin projecting slabs. In contrast, the most dignified use of stone was brought to the area by the fine gentry houses of the C18, Lathom Hall (66) and Parbold (88) which made use of dressed sandstone blocks termed ashlar. At the latter, this is in sharp contrast on the façade to the squared rubble of the late C17 east wing. Adding to the grandeur of these buildings were refined classical details such as pediments and door and window surrounds, all executed in stone to a high standard (plate 95).

Pl. 86
Stonework of several periods at Crawshaw Hall, Adlington, including a blocked doorway in the originally timber-framed solar wing.

BRICK

As a replacement for timber-frame, brick came into use considerably later than stone and its first use in the early C17 appears somewhat tentative. However it found favour as the century progressed in localised areas where the geology made the underlying stone difficult to obtain. This was generally in the fringes of the area where the upland masses descend to meet the plain, so bricks are common around Lathom and Newburgh in the west, and in the northern part of Wrightington; but a band of brick building is also found at higher level in the north and east from Coppull and Adlington to Aspull.

In Lancashire as a whole, the first use of brick in domestic building appears to have been in the south wing of Salmesbury Hall near Preston of around 1545.[9] Its acceptance elsewhere at more minor gentry level was confirmed later by buildings such as Downholland Hall, Downholland of c1600 and Carr House, Bretherton of 1613 both upon the coastal plain. However the gentry of the Douglas Valley largely chose to ignore this material, either opting for stone or retaining timber-frame. What we do have in brick is minimal, occurring towards the end of the rebuilding activity of this class. Allanson Hall, Adlington (2) is the earliest dated brick house in the area, 1618. Not long after it was followed by Coppull Hall, Coppull (31) where a modern datestone reading 1631 adorns what appears to be a brick addition to a pre-existing timber-framed manor house.

After these somewhat hesitant appearances it was left to the yeomanry to make brick buildings more widespread. James Naylor, newly succeeded to his father's freehold estate in Rainford, built the first brick house among the yeomanry in the form of Guild Hall (91; plate 44) dated 1629: what is surprising is that he chose this material in what is otherwise a stone-built area. But we can see at Guild Hall the same type of assertive statement that the 'new gentry' were making with their stone manor houses over a quarter of a century earlier. Here was an ambitious yeoman proclaiming his presence not only with a house of an innovative style, but an innovative building material as well. A similar, but oddly less confident, use of brick in a stone area is Douglas Bank Farm at Upholland (114; plate 47). Here in 1656 freeholder Henry Fisher constructed a substantial brick house — but unusually behind a stone façade. Fisher was hedging his bets between the two new materials, but perhaps chose the brilliant orangey sandstone for the striking effect it had on the façade. Following these pioneers, the gathering momentum of the yeoman rebuilding in the 1660s and thereafter saw an increasing number of brick houses springing up in the north and east of the area.

In this early brickwork the bonding was of the English Garden Wall type, using

Pl. 87
Handmade brick at Webster's Farm, Lathom, of 1682: showing finger prints left in the soft clay before it was fired.

generally between three and five courses of stretchers to one of headers but often the pattern is irregular. During the middle of the C17, as brick grew in use and popularity, the fashion spread for using it decoratively. This expressed itself either in designs using either raised brickwork or vitrified bricks that were coloured bluish-purple using a special firing process. The first dated occurrence of raised brickwork is at Pennington Hall Farm, Aspull (10) where the date '1653' is spectacularly displayed on the façade of the upper wing (plate 89). Other buildings displayed a variety of forms. Douglas Bank Farm, Upholland (114) has a grid of lozenges (plate 90) on the lower wing and a cross on the stair tower. Aspinwall's Farm, Lathom (61; demolished) had a heart pattern and its near neighbour Webster's (73) of 1682 has a central rectangular design on the range along with a course supported on dentilled headers. The fashion continued into the 1690s, but in a more minimalistic way. At Mill Bridge Farm, Worthington (127) of 1694 the decoration was restricted to a simple dogtooth-style course above the windows, a similar trait occurring nearby at Coppull Old Hall (32) of c1700. Of that date also is Darbyshire Farm, Lathom, (64) where the bold lozenge pattern on the large chimney stack is a final exuberance of the practice. The versatility of brick was demonstrated in other ways. In areas where stone was scarce, bricks were frequently cut and shaped to form mullions as at Willow Barn (144) and Copyhold (131) in Wrightington.

A more polite approach to brickwork coincided with the progression towards classicism in the early C18. One aspect was the introduction of Flemish bond in place

Pl. 88
Decorative brickwork became fashionable in the third quarter of the C17: Willow Barn, Wrightington employed vitrified headers in a lozenge pattern.

Pl. 89
Raised brickwork was another technique that flourished. Pennington Hall boldly declares its date of 1653.

Pl. 90
Douglas Bank Farm displays a multi-lozenge brickwork pattern of 1656.

of English, which produced a more consistent and decorative effect using alternating headers and stretchers. This was in use by 1719, when it contributes greatly to the refined appearance of Woodcock Hall, Newburgh (83; plate 70) of that year. Flemish bond then became more of less standard for the rest of the century, in houses such as Moorcroft House, also Newburgh (80; plate 75) of 1741 and Otterheads, Lathom (69) of 1770.

NOTES

1. University of Manchester Archeological Unit, 'A survey of the Cruck Buildings of Tameside' 1998 page 49. The houses are: Apethorn Fold, Hyde (II; AD 1212); Newton Hall, Hyde (1315); Taunton Hall, Ashton-under-Lyne (II; 1315-20); Woodfield Farm, Ashton-under-Lyne (II; 1338).
2. N W Alcock, 'Cruck Construction', Council for British Archeology Research Report no. 42, 1981.
3. Alcock, Cruck Construction; the only crucks recorded in this area were non-domestic examples at barns at Bogburn Hall, Coppull (29) and Elmhurst Farm, Coppull.
4. UMAU, Tameside, p56.
5. UMAU, Tameside, p49
6. Pevsner, South Lancashire, 1969 p344
7. Colum Giles, 'Rural Houses of West Yorkshire 1400-1830', RCHME (1986), p21-22
8. Pevsner, North Lancashire, 1969, p216-7

CHAPTER VII

Exterior Elements and Ornament

The outward appearance of houses reveals much about the people who built them. Their affluence (or otherwise), their awareness of architectural fashions, and their desire to impress neighbours or elevate themselves socially are reflected in their buildings: and in particular the way they were embellished.

In most, the basic structure had some form of decoration applied to it. This usually takes the form of enrichment around essential functional elements such as doors and windows but sometimes also involves the addition of substantial but non-essential appendages such as porches and stair towers, whose role was frequently glorified into a status symbol.

During the C17 and early C18 there was a radical change in the architectural inspiration behind these decorative features with the transition from Gothic to classical ornament during the yeoman rebuilding. This was not a smooth or straightforward process. Its progress was hindered not only by a lack of aesthetic awareness in this remote northern county but also by an innate conservatism which perpetuated Gothic forms well into the C18. By copying the gentry homes built earlier in the C17, certain yeomen were more concerned with furthering their own 'gentrification' than the fact they were perpetuating a style that by now was outmoded. Yet others were clearly more inspired, and after some early and semi-literate attempts, classical detailing gained sufficient favour to become the norm by 1720. But by this time the rebuilding had more or less run its course, so it was left to the substantial C18 gentry houses of Lathom and Parbold that followed to demonstrate classicism in its more refined forms.

DOORWAYS

External entrances lend themselves readily to decoration as a means of emphasising their significance. This is particularly so in classical buildings where the central doorway acted as the focus of the symmetrical façade and thus it frequently received special decorative attention.

In the earliest surviving buildings, the doorways have lintels in the form of a four-centred arch, a form derived from the Perpendicular phase of Gothic which was current in England from the early C15 to the reign of Henry VIII but hung on in a debased manner at vernacular level in remote areas such as Lancashire. Doorways of this type span the transition from timber to masonry, and thus appear in wood at Worthington Hall, Worthington (124) in 1577 and in stone at Birchley Hall, Billinge (12) in 1594. The style continued into the early C17 as the re-used door lintel at Widdows Farm barn, Dalton (50) dated 1625 and the original entrance at Guild Hall, Rainford (91) of 1629 demonstrate. An interesting deviation from this form occurs at Maggot's Nook, Rainford (93) where the crosswing of early C17 date has a blocked external door with four-centred head beneath a lintel that is of steep triangular shape: a real oddity (plate 91).

By this time though a simplified form, where the arch is flattened out to a depressed triangular shape, had appeared, first at South Tunley, Wrightington (139) of 1622 and subsequently made other dated appearances including Douglas Bank Farm, Upholland (114) 1656, Copyhold Farm, Wrightington (131) 1659, Bogburn Hall, Coppull (29) 1663, Leveldale, Lathom (67) of 1664 and Lower Wrennall, Wrightington (136) of 1673. The latest dated example of this type is at Lower Tower Hill, Upholland (119) a modest cruck-framed yeoman's house rebuilt in 1684. These triangular arches were therefore a standard form throughout much of the C17.

By the 1680s, doorways of more conventional style had entered the scene where the arch had given way to a plain, square-headed type as at Webster's, Lathom (73) of 1682 and Ivy Cottage, Newburgh (76) 1690. Both are relatively modest houses. In more affluent buildings the doorway soon became the subject of considerable embellishment as classicism spread in the early C18. Some of the earliest classical treatments, as at Bispham Hall, Bispham (24) of c1700-1710 and Fir Tree House, Billinge (16) of 1704 were applied to the door surround. In both cases the doors have a moulded architrave and at Bispham a false keystone is applied to the door-head. Other houses went further, combining these classical surrounds with decorative emphasis above the doorway. These take the form of pediments or straight entablature, both refined classical devices but not overly refined in their execution at this vernacular level. Stone Hall, Dalton (48) of c1700 introduces the pediment to this area: it is of the scrolly type, but is clumsy in appearance and suggests unfamiliarity with the handling of these details (plate 92). That at Darbyshire House, Billinge (15) of 1716 is better, but is spoiled by the shapeless date plaque which sprawls uncomfortably within the tympanum (plate 93). A finer, later rendering is

Pl. 91
Four-centred arched doorway at Maggot's Nook, Rainford, with unusual triangular lintel: early C17.

A variety of classical doorways:

Pl. 92 (top left) Innovative but somewhat unrefined handling of classical details, as witnessed by the scrolly pediment at Stone Hall, Dalton, c.1700.

Pl. 93 (top right) Dominating the façade of Darbyshire House, Billinge, is this fine pedimented doorcase of 1716; pictured in 1987 before restoration.

Pl. 94 (bottom left) Canopies found favour in the early-to-mid C18 and this example of 1719 on scrolly brackets is at Woodcock Hall, Newburgh.

Pl. 95 (bottom right) An idea of the magnificence of the now-demolished Lathom House, Lathom, is given by this fine pedimented doorway with Gibbs surround in the surviving stable block.

that at Otterheads, Lathom (69) of mid-C18 date. Entablatures, meanwhile, made appearances at the now-ruinous Lyme Tree House, Billinge (20) a fine example with moulded architrave and a pulvinated frieze inserted perhaps c1715-20 into an earlier house. It is now sadly crumbling away. A simpler form, really only a moulded cornice, adorns Manor House, Crawford, Upholland (120) of 1718.

Towards the middle of the C18 a further doorway embellishment makes its debut, the canopy. These came in either triangular or semicircular shape and were supported on stone or wooden brackets. The earliest example is Woodcock House, Newburgh of 1719 (83, plate 94) and of the semicircular type, as is Moorcroft House, Newburgh (80) of 1741. The interior of both is plain, but a more inspired approach was to use a scalloped pattern to imitate a seashell as at the exceptionally pretty doorway to Cockleshell Cottage, Windle, of 1742, just outside our area. Possibly the earliest canopy of triangular form is that at Billinge Hall, an almost barbaric rendering which is just one ambiguity in a very ambiguous building. It is merely two angled slabs supported on crude brackets. That at Greenhill Farm, Newburgh (83), is dated 1748 and is somewhat better in execution.

In the two great C18 gentry houses of Parbold and Lathom halls, classical doorways were demonstrated in a more expansive and scholarly way. At Parbold (88) the north front has the central entrance bay projecting beneath a gable pediment within which is the crest of the Crisp family. The doorway is surmounted by a broken triangular pediment within which rises a semicircular fanlight and the door itself is flanked by narrow windows on each side framed by pilasters. Parbold (1740s?) took its inspiration from the now-demolished Lathom (66; 1725-1730) where similar treatments were pioneered.

PORCHES

Those who could afford it took the idea of emphasising the doorway a stage further. Porches dramatically expressed the height of a building at a time when men wanted to affirm their superiority over homes that were merely single-storey. The minimal practical benefits – of draught protection and provision of a small room on the upper floor – were secondary to their principal function as a status symbol.

Consequently, we find full-height porches appearing in gentry homes of the C16 and early C17 and subsequently employed by yeomen eager to 'gentrify' themselves. The pattern was established by the trio of stone manor houses built southwest of Wigan in the last quarter of the C16. Birchley (12), Winstanley (124) and Bispham (13) halls all had more or less identical facades in which the porch was a key element. It was sited in the inner angle formed by the recessed hall and the projecting lower wing, with a similar projection (without doorway) in the opposite angle to balance it out into a symmetrical, five-gabled front. At Harrock Hall, Wrightington (134) a similar arrangement of c1600 exists with porches at either end of the recessed hall, but only the lower one, leading to the screens passage, is original. But the upper porch may be a faithful C19 replica of a C17 predecessor in a symmetrical façade. Both

Porches of varying style:

Pl.96 (top left)
Harrock Hall.

Pl. 97 (top right)
Prior's Wood Hall, Dalton.

Pl. 98 (bottom left)
Mill Bridge Farm, Worthington.

Pl. 99 (bottom right)
Manor House, Crawford, Upholland, 1718.

Harrock and Bispham have a style of entrance which became virtually synonymous with porches in the C17. It consists of a semi-circular arch springing from moulded responds (plate 96), and was copied subsequently by yeoman houses throughout the C17 such as Halliwell's Farm, Upholland (115), 1671, Digmoor Hall, Upholland (113), Prior's Wood Hall, Dalton (45, plate 97) and even into the C18 with stragglers such as Newgate Farm, Upholland (122) of 1707.

In the Birchley trio and at Harrock, the porches are coupled to the lower wings, and this occurs also at yeoman level also at Douglas Bank Farm (114) of 1656 and Digmoor Hall (113) both Upholland. Where no lower wing existed the porch became an independent element and thus dominates the facades of houses such as North Tunley, Wrightington (137) of c1620, Copyhold, also Wrightington of 1659 (131) and Belle Vue Farm, Dalton of 1683 (37).

With the progression in the C17 towards centralised and double-pile forms, the use of porches began to diminish: they were not a required element of classical planning. For a time in the late C17-early C18, full-height porches were joined by ones of single-storey only, such as those at Scythe Stone Delph Farm, Rainford (94; porch after 1682), Cock Farm, Lathom (63) of 1708, Harsnips, Dalton (42) and Maddocks, Billinge (22) the latter two both early C18. Nevertheless even in 1718 a sizeable house such as Manor House at Crawford, Upholland (120) still retained a full-height porch (plate 99) and so did Needless Inn, Lathom (68) of similar date. More astounding still is Barker's, Dalton (35), still clinging on to a two-storey porch long after they had ceased to be current; to the extent that one doubts whether the 1742 datestone really can apply.

STAIR TOWERS

The philosophy behind these was similar to that regarding porches: their purpose was generally one of display. Again, it was a means of emphasising that a building was of more than one storey and thus of superior status. Unlike porches however, their role was a less visible one as stair towers are normally sited to the rear.

Also, their use was less widespread. Not every householder chose to provide a dedicated expensive structure to house the staircase, most preferring to accommodate it within the main body of the building. Despite this, stair towers, especially north of the river – around the Wrightington area – did attract a following.

To those who could afford them, they offered the practical advantage of minimal intrusion into living space. Therefore they tend to be associated with gentry or upper yeomanry houses. Their use appears to have been pioneered at Gidlow Hall, Aspull (7) of 1574 in the early stages of the gentry rebuilding, followed afterwards by

Harrock Hall, Wrightington (134) c1600. The substantial early yeoman houses of North Tunley (137) and Sanderson House (138), both Wrightington, followed suit. In the former the tower is coupled to the upper wing but gabled independently; at Sanderson the tower assumes the unusual form of a porch-like projection.

In these, as in most other cases, the tower is sited at the rear of the housebody with the stairs therefore leading off that room. An exception though is Bannister House, Wrightington (129) where the tower is located in a side wall of the upper crosswing of c1600, with the stairs accessed from the parlour.

The occurrence of stair towers declines after the mid-C17 as yeomen generally chose to accommodate stairs initially within the upper crosswing and subsequently within the main body of centralised or double-pile houses. Predictably though we have stragglers still employing stair towers in the early C18: Holland's House (43) Dalton, and Toogood Hall (143) of 1708 and Stoney Lane Farm (142) both Wrightington. However each of these shows evidence of reconstruction from earlier timber-framed origins so it is possible their towers are a perpetuation in stone of an earlier form.

WINDOWS

Of all architectural details, windows were subject to the greatest transformation. In the late C16 and early C17 they were horizontal grids of many mullions and occasional transoms; by the mid-C18 they were tall, vertical sashes of finely-balanced proportions.

Windows of mullioned form were long in favour. They are found in inconspicuous parts of otherwise classical houses of the mid-C18. The type spanned the transition from timber to stone and brick with very little modification. Few original wooden mullioned windows survive from timber-framed buildings: all we have are the former three-light fire window uncovered from the earliest phase of Club House Farm, Shevington (97) and a window of at least three lights removed from Rose Cottage, Newburgh (81, plate 101).[1] In both the mullions are of simple diamond section tenoned into their sills and lintels. At Club House there are signs of intermediate wooden glazing bars onto which small panes of glass would have been fastened, but that at Rose Cottage shows no signs of having had glazing. In this and other cases these windows may simply have had internal shutters to be opened or closed as required.

These windows are small fry compared to those that existed in more affluent buildings of the timber-framed era. The now-demolished Standish Hall, of around 1574 (103) had a spectacular wooden mullioned window of no less than 20 lights that once illuminated the first-floor gallery (plate 29). Lighting the hall below, modest by

Pl 100
Thomas Gidlow's reconstruction of a C15 hall-house incoporates a powerful stair tower, symbolising the height and importance of the building: Gidlow Hall, Aspull.

Pl. 101
One of the earliest forms of window is represented by this unglazed, wooden mullioned example removed from Rose Cottage, Newburgh.

comparison, was a 10-light window with a transom.

Displays such as these would have been a marvel to the more impoverished householder. Glass itself was an expensive status symbol, so those who could afford to made a show of it. Nowhere is this more evident than at the stone gentry houses of Bispham (13), Birchley (12), Winstanley (124) near Billinge and Harrock (134) at Wrightington where the fenestration is nothing short of flamboyant. The last of these in particular displays almost as much glass as wall. The centrepiece is a spectacular five-sided bay window rising the full height of the building, lighting the hall and, presumably, the gallery above. In using this, the Rigbys had created a tour-de-force out of a feature which had been introduced probably slightly earlier by Bispham Hall. Here, however, the bay has less effect as it is on an end wall and not the front (plate 102). Nevertheless, the fenestration at Bispham makes a powerful statement. But unquestionably it was overpowered by that at Winstanley, where the hall window is a huge transomed affair of 20 lights with a king mullion (plate 25).

Another gentry house making an equally impressive display of glass was the early C17 rebuilding of Haigh Hall, Haigh (52), for which we have evidence in the form of paintings and the building accounts (see plate 27). Birchley Hall appears to have been used as the role model for this, with one entry reading: 'For goodness in workmanshipp the example to be a transomed window in the Parler at Birchley ...'.[2] Haigh however appears to have surpassed Birchley because a view of one front shows two five-sided bays of three storeys plus basement in height with windows set between them of up to 16 lights and three transoms.[3] The Haigh building accounts give the cost of non-transomed windows as 3s.6d. per light and transomed windows 3s per light. So it all added up to a very expensive spectacle.

Windows with transoms were generally a prerogative of the more wealthy, and so the majority of houses had windows that were mullioned only. Usually the largest window was that of the hall, which could frequently have between three and six lights. But parlours had high-ranking status too and at Guild Hall, Rainford (91) of 1629, its parlour window of six lights matched that of the housebody. At Scott's Fold, Dalton (37), 1683, there was the unusual occurrence of a parlour window being the largest in the house: seven lights compared to five for the housebody. This is a north-facing building though, and the parlour was at the southern end of the wing in the sunniest position.

The better-off yeomen did occasionally fit transomed windows, but generally this form is associated with their gentry predecessors we have already examined. Their use in some numbers therefore at Halliwell's Farm, Upholland (115) in 1671 and Ackhurst Hall, Orrell, in 1686 (84) is belated and retrograde and was probably intended as a means of gentrification. In other buildings, slightly lower on the social

Pl. 102
This fine bay window at Bispham Hall, Billinge, lights and emphasises the great parlour and chambers above.

Pl. 103
Simple mullioned window lighting the housebody of Cicely's Cottage, Dalton, of the late C17. The fissile nature of the local sandstone renders detailing impossible and the horizontal hoodmould above is merely a series of slabs, with dropped and returned ends.

scale, transomed windows were restricted to use as stairlights, such as the virtually-identical Belle Vue Farm (37) and Prior's Wood Hall (45, plate 104), both in Dalton. The effect however is incongruous among windows that are otherwise mullioned only.

The mullions themselves, and transoms for that matter, are generally hewn from stone and their edges chamfered. Sometimes, as at Bispham Hall, Billinge (13) the splay is replaced by a more decorative ovolo moulding, which is also found on a far more modest scale at the now-derelict Lyme Tree House, Billinge (20). Brick buildings on the fringe of stone areas such as Guild Hall, Rainford (91) made use of stone for the windows, but in localities where it was more scarce an improvisation took place. Shaped bricks were used to form the mullions and then plastered over to give the effect of stone: these are found, now without plaster, as Copyhold, Wrightington (131) of 1659 and nearby Willow Barn (144) of slightly later date.

The glass used within them consisted of small panes of diamond or square shape, set within lattices of lead bars called 'cames'. These were fixed to iron glazing bars set between the mullions, some of which still survived at Belle Vue Farm (37) before dereliction became advanced. An 1899 photograph of this building shows the leading painted white, which may represent the continuation of an old tradition (plate 49). Surviving original glass is rare: it is greenish in colour and its translucency not of the highest quality which explains why so little remains. Rarer still are examples of stained glass within domestic buildings: yet among fragments of original glazing at Club House Farm, Shevington (97) is the unique occurrence of a piece decorated with the initials of yeoman Seth Prescott, his wife Frances and their son Thomas and the date 1663 (plate 105). It is found in the 10-light transomed window inserted into the housebody of this previously timber-framed building during stone cladding that probably occurred in that year. As Prescott was a yeoman of average wealth (inventory totalling £93.08.07; LRO WCW 1672) then this was a form of decoration that would have been within the means of many of his contemporaries. Whatever their efforts, they have failed to survive into our era.

The move to classicism in the later C17 caused a gradual shift in the shape of windows from horizontal to vertical. The beginnings of this can be seen at the wing of Kirklees Hall, Aspull (9) which was clad in brick possibly in 1663 and was fitted with unusual windows of upright proportions and semicircular heads. Most are now blocked or altered so it is not possible to ascertain their original form, but they may be of a type known as 'cross windows' which came into widespread use in more progressive buildings from c1700. The name derives from the fact they have one mullion and one transom thus forming a cross pattern. They occur in both stone and wood at first in superior houses such as Bispham Hall, Bispham (24) and Holland's House, Dalton (43) both of c1700 and later in yeoman's dwellings such as Stannanought, Dalton (47) of 1714, Darbyshire House, Billinge (15) of 1716 and Ambrose Cottage, Upholland (106) of c1710-1720. Where these were executed in stone, the profile of the mullion and transoms became square in section instead of being splayed as previously.

Typically, though, there were those who still clung to their mullioned windows in the face of these advances, and Newgate Farm, Upholland (122) of 1707 and

Pl. 104
A belated use a transomed window at Prior's Wood Hall, Dalton, c.1680, where it lights the stair.

159

Pl. 105 (above left)
This delightful stained glass pane within the housebody window at Club House Farm, Shevington, suggests this form of decoration may have had a wide use among the yeomanry. It carries the inititals of Seth and Frances Prescott, their son Thomas and the date 1663.

Pl. 106 (above right)
Wooden cross windows and an horizontal sliding sash at Stannanought, Dalton, 1714. By now, hoodmoulds had become simple monoliths with angled ends.

Gathurst Fold, Orrell (85) of the following year demonstrate this staunch conservatism. Even more remarkable are those which retain transomed windows of which the most graphic example is Manor House, Crawford (120) of 1718, whose display of these windows rivals anything seen at the halls of Bispham and Winstanley. Yet, in comparison the use of similar windows on the façade of Lyme Vale Farm, Billinge (21) seems almost brazen occurring as late as it does in 1733.

The next stage in the evolution of the window was the progression from crosses to sashes, the most refined window form associated with classical buildings. The earliest occurrence is at the east wing of Parbold Hall, Parbold (88) remodelled c1700. These may have been pre-dated though by a late C17 reworking of Wrightington Hall, Wrightington (145) which was said in 1795 to be 'the first sash-window house in Lancashire and the first north of the Trent'.[4] Also, a painting of Haigh Hall after its early C18 rebuilding, shows a completely sash-windowed façade.[5] These examples show an association of sashes with gentry houses. Few yeoman houses employed them in the early C18: the first use may be at Knight's Hall, Upholland(168) of 1716.

By 1741, yeoman buildings such as Moorcroft House, Newburgh (80, plate 76) had adopted sashes as conventional elements of classical language. In lesser buildings however windows of horizontal shape remained in favour for some time: either of wooden mullioned type or a form of sashes wherein one of the lights opened by sliding sideways. An original example of the latter type survived at Stoney Lane Farm (142) Wrightington, inserted in the early C18 into an earlier and subsequently blocked opening. Windows of wooden form are frequently associated with brick buildings as several in the township of Lathom demonstrate, from Jump's Farm (65) of 1690 through to Cock Farm (63) of 1708 and subsequently Wainwright's Farm (71) perhaps 1720. The early C18 occurrence of horizontal windows can be interpreted as conservatism, but their use in the mid C18 – when vertical sashes were the accepted, polite form – can perhaps be seen more as an indicator of a builder of limited means and lesser status.

Pl. 107
Finely-proportioned sashes in the west wing of Parbold Hall, the epitome of clasical fenestration.

161

NOTES

1. Two originally timber-framed Wrightington houses, Willow Barn (144) clad in brick c1660-1680 and Stoney Lane Farm (142) stone-clad early C18 still retain within their later masonry several wooden-framed windows from the earlier phase, but with mullions removed.
2. Photographs taken during renovation of Calico Wood Farm, Shevington (95) show what may have been an early wooden mullioned window of four lights (subsequently removed).
3. Illustrated in Donald Anderson, 'Life and Times at Haigh Hall', (1991), p110.
4. J. Aitken, 'Description of the Country from Thirty to Forty Miles Around Manchester' (1795), p293.
5. Illustrated in Anderson, (1991).

CHAPTER VIII

Interior Elements and Ornament

As with the exterior, the manner in which the interior was appointed was a reflection of the standing and aspiration of the occupier. The nature of fixtures and fittings however makes them more subject to alteration or replacement by later generations. Functional features such as fireplaces and stairs are more likely to remain. More ephemeral are merely decorative elements, such as wall painting and plaster panels, which subsequent eras came to despise and largely eradicated.

SMOKE BAYS, FIREHOODS AND FIREPLACES

To light your fire beneath a chimney, when the majority of your neighbours made do with an open hearth and its attendant smoke-laden atmosphere, was a great status symbol in the C16 and early C17. Open hearths ended with the decline of open halls and thus from the middle of the C16 a number of solutions were employed to provide a dedicated location for the fire to funnel its smoke effectively out of the building.

As with other things these innovations occurred first at the privileged end of society and probably the earliest such structures were the lateral hearths appended to pre-existing open halls of gentry status. At both Kirklees Hall, Aspull (9) and Bannister Farm, Wrightington (129) masonry stacks were fitted to the rear walls of cruck halls of probably C15 date, most likely at the same time as the halls were ceiled. The date of this would have been the second half of the C16. Meanwhile, 'new' gentry houses of this period, such as Gidlow Hall, Aspull (7) of 1574 were built with lateral hearths as an integral part of the structure.

Where a lateral hearth was not possible an alternative was pursued. With the end of the open hall tradition, the screens passage became outmoded and instead was given over to the fireplace. The earliest form was probably the smoke bay, a compartment defined by timber-framed walls at either end beneath which the fire was lit. Early timber-framed yeomen's houses of late C16-early C17 date show smoke bays in use at this time. They are sited axially in the space which a generation or so earlier would have been occupied by the screens passage: instead only a small entrance lobby remains, formed by the side wall, or spere, of the hearth and thus creating the baffle-entry arrangement that dominated house plans throughout the C17. At Willow Barn, Wrightington (144) the bay again served back-to-back hearths heating housebody and kitchen and was some 10½ feet deep; but where the range contained housebody only, as at Club House Farm, Shevington (97) and Newgate Farm, Upholland (122) it was accordingly shallower and set against the end gable wall. Although associated with timber-framed buildings, smoke bays may also have translated across into early brick and stone houses of the yeomanry such as North Tunley, Wrightington (137) and Douglas Bank Farm, Upholland (114) of 1657.

By this time another structure had evolved to gain widespread use. This was the firehood or smokehood, a funnel-shaped structure – initially timber-framed, but later of stone or brick – which sat above the hearth and tapered upwards where it was located beneath the chimney. The timber ones were in themselves probably a fire hazard. This explains why most have not survived, being soon rebuilt in brick or stone when these materials gained general acceptance. A remarkably well-preserved example of a firehood, its sides composed of wattle-and-daub panels within a timber framework, remains at Parker's Farm, Rishton near Blackburn, outside the area; but at Johnson's Farm, Upholland (117) parts of the structure remain to show it once possessed a firehood of this type (plate 109).

Pl. 108
Shaped timber heck post of the early C17 at Giant's Hall.

The hearths associated with firehoods had evolved with smoke bays and are of the distinctive type often termed 'inglenook fireplaces'. They are a rectangular compartment spanned by a heavy beam – the bressumer – which is carried at one end by the spere and at the other. This created an area beneath which the fire was lit upon an iron basket termed a 'grate' or a 'chimney'. These items were often regarded as heirlooms. In his will of 1623, John Haydock of Bogburn Hall (29) left to his son Roger 'one iron chimley with all iron geare belonging to he same'. The usual depth of the firehood was around four to six feet and thus it was almost a room in itself where the occupants could sit upon particularly cold days or nights: at Johnson's is the rare survival of a settle incorporated specifically for this purpose. Early timber-framed houses such as Giant's Hall, Standish (102, plate 108), Manor House, Worthington (126) and Newgate Farm, Upholland (122) have wooden speres terminating in shaped timber heck posts but elsewhere stone quickly superceded them. At Johnson's, Club House Farm, Shevington (97) and Higher Barn, Wrightington (135) the stone hecks are decorated with a moulded capital. Sometimes the space beneath the firehood is illuminated by a 'fire window' in the rear wall of the housebody (Copyhold Farm, Wrightington, 1659 (131); Derbyshire Farm, Lathom (74) c1700 or in the reredos of the firehood itself (Club House Farm; Rose Cottage, Newburgh (81), Furthermore, Derbyshire Farm had a peephole within the heck through which anyone sitting beneath the firehood could see who was entering the front door.[1]

Changing lifestyles during the later C17 and the declining importance of the housebody meant firehoods gradually became anachronistic. By the early 1700s, advanced early classical houses such as Bispham Hall, Bispham (24) and Fir Tree House, Billinge of 1704 (16) had replaced them with stone fireplaces with masonry flues (plate 110). Most others quickly followed suit, but the less adventurous still clung to firehoods, Gathurst Fold, Orrell (85) of 1708 and Stannanought, Dalton of 1714 (47) being the latest examples.

Stone hearths had in fact been in use elsewhere in buildings – other than the hall or housebody – since the late C16. Massive segmental-arched fireplaces used for cooking dominated the kitchens at Bispham Hall, Billinge (13) of around 1600 and Fairhurst Hall, Wrightington (133) of slightly earlier date. Parlours, when heated, used fireplaces of more modest form. The earliest have four-centred arches, such as at Ackhurst Hall, Orrell (84) of the late C16 – a superb example with moulded surround – Bispham Hall and, at yeoman level, Giant's Hall, Standish (102). Later these are simplified to triangular form as Copyhold, Wrightington of 1659 (131) demonstrates. By the early C18 hearths in classically-inspired houses were generally of simple segmental-headed form as those at Fir Tree House and Holland's House, Dalton (43) indicate. Subsequently fireplaces in their most refined classical form are seen at Parbold Hall (88) of the 1740s, where that in the garden hall is flanked by pilasters and surmounted by a pediment with a bust in the tympanum (plate 111).

Pl. 109
Interior of former C17 wattle-and-daub firehood at Johnson's Farm, Upholland and later brick stack.

Pl. 110 (far left)
By the early C18, more advanced houses replaced firehoods with fireplaces, as Fir Tree House, Billinge, of 1704 demonstrates.

Pl 111 (left)
This fireplace of the 1740s at Parbold Hall represents a grandeur and awareness of refined classical forms.

STAIRCASES

During the C16 and C17 the staircase developed from relatively simple, functional origins into an elaborate centrepiece frequently displayed – both internally and externally – in a prominent position. In their simplest form they are basic, straight-flight arrangements as at Giant's Hall, Standish (102) and Coppull Old Hall, Coppull (32). Where space was more limited a different arrangement was employed: the spiral stair, where wooden treads ascend around a central newel post. Some of the earliest stairs are of this design. The type occurs in the late C16-early C17 at Balcony Farm, Upholland (107), Ackhurst Hall, Orrell (84) and the attic of Fairhurst Hall, Wrightington (133) in the late C16 and subsequently at Copyhold Farm (131) in the north of that township, dated 1659, and possibly the latest example.

Both these variants gave little opportunity for display however, and stairs – at a time when most buildings were single-storey – were something proud householders wished to accentuate. For this reason, as we have seen, the gentry – and some yeomen – went to the trouble of constructing towers to specifically house their stairs especially if they were added to previously-open halls. This created a forceful presence externally, but required internally something more than a mere series of steps. The type that evolved to accommodate these towers involved a series of flights rising to landings around an open well, which gave considerable opportunity for display. The stair tower at Parbold Hall, Parbold (88) houses this kind, although it is a replacement inserted c1700.

In the more confined space of yeoman's houses, where the stair was frequently sited in a lobby in the upper wing, simplified versions were required. Two neighbouring houses at Standish demonstrate early solutions to the problem of fitting a decorative stair into a limited space. At Upper Wood Fold (104) of the early C17 the stair located in the parlour, is of the quarter-turn type, ie rising to a landing with the next flight at 90 degrees. Next door, at Upper Wood Farm (105), which is later in date, the stair is of a 'dog leg' type where, the turn from the landing is 180 degrees. From the second half of the C17, this type gained universal acceptance throughout the area and at all levels.

These two houses, built perhaps half a century apart, also demonstrate evolving decorative treatment applied to staircases. The stair at Upper Wood Fold is fairly simply decorated, in which the balusters are of cut-and-pierced type ('splat' balusters being the correct, if somewhat odd, term). Upper Wood Farm demonstrates the later, more elaborate and therefore more expensive treatment whereby the newel and balusters are turned and the handrail has a moulded grip. The fact that the newel is also decorated with a carved rosette – and extends full-height to the ceiling – is

Pl. 112
Delightful carved flower on the newel post of Upper Wood Farm, Standish; probably mid-C17.

Fine late C17-C18 dog-leg stairs demonstrate the attention given to detailing this important feature.

Pl. 113 (left) Lowe's, Lathom.

Pl. 114 (centre) Bispham Hall, Bispham (detail of baluster).

Pl. 115 (right) Guild Hall, Rainford.

unusual and indicates this is an early, mid-C17, example of a dog-leg stair (plate 112). Generally, later ones were simpler with square newels, although many early C18 examples incorporated a similar sunken panel motif (Stannanought, Dalton (47) 1714; Manor House, Upholland (120) 1718; Woodcock House, Newburgh (83) 1719, Maddocks, Billinge (22) c1710-20). One of the finest stairs is that at Lowe's, Newburgh (78, plate 113) where the upper portion of the newels are carried on coupled balusters and the quality of the design continues even on the attic floor. The balusters themselves are elegantly shaped like classical columns. Those at Fir Tree House, Billinge (16) were more fanciful, twisted in the 'barley sugar' style (although they are now modern reproductions of the originals). Other renderings were less extrovert: despite its candid exterior, the stair at Stone Hall, Dalton (48) has plain balusters of simple, square section.

The double-pile plan saw the staircase take on a new significance. Its position in a lobby at the rear meant it could be reached from all rooms and in this respect it bonded the entire household. This accessibility from all quarters also removed the need for a separate stair for servants which had existed in some of the homes of the better-off yeomanry. From its earliest phase of 1629, Guild Hall, Rainford (91) had a service stair in its kitchen (straight-flight, splat baluster) and Copyhold, Wrightington (131) in 1659 had a second spiral stair in its outshut behind the kitchen. The stair lobby in double-pile houses meant master and servant could use the same staircase without the latter encroaching upon the former's territory. However the distinction remained in the more grandiose exponents of this plan. Two of the large, tripartite double-pile houses of the early C18 retained service stairs: Manor House, Upholland (120) of 1718 and Woodcock House, Newburgh (83) of the year after. At the former, both were of dog-leg style but the service stair, as we would expect, is notably inferior in execution.

BEAMS

Exposed timbers supporting a ceiling were almost always given a decorative treatment, although as in other respects this was usually in direct proportion to the status – and pocket – of the occupant. The main beams – and occasionally the joists – were chamfered along the edge in a variety of styles, terminating in a 'stop' which also took a number of forms. Usually, the earlier the date, the more elaborate the treatment.

Medieval beams were often heavily moulded in a variety of concave and convex curves as one at Bradley Hall, Langtree (57) and those found re-used within Prior's Wood Hall, Dalton (45) – possibly from the predecessor of this building – demonstrate, this still had a bearing into the C16 as the spine beam inserted to support the ceiling in the cruck hall at Banisters Farm, Wrightington (129) shows, possibly of the 1570s and unique in the area for carrying a shield with the initials of its builder (plate 28). By 1600 these intricate curves had largely been superceded by a simpler style which became virtually standard – in superior houses especially – for the next century. This consisted of a deep convex chamfer which gives the term 'quarter round' to the type. Bispham Hall, Billinge (13), Knight's Hall, Upholland (118), Bogburn Hall, Coppull (29) and Holland's House, Dalton (43) all of the early C17 make use of them, and the type continued in vogue in the middle of the century, at Douglas Bank Farm, Upholland (114) of 1656, Copyhold, Wrightington (131) of 1659 and Leveldale, Lathom (67) of 1664.

Another distinctive early type, which found a much more limited distribution, is

Pl. 116
Superb plastered beams, probably of the 1740s, at Parbold Hall, Parbold. Beneath the embellishmnet are the quarter-round beams of the original house of c.1600.

one employing a pyramid or broach stop. This would appear to be late C16 and is associated with buildings of higher status. In a clearly re-used form (as they are too grand for the location) they occur in the cellar of Parbold Hall, Parbold (88) with a double chamfer, and in simpler style at Felton's Farm, Dalton (41) and Johnson's, Upholland (117).

Later in the C17, decoration became more minimalistic with a simple chamfer and tongue or cyma stops. The 1679 wing of Yew Tree House, Dalton (51) illustrates this on a modest scale, and by 1718 the substantial Manor House at Crawford, Upholland (120) had followed the trend. Yet in 1703, Hydes Brow Farm at Rainford (92) was still featuring quarter-round beams; but this is a modest yeoman rebuilding of a cruck house and the owner may have been using them as an attempt to gain status.

By 1700 though a new treatment of ceilings had begun to be used, one which saw exposed timbers as somewhat uncouth, preferring them to be plastered instead. The roughly-adzed surfaces of those at Bispham Hall, Bispham (24) indicates they had once been prepared in readiness for this treatment. The finest examples are at Parbold Hall (88, plate 116). Later, by 1748, small farmhouses such as Greenhill Farm, Newburgh (75) could boast plastered beams. Subsequently in the C19, many fine beams suffered the indignity of being boxed in. Victorian society regarded these naked timbers with the same distaste as the exposed legs of chairs and tables.

DOORS

Early doors were quite crude compared to the forms that began to supersede them in the later C17. Basically, they were a series of vertical planks fastened to horizontal battens at the rear and secured by means of large hinges to gudgeon pins on the door jamb. Board doors are found in the late C16 and early C17 at houses such as Spring Bank, Wrightington (141), Upper Wood Farm, Standish (105, plate 117) and Lower Wrenall, Wrightington (136), the latter dated 1673.

The surrounds went through the same metamorphosis as their external counterparts, the earliest form being four-centred. Frequently this form was taken a step further by having a 'nicked' lintel, which was a four-centred arch with a vertical cut in its apex. This can be seen as the last vestige of the medieval ogee arch, a C15 example of which is the door from screens passage to service wing at Bradley Hall, Langtree (57). Nicked lintels are characteristic of the late C16-early C17, and are found at Spring Bank (141) and Stoney Lane Farm (142) both Wrightington, Holland's House, Dalton (43) and Bogburn Hall, Coppull (29, plate 118).

Later in the C17 a new type of door of more refined appearance was introduced, of framed construction and incorporating a series of fielded panels. That at Upper Wood

Pl. 117
Early C17 boarded doors frequently had strap hinges ending in a lys design and supported on gudgeon pins on the jamb, like this example at Upper Wood Farm, Standish.

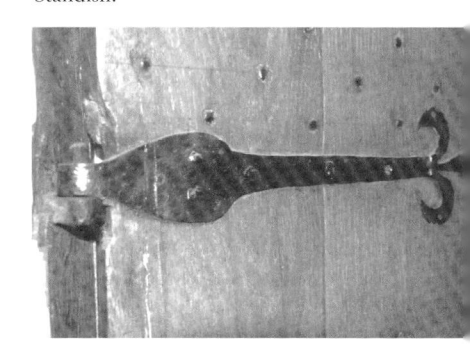

Pl. 118
Nicked lintel of chamber doorway at Bogburn Hall, Coppull.

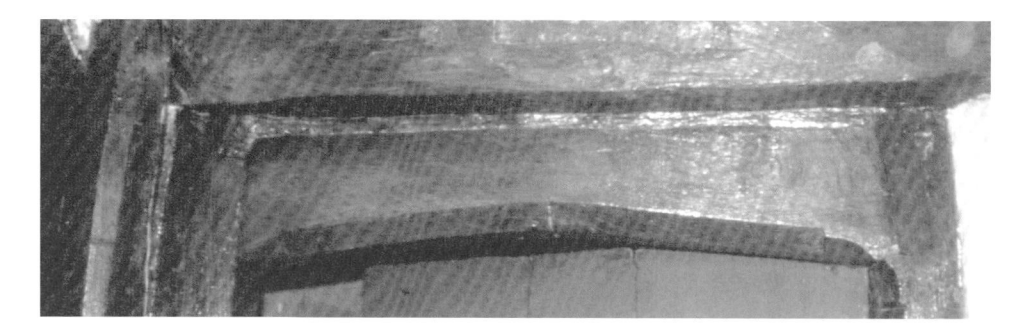

Farm, Standish (105) in the parlour chamber has no less than eight panels, and a similar example at nearby Giant's Hall, again Standish (102), has six. These early examples, both perhaps of the 1670s, are relatively elementary, in which the panels are sunken, but later classically-inspired doors became more elaborate with panels that were raised and moulded and the door surrounds themselves featured moulded architraves. The doors to the parlours at both Ackhurst Hall, Orrell (84, plate 119) and Darbyshire House, Billinge (15) of 1716 have architraves with a prominent bolection moulding. The doors themselves, in the case of the former, have two large panels and at the latter, six. Naturally, the trend was taken further in gentry houses, and particularly inspired doorways can be found in the garden hall at Parbold Hall (88), which have Gibbs surrounds, usually an external feature (see plate 95), in a particularly extrovert display of the 1740s.

Fine C18 doors of panelled form.

Pl. 119 (right)
Ackhurst Hall, Orrell.

Pl. 120 (far right)
Greenhill Farm, Newburgh.

WALL DECORATION: PLASTER, PAINTING AND PANELLING

Evidence, both physical and documentary, has survived to show that the rooms of both gentry and yeoman houses had walls which were not simply left plain but adorned in a variety of ways. This decoration took the form of wooden panelling, plasterwork or paintings.

Panelling – or 'wainscoting' – is referred to in documents relating to several gentry houses, so must have been fairly standard at this level. Parbold Hall (88) had its hall wainscoted at one end and Langtree Hall (59) two wainscoted chambers and a dining room when both buildings were surveyed by Commonwealth authorities in 1653. At Chisnall Hall, Coppull (30) a fragment of panelling, with fine carved decoration, survives upon the chamber floor. Few yeomen would have been able to afford this extravagance, but a panelled screen in the housebody of Guild Hall, Rainford (91) shielding this room from the entrance lobby, shows it was within the reach of the more wealthy. This example dates from c.1688, when the house was enlarged by its new owners, the Gill family, who clearly aspired to gentry status.

Decorative plasterwork was used widely on walls and ceilings of gentry homes in the late C16 and C17. Displays that survive in the great houses of Gawthorpe and Speke in Lancashire illustrate this art at its highest level. Sadly no early plaster has survived in the gentry houses of the Douglas Valley, but one of the chambers at Standish Hall, Standish (103) once had a plaster panel above its fireplace with the Standish arms and crest with cherubs' heads as supporters.[2]

Pl. 121 (left)
This remarkable plaster mural at the dais end of the housebody at Copyhold Farm, Wrightington, suggests this was a form of decoration readily employed by the yeomanry.

Pl. 122 (below)
Detail of the centrepiece.

Fig. 38
Copy of the stencilled frieze discovered in the housebody of Greenslate Farm, Billinge, possibly early C18.
(Mrs Jane Fairhurst)

What has survived however is a remarkable gem which supports the view that the yeomanry of the C17 practised this form of decoration too. At Copyhold Farm, Wrightington (131) is a plaster panel measuring 10ft wide and 8ft high and covering most of the crosswall at the dais end of the housebody with a wild, crude and fanciful arabesque design.[3] The central motif is a fleur-de-lys in a garnished cartouche with a grotesque animal head above and a bizarre human face below with others in profile. Vines flow between all these elements and extend above the entrance to the crosswing and the door in the rear wall of the housebody; the main design is supported upon a panelled plaster dado some 2ft high. Copyhold was built in 1659 and the design would appear to fit that date. Its builder was Oliver Halliwell, schoolmaster at nearby Heskin. He may have been described as 'gentleman' in the Eccleston parish registers but he was not the highest ranking member of local society by any means; his inventory (LCRO WCW 1668) totalled £82 14s 10d, a figure surpassed by other yeomen. Therefore these could presumably have afforded plasterwork of similar standard and what we see at Copyhold may be the remnants of what was once commonplace.

Similarly, wall painting appears to have been once widespread, with examples throughout Lancashire coming to light in recent years and possibly more awaiting discovery beneath layers of plaster and wallcoverings.[4] We know too from inventories that this decoration existed; such as the reference in the inventory of John Haydock to the 'painted chamber' at Bogburn Hall, Coppull (29) in 1623. The surviving examples date from the C16 to the C18. Designs were initially painted freehand and executed mainly in black on white, but from the late C17 colours began to be used, along with stencils. It was this type of stencil work that was discovered in 1996 in the housebody of Greenslate Farm, Billinge (18), a small double pile house of c1715-1725. This took the form of a geometric frieze along the top of the walls, in indigo on a white ground. Similar designs were also found on the inner jambs of the door from that room to the stair lobby. On the walls themselves were traces of a 'rose and honeysuckle' pattern which appeared to be later.[5]

Geometric patterns were in vogue in the early C17, for a freehand painted design of this type, with interlinked crosses and circles, was discovered in 1989 at Hesketh Farm, Penwortham, north of the area and dated 1700.[6] But nothing compares with the startling rendition in the housebody of a small, disused farmhouse of c1700 at Cock Hall, Whitworth, in the Rossendale uplands of East Lancashire.[7] Crumbling plaster revealed in 1989 a series of crude classical columns painted on the walls supporting a frieze of zig-zag pattern, again in black on white.[8] Given that this is an isolated farm in a remote upland area, there is every reason to suppose that its contemporaries in the more prosperous Douglas Valley, and throughout Lancashire as a whole, were once similarly decorated.

NOTES

1. At the time of listing, c.1990. By the time it was surveyed for this book, August 1999, it was concealed.
2. VCH VI, p196.
3. First recorded by Garry Miller, June 1987.
4. For several examples on the Lancashire coastal plain, see M E McClintock and R E Watson, 'Domestic Wall Painting in the North West' in Vernacular Architecture 14, 1983.
5. Unfortunately, none of the paintings were in a condition that allowed them to be preserved. Fortunately, they were copied by the owner Mrs Jane Fairhurst, who has supplied her drawings.
6. Recorded by Garry Miller, March 1989.
7. Recorded by Garry Miller, September 1989.
8. Representations of structural features are known elsewhere: a house at Pilling in the Fylde had crucks painted upon a crosswall and one at Ainsdale, a depiction of timber-frame. McClintock and Watson, Vernacular Architecture 14.

Inventory of Houses in the Douglas Valley

The author is deeply grateful to the owners and occupiers of these houses for granting permission for them to be surveyed. Please note, however, that none are open to the public and readers are therefore asked to respect their privacy.

ADLINGTON

Township of 1,064 acres bounded by narrow valley of Douglas to SE and rising towards West Pennine Moors in E. Adlington family owned part of manor since C13, another initially held by Duxbury family but relinquished early C14 and subdivided between several families including Allanson of Allanson Hall and and Worthington of Crawshaw. Manor acquired before 1700 by merchant Thomas Clayton, of London and Liverpool, whose family held until late C19. Four freeholders 1600. 1664 Hearth Tax records 47 households.

(1) ADLINGTON HALL
Fine classical mansion house built 1770; demolished. Brick, seven bays, with 3-bay pedimented centre on four pilasters above central three. Two-and-a-half storeys, hipped roof; tall sashes and first floor balcony in centre. Built by Sir Richard Clayton, 1st Baronet (d.1828), replacing earlier timber-framed structure probably of C16-17.

(2) ALLANSON HALL SD597134
Minor gentry house dated 1618, extended and altered. Brick, facade renewed in C18 Flemish bond but older English garden wall bond at rear. Originally three-unit plan with porch, but first bay (service) demolished. Lateral stack to rear of hall; inner doorway in porch has triangular-headed arch with fine moulded surround. Later C17 2½ storey brick extension, on stone base, to rear of third bay. Fine late C17 dogleg stair sited unusually in outshut to rear of hall. Worth detailed investigation.
HISTORY: Allanson family became one of the holders of the moiety relinquished by Duxbury family in C14. Roger Allanson d.1598 holding messuage in Adlington and lands in Heath Charnock; son George a freeholder 1600, his initials on stone reset on porch. Robert Allanson taxed on four hearths 1664. Will of John Allanson of Adlington, esquire (LCRO WCW 1732) refers to capital messuage and lands held in Adlington, Longton (near Preston) and elsewhere in Lancashire.
*VCH VI, p219.

(3) CRAWSHAW HALL SD592116
Surviving solar wing of minor gentry house, originally timber-framed, attached to short range to W dated 1906. Probably early C16, added to hall range (possibly pre-existing) now replaced by 1906 work. Inside fine windbraced roof trusses of principal rafter type with angle struts; blades meeting at ridge above yoke (similar to apex of crucks at Peel Hall, Ince (56) and Kirklees Hall, Aspull (9). Ground floor has sequence of seven massive stop-chamfered beams. Wing clad in stone of exceptional thickness – 3 feet – probably early C17: use of random rubble remarkably coarse for house of gentry status. Crude blocked door in E wall. External stack to S room of wing denotes use as parlour by this time.
HISTORY: Crawshaw held by Worthington family possibly since C14. Lawrence Worthington of Croweshaw, gentleman, recorded as freeholder 1600; son Thomas d.1626 holding capital messuage and lands of Hugh Adlington and lands in Chorley and Thornton in the Fylde. Inventory (LCRO WCW 1626, total £130 19s 10d) records: outer parlour, chamber at stairhead, new chamber, little parlour, stone chambers, hall, servants chamber, brewhouse, kitchen, little larder, buttery and deyhouse (last two both with chambers above). 'New chamber' implies recent building; 'stone chambers' may refer to the wing and suggests some, if not remainder of house, still timber-framed. Lack of reference to chamber above hall suggests latter was still open, possibly cruck-framed? His son Lawrence, aged 42 in

1641 taxed on five hearths 1664; said to have been succeeded by three daughters, Agnes, Dorothy and Anne.
*VCH VI, p219-220.

(4) RIGBY HOUSE FARM SD590125
Early C17 brick yeoman's house on stone plinth, with stone mullioned windows. Three-unit rear baffle-entry plan with wings at either end, stair turret to rear. Housebody firehood and quarter-round beams, spiral newel stair. Photograph c1900 (M D Smith) shows unusual large multi-flue main chimney.
HISTORY: Rigby yeoman family recorded in Adlington C17. Roger Rigby assessed on two hearths, 1664; his inventory (LCRO WCW 1676) records 'oulde house' (predecessor that still stood?), parlour, chamber over house, maiden's chamber, cheese chamber, nearer and further kitchen chambers.

ASPULL

Township of 1,905 acres east of Wigan, with ground rising from valley of Douglas in W to 147m in NE near Haigh boundary. Manor held along with that of adjacent Ince from early C14 by Ince family and subsequently by Gerard family until C19. Several minor gentry families recorded as freeholders from early date including Gidlows of Gidlow Hall and Houghtons of Kirklees: total of eight freeholders in 1600. Hearth tax records 108 households 1664.

(5) BUTTERFLY HALL
Fine stone two-unit end-baffle-entry house with parlour wing and full-height porch; demolished. Photograph c1900 (WRO) shows mullioned windows of up to five lights and triangular arched lintel reading EB TW LP 1660. Lower bay to R with outshut appears to be later addition.

(6) COLLIERS ARMS SD604074
Earliest surviving dated building of double-pile plan in area: 1700. Inn, possibly house originally. Symmetrical front with horizontal windows on facade, probably originally mullioned; mullioned windows surviving at rear; gable chimneys.

(7) GIDLOW HALL SD625071
Fragment of substantial minor gentry house on moated site: dated 1574 and thus earliest dated stone building in area. House drastically reduced in size and remodelled 1840 to rectangular two-unit plan with outshut. Of 1574 is masonry on front wall and powerful 2½ storey stair tower to rear; lateral hearth on former rear wall and evidence of former timber-framed partition by blocked earlier entrance suggesting original screens passage. Over stair turret is fine roof truss of originally arched-braced form along with four inferior principal rafter trusses with queen struts and collars over main range. These probably re-used from earlier, possibly C15 house during 1574 rebuilding. One truss with carpenter's mark X suggests 10th in series of frames; this plus decorative nature of arched-braced truss indicates earlier building was of some size and quality. Drawing of September 12 1826 (LCRO DP291/34) by Will Lathom shows form prior to 1840 reconstruction: tall 2½ storey wing at lower end with transomed windows, and projection which may be porch (or another stair tower); main range with outshut as at present.
HISTORY: Gidlow family recorded as freeholders in Aspull from 1291, subsequently also holding lands in Ince, Langtree, and Coppull. Initials on ornate datestone are of Thomas Gidlow, elected coroner of Wigan 1586, recorded as freeholder 1600. Died 1606 holding capital messuage and 280 acres in Aspull of Miles Gerrard of Ince by rent of 14s and 12d; also 12 acres plus watermill of the king, and formerly of the late Hospital of St John of Jerusalem. As convicted recusant, Thomas Gidlow paid double in the subsidy of 1626.
*GMAU report, 1996; VCH IV, p120-121.

(8) HIGHER HIGHFIELD SD612084
Yeoman house of 1714. Highly conservative plan: three unit baffle entry with 1st bay as projecting wing. Brick, irregular English garden wall bond on stone base; later outshut to rear of main range. Plan compares with similarly-conservative Stannanought, Dalton (47) and Dial House, Upholland, (112) both 1714.

(9) KIRKLEES (now KIRKLESS) HALL SD603064
Substantial cruck framed open hall of medieval freeholders, C15 or earlier with complex sequence of alterations and extensions from later C16 to C18. Former cruck range of probably four bays, with two-bay hall; blades all of medium to heavy scantling and overall height of structure 22 ft. Three trusses surviving: former central truss of hall has smoke blackening from former open hearth at apex and yoke with carved roundel with initials facing dais end. Remaining trusses define narrow service end, with high stone plinth partly remaining on facade.

First stage of rebuilding was addition of massive stone lateral chimney stack to rear of hall mid-C16. Ceiling inserted in hall at same time: central cruck had blades removed below ceiling level with fine roll-moulded beam, partly supported on stack, inserted to carry upper portion of truss. Upper bay rebuilt c1600 as two-storey parlour wing of post-and-truss construction with stair turret added to rear of hall adjacent to stack. Main range possibly also rebuilt in timber-frame at this time (see below). Wing clad in brick and heightened to 2½ storey mid-C17 (modern datestone 1663) with fine raised brick lozenge decoration and unusual segmental-headed vertical windows (possibly cross windows originally). Cladding of rest of structure piecemeal: front of hall in early-mid C18 Flemish bond but third bay and added fourth bay in inferior English Garden Wall bond of early C18. This suggests building possibly subdivided from early date. Drawing in LCRO by Will Lathom (DP291/13) of 1820s shows wide timber-framed porch with decorative panels and kingpost truss in gable, along with diagonal bracing on range to R of porch. This indicates main range may have been rebuilt c1600 at same time as parlour wing added. Hall windows then of cross-type, and tall, unusual multi-flue stack to rear of hall.

HISTORY: Kirklees held by Houghton family, originating from neighbouring Westhoughton near Bolton, from early C14: John de Houghton held two messuages and land in Aspull in 1317. Richard Houghton acquired lands in Aspull, Ince and Wigan in 1572; son Ralph a freeholder 1600. Family were convicted recusants, Ralph Houghton paying double the subsidy of 1626; another Ralph renouncing his faith in order to avoid confiscation of his lands in 1653.

*VCH IV, p121-122.

Pl. 123   Kirklees Hall in 1820s (LCRO DP291/13).

(10) PENNINGTON HALL SD622067

Large brick yeoman's house of 1653 of three-unit, former baffle entry plan with crosswings at either end. Date in raised brickwork on front of upper wing, brickwork of range and lower wing renewed C19, probably at same time as additions to rear and removal of former firehood. '1847' scratched on beam inside housebody probably dates these alterations.

HISTORY: associated with Pennington yeoman family: Robert Pennington recorded as freeholder 1600.

BILLINGE

Elevated township of 2,732 acres with Billinge Hill at 157m forming highest point among the hills flanking the Douglas. By 1212 manor had been 'long divided' into three portions, two of which were held by Billinge and Winstanley families (the latter of that manor). By 1374 it was further subdivided into four, one of which, Birchley, was acquired by the Anderton family of Lostock in the C16; the Bispham portion was held by family of the same name. Six freeholders 1600; 76 households indicated by 1664 Hearth Tax.

(11) BILLINGE HALL SD513026

Much-remodelled house of fallen status, analysis problematical: core probably gentry house of early-mid C17, form obscured by inferior adaptations of early C18. Stone, two storeys with low central range between unequal wings: that to S narrower and projecting front and rear, N wing projecting to front only. Both wings have tall mullioned windows, two external stacks each, and appear C18; range and rear wall has low mullioned windows and earlier masonry. Off-centre in range is C18 entrance with fine moulded surround but crude triangular hood on brackets, L of which is shallow projection with blocked three-light window which may be remains of porch.

Unique internal layout in this area: entrance leads to transverse passage connecting wings with central unheated service room occupying main range where one would expect housebody (comparisons, see Brunskill, 'Handbook of Vernacular Architecture' p108-109). This room has six-light window. Modern stair occupies what may have been former through-passage. Wings have two rooms, functions uncertain; all heated except for one at W end of N wing, which was formerly at lower level and probably a dairy. Room at front of S wing has quarter round beams.

HISTORY: Billinge family recorded from 1212. Richard Billinge a freeholder 1600; inventory LCRO WCW 1626) records parlour and chamber above, buttery, milkhouse and 'soot loft' (implying ceiling-in of former open hall?). Grandson Richard's estates sequestered 1652 as a papist. He was assessed on five hearths 1664 and inventory (LCRO WCW 1676) indicates substantial rebuilding had taken place, with 15 rooms: hall, parlour, green parlour, kitchen, larder, garner, brewhouse, parlour chamber, stowhouse chamber, little ground chamber, brewhouse chamber, milk-house chamber, porch chamber, gallery. Son John and wife Margaret (initials on relocated datestone of 1683 on barn) sold estates to Bispham family of Bispham Hall, 1691. Inventory of yeoman Robert Billinge (LCRO WCW 1729, total £102 6s 5d) records house, buttery, kitchen, milkhouse, parlour chamber, chambers over cellar and milk-house, and 'shop' which contained looms. Uncertain if his house was Billinge Hall but six-light window in central service room would suit loomshop: therefore possibly early example of domestic building designed for industrial purpose also.

(12) **BIRCHLEY HALL** SJ525998
Trend-setting stone manor house of 1594, style subsequently imitated by Bispham Hall (13) and Winstanley Hall (124). Powerful, symmetrical five-gabled facade with recessed hall and projecting wings and smaller projections in internal angles, one on R is porch with four-centred arched doorway with initials T A and date 1594 in spandrels. Two-and-a-half storeys. Principal windows with transoms, now mostly altered or blocked and replaced by sashes. Entrance would probably have led to screens passage; lateral chimney stack at rear of hall.
HISTORY: by 1581 manor of Birchley had been acquired by the Anderton family of Lostock Hall, near Bolton, from the Heatons, its owners since C14; Andertons recorded as freeholders in Billinge 1600. Initials on door those of Thurstan Anderton, second son of Christopher Anderton of Lostock; elder brother James died 1613 holding capital messuage of Birchley among other properties. Fourth son Roger (d.1640) had Birchley by arrangement with brother Christopher of Lostock (third son). Roger's eldest son James (1617-1673) inherited Birchley and was assessed on 16 hearths in 1664.
 Description of Hall in 1778 (LCRO DDX 1046/1) records:
'A Courtyard and sevral steps up to the House on one side walled. When you come in the House on the left a goodish Parlour & three Bed Chambers 2 very small a kitchen underneath the Priests Chamber wh(ich) has a light Closet to it. On the right the old Hall partitioned off from the Passage (screens passage?) & through the Hall a large Parlour & over it a large Bed Room. Staircase out of the Hall - on the left of stair Case 2 large rooms one over the Parlour (illegible) another stair case in the Passage to another Passage ... with 2 or 3 small Rooms now in Ruins and a Passage to a (illegible) and the same from the lower Parlour & many old Books piled up it. Staircase out of the Passage at Front a staircase into Kitchen a very good Room & what I suppose the Ser(vants?) Hall now a Bedchamber & dairy. What was the old Dairy now a Miller's Room and what was Lady G's Dressing Room let to 2 women. Offices just behind Back Door and a stream running into a Mill Pond.'
VCH IV, p85

(13) **BISPHAM HALL** SD524025
Later replica of Birchley: c1600 but possibly incoporating earlier remains. Again, two-and-a-half storey symmetrical front with recessed hall between flanking wings and short projections in internal angles. That on R contains porch, semi-circular arched entrance of which indicates later date c1600; inner door has four-centred arch. Most windows transomed. Interior altered following fire of 1977. Porch presumably led to screens passage, hall heated by lateral hearth stilll in situ. Upper wing to S probably contained two heated parlours, larger with handsome full-height 5-sided bay window. Service wing incorporates kitchen at front with large segmental-headed hearth served by gigantic external stack. Site of stair uncertain; first and upper floor each had gallery. Early additions to N; further C17 extensions to rear largely demolished but formerly accessed from hall by fine archway with moulded capitals and dropped false keystone. Survey by GMAU 1990 suggested service wing incorporated remains of earlier C16 stone structure.
HISTORY: seat of Bispham family, lords of fourth part of manor of Billinge possibly since 1346. Building of earlier timber-framed structure may have occurred 1559: in that year Thomas Bispham conveyed messuage to his son upon his marriage and agreed to deliver 'sufficient wood and timber as well to erect and build the same'. Thomas (the son) recorded as freeholder 1600. Heir Edmund sold inheritance to brother William 1610 – latter, who acquired Rivington manor 1602 and held lands in Essex, is most likely builder of hall. Thomas Bispham assessed on 12 hearths 1664. Inventory of Samuel Bispham (LCRO WCW 1678, total £965 7s 6d) records hall, great parlour, little parlour, great staircase, dining room, 'compassed chamber', green chamber, passage room and stairhead , little green chamber, nursery, kitchen, study.
VCH IV, p85; Savigny, Bispham Hall (1976 reprint).

(14) **CROW NEST FARM** SD512014
Significant early yeoman's house in stone dated 1635, demolished 1970s. Photograph c1900 shows two-storey main range and wing and possibly stair tower. Home of Darbyshire family, leaseholders of Bankes family of Winstanley Hall. Will of Lawrence Darbyshire (LCRO WCW 1632; total £123 6s 6d) records buttery and new chamber (latter created by inserting floor in open hall?). Builder of house was son William whose inventory (LCRO WCW 1640, total £147) mentions new house, old house (predecessor?) buttery, old buttery, new chamber, old chamber, new loft, further new loft, little chamber. Son Lawrence assessed on four hearths 1664, paid 29s annual rental to Bankes family, 1670-1675; will of his son William (LCRO WCW 1719) states he leased 40 acres from Thomas

Bankes of Winstanley for £5 from 1705; most expensive item in inventory 184 hides at £120 6s 10d indicating extensive tanning business.
F R Pope, private report, 1980; Bankes and Kerridge, (1973) p93-98.

(15) DARBYSHIRE HOUSE   SD511025
Superb classical yeoman's house of 1716. Stone, two-and-a-half storeys with symmetrical façade, gable chimneys and considered detailing. Fine entrance has moulded surround and triangular pediment supported on pilasters; stone cross-windows on façade, but sides and rear revert to mullioned. Inside, two-panelled door from housebody to parlour has architrave with bold bolection moulding. Hybrid roof structure: front purlins carried on crosswalls, those at rear on unusual half-trusses above timber-framed walls flanking dog-leg staircase (as at Greenslate Farm (19) and Cock Farm, Lathom (63). Front attic rooms unwindowed, therefore used for storage only.
HISTORY: oval datestone in tympanum of pediment refers to Thomas Darbyshire, alternatively described as yeoman (Upholland PR) or linen webster (LCRO WCW admon 1718). Nature of house indicates profitable business. Member of prominent Darbyshire yeoman family whose principal residence was at Crow's Nest Farm (14)
Pevsner, South Lancashire (1969), p76.

(16) FIR TREE HOUSE   SD506014
Early double-pile classical house, 1704, with idiosyncracies; retains baffle entry (albeit against back-to-back stone hearths instead of firehood) and stair sited not at rear but mid-way between parlour and buttery. Symmetrical façade: central doorway with moulded surround, string course, and windows that would originally have been of cross-type. In contrast, rear has mullioned windows to buttery and chamber above. Main beams with unusual scroll stops. No roof trusses: purlins carried directly on crosswalls. Earlier origins suggested by re-used cruck blades as lintels to windows in both buttery and chamber above.
HISTORY: datestone initials may refer to John Howard, gentleman (d. 1717) and wife Elizabeth (d. 1714).
Pevsner, South Lancashire (1969), p76.

(17) GANTLEY HOUSE   SD523029
Stone later C17 yeoman house with recessed centre and two projecting wings, incorporating evidence of earlier timber-frame. Low, two-storeyed with mullioned windows. Wall between housebody and upper wing to R timber-framed with jowelled wallpost supporting principal rafter truss at this point; internal wall beneath truss also timber-framed. Dog-leg stair at rear of wing. Lower wing also contains principal rafter truss of heavy scantling with collar, beam in room to front with deep run-out chamfer. Other beams plain with stops seemingly buried in walls: further evidence of cladding. Entrance to housebody at opposite end to hearth; no firehood. Stonework suggests date c1670-1690, but joint between rear of parlour wing and housebody indicates alternate rebuilding possible.

(18) GREAT HOUGHWOOD   SD520008
Superior early yeoman house in stone c1600 with added mid-C18 cottage. Earliest build comprises hall heated by large segmental-headed lateral hearth, in imitation of gentry style, with massive external stack; projecting wing to N with parlour. S end of hall now an external gable with fine four-centred arched doorway; but photograph c1900 shows part of gabled projection here, possibly porch, subsequently demolished. Wing contains principal rafter truss of heavy scantling with collar and windbraces.

Cottage added unusually as continuation of wing, probably 1750-1770, with facade at right angles to that of house. Asymmetrical front with doorway in 1st bay with Doric pilasters supporting broken pediment, sashes. Originally 2½ storeys but attic removed following fire.
HISTORY: uncertain. Winstanley family of Hoge Woode recorded 1616 (Wigan PR); John Billinge assessed on six hearths 'for the Houghwood' in 1664.

(19) GREENSLATE FARM   SD531031
Small stone double-pile house c1715-1725, significant for discovery of wall painting in housebody: geometric frieze along top of walls in indigo on white ground, with similar design on inner jamb of door to stair lobby. Traces of rose and honeysuckle pattern also on walls which appeared to be later. Stair flanked by timber-framed walls supporting half-trusses similar to Cock Farm, Lathom (63) of 1708 and Darbyshire House, also Billinge (15) of 1716.

(20) LYME TREE HOUSE/WIDDOWS   SD514019
Fragment of C17-early C18 house: destroyed by fire and now only façade and little else remaining. Three-bay linear plan possibly with outshut behind first. Fine but now eroded classical doorway with moulded architrave and cornice and entablature above, probably c1710-1720 and inserted into pre-existing house of later C17 on evidence of remaining mullioned windows. Named as 'Lyme Tree House' on 6" OS Map 1846, and 'Widdows' on 1909 edition.

(21) LYME VALE FARM   SJ522995
Large double pile house dated 1733 added to lower, pre-existing wing of earlier house which now projects oddly from front of first bay. Stone, two-and-a-half storeys.

Windows of wooden mullioned and transomed type and semicircular hood above entrance on moulded brackets. Not surveyed internally.

(22) MADDOCKS SJ 505022

Small double-depth house of c1710-1720, subsequently extended and barn added laithe-house style. Original building of two-unit, end-baffle-entry type with gable chimneys and splayed mullioned windows, similar to Holmes House Farm, Blackrod (28). Later bay to W, with mullioned windows of square section added at same time as single-storey porch. Outshut to rear of this bay is later C18, along with barn and shippon added at E in watershot masonry. Interior has crude beams but fine dog-leg stair.

BISPHAM

Small township of 926 acres with ground falling westwards from 45m on lower slopes of Harrock Hill to 7m on wide, marshy floodplain of Douglas stretching northwards towards Ribble estuary. Manor initially held by Bispham family in C13 then Daltons of Dalton township from late C13-early C14; subsequently sold to Stanleys of Lathom mid-C15 and remained with Earls of Derby. Separate estate, including Bispham Hall, acquired by Ashurst family of Dalton 1610. No freeholders listed in 1600; 24 households only in 1664 hearth tax.

(23) ANDERTON HOUSE SD494127

Early C18 crosswing house, product of staggered rebuilding. Three units, two low storeys, thin coursed grey sandstone. Crosswing added c1700 to pre-existing range (probably cruck-framed) in turn rebuilt early to mid C18. Section of fine moulded beam, early-mid C16, discovered during restoration, used as lintel over window. Adjacent barn dated WA 1709.
HISTORY: Anderton yeoman family. Will of William Anderton (LCRO WCW 1760) bequeathed leasehold lands in Mawdesley and Bispham to grandson, also William.
Garry Miller, private report, 2000.

(24) BISPHAM HALL SD485130

Minor gentry/upper yeomanry house of c1700-1710 of transitional style showing classical modification of traditional plan. Stone. Three-unit central-entry plan with rear wing at upper end. Symmetrical front with moulded doorway with false keystone flanked by pilasters supporting pediment-style gable at eaves (similar to Stone Hall, Dalton, 48) containing sundial. Windows probably cross type originally; storey band; chimneys at ridge set at angle. Entrance into centre of housebody, not against hearth; heated kitchen and parlour. Wing to rear of latter contains fine dog-leg stair and buttery. Infill in upper portion of timber-framed wall between stair and buttery composed of staves only with no wattles.
HISTORY: Owned by Ashurst family as lords of manor, which explains similarities to Stone Hall; probably on site of earlier house referred to as capital messuage in 1610 on acquisition by Ashursts. This predecessor may be that of 'Anne Holt, tenant to Mr Ashurst' recorded as having three hearths 1664.

(25) ECCLES HOUSE SD487129

Small two-unit main range of c1710-1720 grafted on to pre-existing wing of c1670-1690. Thin coursed grey sandstone. Two storeys; main range has symmetrical front, semicircular doorway hood on moulded brackets and probably cross-windows originally. Not of double depth plan however: instead, single-depth housebody in 1st bay with outshut to rear of subdivided 2nd bay. Roof carried on upper cruck. Wing, despite being earlier, uses load-bearingwalls throughout; formerly-unheated parlour sited unusually to rear with buttery to front.

(26) GREYSTONE FARM SD489124

Three-unit baffle-entry house dated 1698. Stone. Two low storeys with dormers at eaves level above 2nd and 3rd bays. Former firehood in housebody removed, with recesses for salt cupboards remaining. Redundant water-tabling on chimneys indicates roof formerly thatched. Later C18 extension to rear.

BLACKROD

Upland township of 2,388 acres bounded by Douglas on N, E and W: village with church of C16 origin sited on steep ridge reaching maximum height of 158m. Manor owned by Bradshaigh family from late C13, then subdivided from early C16. Sub-manor of Arley in north recorded from C13; present C19 Arley Hall exists on fine moated site. Two freeholders recorded 1600 and 86 households 1664.

(27) GREEN BARN SD 622102

Progressive house of 1704, one of earliest to use true double-depth plan. Two storeys plus attic; symmetrical front with later single-storey porch, gable chimneys. All windows originally horizontal mullioned of up to five lights; attic has dormers to front. Interior includes fine dog-leg stair, five-panel doors on chamber floor, beams with ovolo moulding and stop. Hybrid roof: central structural crosswall augmented over 2nd bay by principal rafter truss of poor scantling with collar. Inferior addition to W, prob-

ably agricultural/industrial use.
HISTORY: initials on datestone probably those of Gregory family (Blackrod parish registers).

(28) **HOLMES HOUSE** SD603108
Small double-pile house with conservative tendencies, dated 1721. End-baffle-entry; mullioned windows of square section with housebody having four lights on facade and rest three. Storey band to front, individual monolithic hoodmoulds at rear. Distinctive sandstone of orange-brown hue, watershot on W gable facing prevailing wind. Fine salt cupboard in housebody with carved door dated 1688, probably re-used. Simple dog-leg stair with undecorated newels. Purlin roof. Similarities to Maddocks, Billinge (22).

COPPULL

Township of 2,280 acres at northern extremity of Parbold-Harrock landmass with ground rising to 93m. Coppull family owned manor since early C13 at least: Richard, lord of Coppull, a benefactor of Burscough Priory c1230-1264, granting land called Perburn. Family sold manor to Sir Thomas Stanley of Lathom Hall (66) in 1461; sold again 1600 to Rigby family of Burgh in Duxbury. Sub-manor of Chisnall in west held by family of that name from C13; Blainscough in north by Worthingtons; Perburn (later Bogburn) in south by Perburn family from C14, and by Haydocks from early C16 at least. Three freeholders in 1600. Hearth tax 1664 records 66 households.

(29) **BOGBURN HALL** SD561124
Significant but problematical gentry/yeoman house of C16-17. Present form dates from 1663 in brick: pioneering example of symmetrical front and centralised plan. Two-unit central baffle-entry main range containing housebody and parlour, with kitchen in wing to rear of bay 2 and stair outshut to rear of bay 1. Single-storey porch with triangular arched doorway. Back-to-back firehoods in housebody and parlour, have fine quarter round beams in both rooms.

Evidence exists however of a remodelled, substantial timber-framed building but exact form uncertain. Set against W gable in attic is principal rafter truss with angle struts: lack of weathering on side facing gable indicates building once extended further; probably this was central truss in two-bay hall. Two similar trusses flank brick chimney stack to form short bay which may once have been smoke bay, or alternatively screens passage, subsequently filled by back-to-back firehoods. Further truss at junction of main range and wing, not in situ and relocated here during 1663 rebuilding. This of inferior quality, but fine scantling of others intimates C16 origins: possibly as open hall, as present quarter-round beams supporting (?inserted) ceiling suggest early C17.
HISTORY: home of freeholding Haydock family since early C16, but site has earlier origins. Hugh Haydock in possession of Perburn estate in 1512, in right of his mother Catherine, one of heirs of Perburn family. John Haydock a freeholder 1600; died 1622 holding messuage and 14 acres in Coppull, six acres in Langtree and three in Heskin. Inventory (LCRO WCW 1622, total £432 5s 2d) refers to following rooms: house, parlour, buttery, old buttery, kitchen, painted chamber, high chamber. 'Old' buttery and reference in will to leaving 'broken tymber made for the use of...the house' to son Roger (b.1615) infers timber-framed house partly rebuilt by that time. Roger Haydock, yeoman, acquired lease of Langtree Hall (59) 1653. Datestone on porch has initials of Roger Haydock and family badge, a sparrowhawk; second stone, on E wall, initials of his son John (d.1719), imprisoned for Quaker beliefs.
VCH VI p224, 228. Porteus, p149, 159.

(30) **CHISNALL HALL** SD539126
Stone minor gentry house of c1600 on moated site, reduced and remodelled c1800. Now 2-bay double-depth plan with symmetrical facade, round-headed entrance and sashed windows. Rear however has earlier masonry with mullioned and mullioned-and-transomed windows. Deep ovolo-chamfered beams with tongue stops. Chamber floor has panelling of later C17 with fine carving and 6-panel doors with fancy hinges.
HISTORY: seat of Chisnall family first recorded as landowners in Coppull and Worthington in 1277. Built probably by Edward Chisnall, who suceeded before 1600, recorded as freeholder that year. As substantial landowner he paid £25 on refusing knighthood 1631; d.1635 holding capital messuage of Chisnall Hall, lands in adjacent townships and messuage in High Holborn, London, called Chisnall's Buildings. Son Edward fought for Charles I in defence of Lathom House and at Marston Moor, as result of which estates sequestered by Parliament. Died 1653; fine memorial tablet in Standish Church. Son, another Edward, taxed on seven hearths 1664; inventory (LCRO WCW 1680) total £93 10s 4d.
VCH VI p226-7.

(31) **COPPULL HALL** SD 579136
Manor house of Coppull on ancient, possibly moated site: probably early C17 brick addition to pre-existing timber-framed structure. Odd L-shaped plan with broad projection containing porch with semi-circular arched entrance and fine moulded dripstone above; modern datestone '1631'. Wooden mullioned window at rear suggests timber-framed

origin. Interior has unusually deep back-to-back firehoods and four-centred arched doorways. Interior not viewed. An important building worthy of detailed survey.

HISTORY: earthwork features suggest possible moated site; medieval stock oval identified to S, shared with Holt Farm (33). Hall occupied by Dicconson family in C16-C17: Jane Dicconson, 'vidua aula de Coppull' buried at Standish 24 March 1603 (Standish PR). Edward Dicconson, gentleman, paid for 10 hearths 1664, second largest number in Coppull: this and inventory (LRO WCW 1680; total £93 10s 4d) reveals substantial building with 21 rooms. They are: hall, great parlour, master's parlour, buttery, larder, kitchen, old kitchen, brewhouse, dairy, west larder, 'boulthouse', kitchen chamber, brewhouse chamber, red chamber, master's chamber, women's chamber, little closet over the sink(?), feather loft, flax loft plus 'great staires head' and 'other staires head'. 'Old kitchen' implies an earlier building, now removed, perhaps to W of present structure; latter probably built as upper wing with parlour.

Department of Culture, Media and Sport, lists of buildings of architectural or historic interest, Chorley BC, parish of Coppull; Crosby, Ellerbeck report, p17-19; VCH VI, p224-225.

(32) COPPULL OLD HALL SD574139

House of uncertain status incorporating timber-frame of c1600 and substantial re-used cruck blade. Present form is three unit central-entry in brick of c1700. First bay has timber post on high stylobate with brace to presumed tiebeam now boxed-in: this at right angles to axis of building, suggesting former wing. Housebody in bay 2 has quarter-round beams and is divided from outshut to rear, containing stair, by timber framed wall with posts braced to purlin. (Re-used as outshut principal is section of heavy cruck blade with run-out chamfer.) Extent of house before remodelling in brick unclear. Façade windows vertical, probably wooden crosses originally, but some mullioned at rear including one with dogtooth brick decoration above. Bay 3 reduced to single-storey following fire; wing at N end added 1900.

History: unclear. Probably of sub-manorial status and not, as implied by name, predecessor of Coppull Hall (31) as latter is on ancient, possibly moated site; referred to as 'Old Hall, Coppull' on 1846 OS map.

(33) HOLT FARM SD581127

Brick exterior of c1700 concealing remains of timber-framed house of C16-early C17 on ancient site. Three-unit baffle-entry with 3rd bay as crosswing incorporating outshut to rear. Timber-frame exists in housebody (bay 2) and wing; both have massive gritstone plinth. Wallposts braced to wallplate exposed on upper floor of crosswall between wing and range; also one jowelled wallpost supporting principal rafter truss which formed former N gable of wing. All timbers of heavy scantling. Further principal-rafter truss exposed above housebody, some four feet from wing, with mortices in soffit for former braces to now-removed wallposts. Latter suggests former open hall of early C16 date at least, to which upper wing was added c1600. No evidence of framing in 1st bay (presumed kitchen) which appears C18; ceiling joists marked with Roman numerals to aid assembly. House restored from 1996.

HISTORY: formerly significant building, perhaps sub-manorial status initially but in wealthy yeoman occupation by early C17. Site of medieval or earlier origin, sharing stock enclosure with Coppull Hall (31) to north. The Holt or 'Haultes' originally held by Chisnall family of Chisnall Hall, (30): Robert de la Holte and John de Chisenale senior witnessed release of land in Standish and Langtree 1315. Holt estate acquired by Standish family 1518; 'capital messuage and the chief house of Holt' referred to in indenture of 1575. Richard Prescott, yeoman, purchased Holt c1610: was he the builder of the wing? Inventory (LCRO WCW 1631, total £222 1s 10d) refers to house, buttery, kitchen, brewhouse, 'boyes chamber', 'his owne chamber', higher chamber, lower chamber and another chamber as well as 'other house.'

VCH VI p228. Porteus, 'Standish Deeds', p11, 72, 126. 'History of Holt Farm' compiled by Janet and David Cole.

DALTON

Hilly township of 2,103 acres with highest point Ashurst Beacon at 170m forming southern slope of Douglas Valley. Manor subdivided from C12; various portions changing hands several times until Ashurst family acquired manor in its entirety c1600. Only one other freeholder recorded 1600; 1664 hearth tax shows 51 households. Nucleus of poorer yeoman houses, several showing evidence of crucks, at Elmers Green on southern slope of Ashurst Hill (now within Skelmersdale New Town).

(34) ASHURST HALL SD496082

House of gentry Ashurst family, modernised but upon ancient site. Stone gatehouse dated 1649 implies presence of substantial building at that time. Inventory of William Ashurst (LCRO WCW 1618) records best chamber, two chambers over the hall, chamber over little parlour, chamber above parlour; 16 hearths recorded 1662, ten in 1664. Ashurst family landowners in Dalton and Orrell from reign of Henry III and were tenants of Knights of St John of the Hospital around 1540; acquired fourth part of the manor around this time and remainder from William

Orrell of Turton around 1600. Estate survey 1750 (LCRO DDHk) states Ashurst demesne lands contained more than 88 acres. Ashursts sold manor in 1751 to Sir Thomas Bootle of Lathom House (66).
*VCH IV, p98-101

(35) BARKER'S FARM SD497074

Extremely late example of centralised baffle-entry plan, dated 1742 but more than likely earlier. Stone, two-storey two-unit main range with rear service wing with outshut to W. Wide, central porch formerly contained stair – unconventional; back-to-back hearths heating housebody and parlour. Rear wing appears partly rebuilt in C19, but probably retaining original form; outshut originally built back-to-earth. Through-purlin roof, but gable of porch supported by kingpost truss; section of porch wallplate possibly re-used cruck tiebeam.
HISTORY: Hatton family. Edward Hatton referred to as shoemaker in Upholland PR 1735. Ashurst estate survey 1750 (LCRO DDHk) refers to 'Edward Hatton's tenement' with 13 acres.

(36) BLACKBIRD'S FARM SD495098

Stone yeoman house of C17-18 containing two cruck trusses probably of C16. Three units, former baffle entry (entrance blocked); recessed housebody with dormer at eaves level between forward-projecting wings of differing date; outshut behind bay 1. Crucks of medium scantling, positioned at either end of housebody indicating original cruck range of at least three bays in length. Firehood positioned between cruck and lower wing (bay 3), suggesting it was inserted in former through-passage. Lower wing may have originated as early C17 timber-framed addition with principal rafter truss forward of junction with range; one roll-moulded beam on ground floor. Upper wing always of stone, with ragged joint in masonry suggesting it was added (probably mid-to-late C17) prior to cladding of range; unheated parlour has quarter-round beam.

Main range and lower wing clad c1700-1710 on evidence of dormer and ceiling probably inserted in housebody at same time; lower portion of blades of cruck at lower end removed when outer walls rebuilt in stone. Both crucks had collars removed to allow circulation on new upper floor and eaves were raised by means of outriders. Outshut may have existed during cruck-framed phase as exposed section of wallplate to between this and bay 1 lacks weathering.
HISTORY: named Berry's Farm on 1846 OS map. Yeoman Berry family recorded in Dalton C17-18.

(37) BELLE VUE FARM (SCOTT'S FOLD) SD5O9072

Fine yeoman's house of 1683: long disused and now appallingly ruinous. Virtually identical to Prior's Wood Hall (45): three-unit baffle-entry plan with crosswing and two-storey porch, later outshut. Northern aspect, resulting in parlour sited to rear of wing with buttery and stair to front. Parlour had largest window (seven lights) and later separate entrance; three-light stairlight on facade is only window with transom. Porch has round-headed entrance on moulded responds. Decay revealed two principal-rafter trusses, that over wing with re-used cruck blades.
HISTORY: datestone (now missing) on porch carried initials of James Scott, yeoman (d.1700) wife Margaret (d.1705) and son Francis (b.1667); family recorded in Upholland Parish Register from early C17. Scott assessed on one hearth in 1666; present house has three (housebody, parlour, parlour chamber) representing tremendous improvement in living standards, replacing building that was probably cruck-framed. Two adjacent stone barns, again ruinous; one dated 1680, indicating Scott's investment in agriculture took precedence over domestic accommodation. Third datestone, of 1685 found among ruins c1982 (information from Linda J Mawdsley); location on building unknown. Referred to as Scott's Fold on 1846 6" OS map and VCH.
*W F Price, 'Places, Traditions & Folklore of the Douglas Valley', Hist. Soc. of Lancs. & Cheshire (1899).

(38) BENTHAM'S FARM SD497092

Stone, three-unit linear baffle-entry house dated 1718 and therefore extremely late occurance of this plan. Single-storey porch. Not surveyed internally. Bentham yeoman family: Ashurst estate survey 1750 (LCRO DDHk) records Thomas Bentham held more than five acres.

(39) CICELY'S COTTAGE SD467067

Small two-unit two-storey end-baffle entry house, probably last quarter 17th century. Roof over second bay treated as cross-gable, as at Heyes Farm, Upholland, 1680 (116) and Crisp Cottage, Dalton (40). Wing contains small heated parlour and formerly buttery. Low height suggests remodelling of cruck-framed structure but no crucks evident; roof timbers now renewed. However change in masonry at first floor level suggests an original single-storey structure subsequently heightened, therefore crucks possibly removed when eaves raised.

(40) CRISP COTTAGE SD509073

Unusual small house of two bays of differing building periods. Stone, two low storeys. Bay 1 earlier, gabled in manner of crosswing but flush front and rear with bay 2; firehood on rear wall, bressumer (ex-situ, possibly) is re-used cruck tie. Within is fine stone hearth of early C18, probably ex-situ. Bay 2 has end baffle entry and dormers front and rear, suggesting date c1710-20; datestone JWJ 1758 probably not original. Overall impressions and low height suggests staggered remodelling of cruck structure, with first bay rebuilt late C17 and 2nd bay thereafter; similarities to Cicely's Cottage (39).

(41) **FELTON'S FARM** SD501066

Fragment of post-and-truss yeoman house probably of late C16, subsequently clad in stone: remnant of what must have been largest and most important house in Elmers Green. Original plan unclear. Present form is two-storey two-bay main range, containing timber-frame, coupled to later two-storey stone range at rear. Former rear wall of main range (now internal) entirely timber-framed, wallplate of front wall has pegs for corresponding posts.

Firehood placed centrally with stone spere facing former rear wall (door in latter may indicate former baffle entrance); however on chamber floor, stack is framed by principal rafter roof trusses suggesting firehood was preceded by smoke bay. Furthermore, stave holes in tiebeam of W truss demonstrates it was formerly enclosed. Beneath E truss is inserted early C17 stone hearth with four-centred arch heating this chamber, indicating smoke bay was quickly superseded.

Housebody in bay 1 has broach-stopped beam. Bay 2 has two four-centred doorways either side of chamber floor hearth and one by spere on ground floor. Trusses are of principal rafter type, that to W with gouged carpenter's mark III, that to E, IIII: indicating timber-framed structure originally longer. At W end of adjacent barn (see below) is re-used principal rafter truss with gouged mark II which possibly stood previously at W end of house: weathering on one side and vacant mortices in tie for wallposts and braces inward of these hint at use on an external gable. Present W gable probably therefore rebuilt in late C17, but thickness and extent of masonry suggests rest of main range remained timber-framed. Secondary range to rear began as outshut at same time, indicated by change in masonry at storey level; may have been heightened when rest of main range clad in C18.

Adjacent barn, with two cruck trusses, probably of late C16 - early C17 date, clad in stone and enlarged later C17 using principal rafter truss referred to above.

(42) **HARSNIPS** SD499067

Yeoman's house with crosswing, showing development from original cruck-framed structure possibly of C16. Stone, three-unit-baffle-entry with later single-storey porch. One truncated cruck truss surviving at junction of range and wing with tiebeam, on secondary posts, added to carry ceiling inserted in housebody early C17 (with quarter-round beam). Main range subsequently stone clad later C17-early C18 (datestone 1667 on range) and walls heightened, involving removal of upper portion of cruck and replacement by principal rafter truss (compare Higher Barn, Wrightington, 135). Wing probably added at same time, but stonework here and at rear of range shows evidence of several building periods.

HISTORY: initials RH refer to Roger Harsnep, yeoman, recorded in Upholland Parish Register in 1660s.

(43) **HOLLAND'S HOUSE** SDSD506094

Large timber-framed house of wealthy yeoman freeholder, 1st quarter C17, possibly c1608; subsequently clad in stone and remodelled late C17-early C18. Now rectangular three-unit baffle-entry plan with stair tower to rear of housebody. but first bay originally crosswing. Latter contains two rooms connected by doorway with nicked lintel, front one a parlour (probably originally unheated). Presence of beam close to rear wall indicated wing once extended further to N. Tower contains modern stair but formerly contained one dated IH 1727 now removed; dimensions suggest stair of open-well or framed newel type originally. Quarter round beams throughout. Housebody and kitchen clad early C18 creating symmetrical composition (round-arched entrance, cross-windows, storey band). Masonry suggests wing not clad until later, when reduced to present size. Large segmental-arched hearth in housebody. Kingpost truss (altered) over main range at junction of 1st and 2nd bays.

History: freeholding Holland family recorded from C16. James Holland also a customary tenant (copyholder) in 1507 (LCRO DDHi); Richard Holland d.1587 holding lands in Dalton, Parbold and Ormskirk. James Holland (son?) d.1605 holding three messuages and 40 freehold acres in Dalton plus lands in Parbold and Ormskirk. Son Richard (?1594-1667) taxed on four hearths 1664. Inventory (LCRO WCW 1667, total £223 11s 4d) records firehouse, buttery, great parlour, little parlour (the rooms in the wing?), kitchen, buttery, green chamber, red chamber, little chamber, another chamber, little room and 'another room' plus garretts.

* Price (1899).

(44) **LOWER HOUSE** SD507093

Problematical minor yeoman house built around cruck-framed core possibly of late C16. Stone, three-unit former baffle-entry with wings at either end. Masonry and details of main range and W (upper) wing late C17, E wing mid-C18. Two crucks of poor, irregular scantling: one in range at junction with W wing (figure 5), other at right angles within W wing (with triangular headed door) implying existence of rare cruck-framed wing. Rear wall of W wing contains remains of post and truss frame suggesting repair or an extension beyond original cruck structure, perhaps early C17. Low housebody remains open to roof. Nature of trusses suggests use towards end of cruck tradition and limited resources for rebuilding.

HISTORY: Name and proximity to Lower House suggests association with latter, perhaps as home of secondary branch of Holland family. A James Holland taxed on two hearths 1671; also inventory of Robert Holland of Dalton (LCRO WCW 1682, total £34 4s 2d) records house, parlour (both heated) and little chamber which seem appropriate for this building.

(45) PRIOR'S WOOD HALL SD502097

Substantial yeoman's house of stone with two crosswings, gentrified in C19 by extensive additions. Datestone illegible; possibly c1680, but may be earlier. Original form three-unit baffle-entry with E crosswing and narrow two-storey porch: virtually identical to Belle Vue Farm (37) of 1683. Unheated W wing added soon after, differing only slightly in external details: conclusive proof of its addition is blocked window in former W. gable in attic over 3rd bay. Apparently no access originally to W wing from main range: may indicate non-domestic function or separate household. Fine stair contemporary but ex-situ. Four principal rafter trusses, all of heavy scantling. W truss over housebody has reused moulded collar, possibly from arched-braced truss; similar moulded timber reused as common rafter over E wing and fine moulded beam reused at stairhead. These appear late C15-early C16 in date and suggest presence of substantial earlier house on site.

HISTORY: probably home of Prescott yeoman family, copyholders in Dalton 1507 (custumal, LCRO DDHi), Richard Prescott tenant-at-will (leaseholder) of Burscough Priory in Dalton at time of Dissolution, paying total of £4 10s implying large estate. Two branches of family recorded in 1664 hearth tax, Richard Prescott senior and Richard Prescott junior each assessed on three hearths. Inventory of Richard Prescott the younger (LCRO WCW 1680, total £140 15s 8d) lists firehouse, parlour, kitchen, buttery, best room (parlour chamber), room over firehouse, porch chamber, little chamber.

(46) SMITH'S FARM SD496067

Unusual yeoman house with two-unit double-depth form created by staggered rebuilding. Earliest element is gabled second bay, which was originally wing added to pre-existing, probably cruck-framed range. This contains buttery and parlour with cross-corner fireplace; principal rafter roof truss; date probably 1670-1690. Main range replaced by present first bay c1710-1720 in pursuit of double-depth layout: housebody to front and further bay containing modern stair to rear. Doorway placed centrally on facade in attempt at symmetry. Main range taller than wing, resulting in oddly-improvised roof structure: roof over wing by means of hip to junction with range, where upper cruck truss sits on crosswall of wing. Also fine combination barn dated 1689.

HISTORY: Darbyshire yeoman family. Will of John Darbyshire (LCRO WCW 1718) states he held 'lands of inheritance' (copyhold) and leasehold estates in Ashton, Bickerstaffe and Dalton, left to son Thomas (who may have rebuilt main range). Also that he was entitled to profits from coal 'yet remaining ungotten' within the lands he 'lately exchanged' with Sir William Gerard of Garswood, which were intended for his younger children.

Garry Miller, private report, 1991/2000.

(47) STANNANOUGHT SD498074

Dated 1714; a late example of crosswing house: compares with Dial House, Upholland (112), and Higher Highfield, Aspull (8) of same year. Stone, three-unit baffle entry plan with receding wing to R; flat asymmetrical front. Northern aspect results in parlour at rear of wing, buttery and stair to front. Ground floor and stairlight windows are wooden cross windows, first floor small sliding sashes. Firehood in housebody replaced, parlour and chamber above have cross-corner hearths. Fine dog-leg stair. Two principal-rafter roof trusses, both having re-used cruck blades as principals.

History: built by Robert Stannanought, yeoman (1657-1729) and wife Sarah (d. 1726), last of family recorded in Dalton from C16. Robert's father John assessed on one hearth 1664, therefore pre-1714 house probably cruck-framed. John Stannanought left goods totalling £26 16s 6d (inventory, LCRO WCW 1671) but had debts totalling £33.4s.2d, which may account for son's belated rebuilding in conservative style. Robert Stannanought churchwarden at Upholland, 1693 (PR). Inventory (LCRO WCW 1729) mentions parlour, buttery, house, kitchen (all with chambers over) cellar and outhousing. Adjacent barn, altered; datestone RS 1690.

(48) STONE HALL SD509077

Fine but eclectic early double-depth classical house: probably c.1700-1710. Two-and-a-half storeys, squared sandstone rubble with rusticated quoins and ashlar stone around doorway. Compact three-bay façade with pediment containing oval window above central bay, supported on pilasters. Moulded doorway has somewhat coarse scrolly open pediment on consoles; ovolo-moulded cross windows. Sides and rear however with mullioned windows.

Unconventional double-depth form. Single-depth main range containing housebody and parlour; services in twin

gabled wings projecting to rear with stair outshut, rising only to second storey, between. Hybrid roof: purlins carried on central crosswall of range and also upon fine upper cruck sited midway along 1st bay. Back-to-back fireplaces located at junction of main range and wings. Inferior mid-C18 extensions to rear. Plan compares with Lowes, Newburgh (78) of similar date; similarities of detail to Bispham Hall, Bispham (24), also owned by Ashurst family.
HISTORY: location suggests ancient site, possibly as earlier manor house of Dalton before manor acquired in entirety by Ashursts of Ashurst Hall (34). 'Stone Hall lands' comprised 40 acres in 1750 survey of Henry Ashurst's estate (LCRO DDHk). Name 'Stone Hall' implies existance of another hall that was not stone, ie timber-framed.

(49) **TYLDESLEYS** (now BEACON VIEW) SD495078
Small stone house aspiring to classicism: double-depth plan but rear rooms beneath outshut instead of full-height. Central baffle entry. Dormers at eaves level on facade, characteristic of date: 1713.

(50) **WIDDOWS** SD498067
Stone parlour wing dated 1680 added to pre-existing, probably timber-framed, main range. Internal walls loadbearing, no roof trusses: progressive. Present main range is inferior, early-mid C18. Barn has fine re-used four-centred arched door lintel inside, dated RB 1625.
HISTORY: Jackson yeoman family. Inventory of William Jackson (LCRO WCW 1704, total £84 2s 6d) identifies firehouse, parlour (heated), buttery, kitchen, chamber over house, chamber over parlour, kitchen loft.

(51) **YEW TREE HOUSE** SD498068
Yeoman's house dated 1679 and 1710. Stone with two forward-projecting wings. Earliest is parlour wing to S dated 1679, originally added to former, probably cruck-framed, main range now replaced by housebody and lower wing of 1710. 1679 wing shows signs of having been shortened to lie flush with rear of housebody. Cross-corner fireplace in parlour. 1710 work attempts to create balanced composition. Symmetrical housebody front with central entrance, upright windows (probably wooden cross-type originally) string course and central dormer above. Housebody had brick hearth from the start, and not firehood. Principal rafter truss above 1679 wing contains re-used cruck blade. Deep early C18 outshut to rear and C19 additions.
HISTORY: Crane yeoman family. 1679 wing built by John Crane, (d. 1709) and wife Jane (d. 1714). Inventory (LCRO WCW 1709, total £39 13s 4d) records firehouse, parlour (unheated), old chamber, buttery, old chamber (indicating rebuilding), room above old chamber, room above parlour, loft over parlour. 1710 remodelling by son Thomas (b.1667).

HAIGH

Large township of 2,135 acres northeast of Wigan bounded on west by River Douglas and rising steeply to E to reach maximum of 156m. Bradshaigh family lords of manor from late C13 until late C18, prospered through mining of cannel-coal from C16. They and one other freeholder recorded 1600; Hearth Tax 1664 indicates 52 households.

(52) **HAIGH HALL** SD595085
Classical mansion house of 1827-40, a reconstruction of predecessors of early C17 and early C18, with remnants of latter probably incorporated within. Building contracts dated 1606 (for up to £140) 1613 (also up to £140) and 1622 (£70) confirm substantial rebuilding in stone by Roger Bradshaigh (1578-1641) who succeeded to manor 1599. Work modelled upon Birchley Hall, Billinge (12) of 1594; Bradshaigh's wife Ann was member of Anderton family of Birchley. C17 building, of three storeys plus basement, with full-height bay windows, transomed windows of up to 16 lights, and steps up to entrance (plate 27). Southeast front subsequently rebuilt early C18 in brick by Sir Roger Bradshaigh (1675-1746): three-storey, symmetrical seven-bay facade with recessed centre, sashed windows, storey bands and scrolly pedimented entrance.
*Anderson, 1991

INCE

Low-lying township south of Wigan, formerly with large tracts of mossland but ground rising to NE at boundary with Aspull; area 2,230 acres. Ince family held manor, along with Aspull, from late C13 and subsequently Gerard family, by marrriage, from early C15 until late C17. Six freeholders in 1600 and 36 households in 1664 Hearth Tax.

(53) **DOWER HOUSE** SD601034
Prodigiously early, eclectic double-pile house of 1686; demolished 1997 after arson attack. Pioneered layout which elsewhere only became standard after 1700, yet ignores any attempt at façade symmetry. Housebody and heated parlour occupied front, rear contained formerly unheated kitchen, stair lobby and buttery. Unconventional however was two-storey porch on E gable and small gabled single-storey

projection to front of housebody, both contemporary; latter possibly small secondary parlour. Brick on stone plinth with storey band (early use) and some raised brick decoration including hearts on porch and small projection. Brick mullioned windows with segmental hoodmoulds; housebody has largest, 5 lights, but parlour chamber originally lit by two three-light windows with additional light subsequently inserted between to make 7-light window. Shallower single-bay addition to W with two heated rooms, possibly intended for separate occupation; weathered date stone read 17—.
HISTORY: Name and proximity to site of Hall of Ince (55) suggests an association with latter.
*RCHM report, 1997.

(54) HALL OF INCE
Demolished; rambling timber-framed gentry hall illustrated in Philips, 'Old Halls of Lancashire & Cheshire' (plate 34), rebuilt in brick late C19. Seat of Gerard family: Miles Gerard a freeholder in 1600 and James Gerard assessed on five hearths 1664.
*VCH IV, p104

(55) INCE HALL (PEEL DITCH) SD599058
Fine timber-framed gentry house of late C16-early C17, destroyed by fire and rebuilt in brick 1854. Drawing by Will Lathom, 1820s, (LCRO DP 291/2) shows symmetrical two-and-a-half-storey, five-gabled facade with recessed centre, projecting wings and central porch. Decorative herringbone bracing and first and attic floors carried on jetties. All ground floor windows with transoms. Date 1601 at rear of present building may refer to its construction. Plaster ceilings said to have existed in hall and other rooms, along with wainscoting.
HISTORY: seat of Brown gentry family, recorded as landowners since 1391. Wiiliam Brown d1596 holding two messuages and various lands in Ince of Miles Gerrard along with 16 messuages in Wigan. Son Roger (c1580-1619) a freeholder in 1600. Ralph Brown assessed on nine hearths in 1664.
*Baines, 1891, p310. VCH IV, p105.

(56) PEEL HALL SD597057
Medieval cruck-framed gentry hall upon formerly-moated site, possibly C14 or earlier: one of the finest of its type in North West England. Rebuilt and altered C15 to C18: present form is three unit, brick, with short forward projecting upper wing and larger wing at service end beyond through-passage; axial firehood. Original cruck structure of at least four bays. Two trusses remain, both of heavy scantling with finely-shaped blades: former central truss of two-bay hall and that which divided hall from upper bay originally containing bower. Former (figure 1) is arch-braced to cranked collar, blades meeting at ridge beneath yoke; smoke blackening at apex from former open hearth. Style similar to (but of finer quality than) Taunton Hall, Ashton-under-Lyne, dendro-dated to c1315-1320 (GMAU). Upper truss similar but originally closed and with straight collar (removed to allow circulation after ceiling inserted); spur to wallpost survives on E wall. First stage of modification occurred late C15-early C16 with replacement of lower bay by two-storey service wing of post and truss construction. This divided on upper floor by timber-frame wall supporting truss with unusual kingpost with forked base (figure 1). Windbrace housing in purlin at W gable indicates another truss formerly stood here before cladding.

Ceiling inserted in hall mid to late C16 upon roll-moulded beam (similar to Kirklees Hall, Aspull, 9) and eaves heightened by means of outriders applied to both trusses. Firehood inserted probably at same time: axial location indicates (along with modest nature of subsequent rebuilding) house had fallen to yeoman status by this time. Upper bay built out to front in manner of short wing containing parlour, early C17: originally timber-framed on stone base then subsequently clad mid-to-late C17 along with remainder of bulding. Extension to rear early C18.
HISTORY: uncertain. Proximity to Ince Hall (55) suggests an association with Brown family, possibly as their earlier residence.

LANGTREE

Small township of 1,568 acres north of Standish and bounded by Douglas to E. Manor held by Langtree family from at least time of Edward II to 1652, when debt-laden Thomas Langtree had lands sequestered by Parliament and family vanished from record. Separate manor of Bradley held by Standish family of Duxbury near Chorley. Edward Langtree only freeholder in 1600; 40 households recorded in Hearth Tax 1664.

(57) BRADLEY HALL SD570110
Timber-framed manor house of two periods, clad in brick early C19. Earliest element is narrow hall, originally open and now of three bays but formerly of four: possibly late C15-early C16. Three kingpost trusses with curved struts on jowled wallposts. Former central truss has cranked tiebeam; position indicates fourth bay of hall once existed at upper end. Lower end has screens passage with one doorway with depressed ogee arch accessing service end. Ceiling inserted in hall mid-to-late C16, when stair tower added to rear of screens passage.

Service wing apparently a remodelling c1600 of earlier structure: extends beyond rear of range in manner which suggests possible courtyard plan. Five bays: mostly principal rafter trusses with angle struts, but that at S gable has kingpost, and truss between first and second bays, largely concealed, appears to have been of arch-braced form denoting superior room and probably C15. Bays 1-3 have massive quarter-round moulded beams and wallposts: latter with unusual carved capitals (plate 84), again denoting building of high status. Doorway on chamber floor indicates wing was formerly coupled to two-storey porch. At upper end of hall is small parlour built forward of 2nd and 3rd bays, probably late C16-early C17 with four-centred arched fireplace, served by external stack, and fine moulded joists. House clad in brick of C18-19 and extended to rear.

History: manor of Bradley owned by Standish family of Duxbury possibly since early C14. Christopher, son and heir of James Standish owned Bradley in 1471 and in 1517 the manor of Bradley was held by Thomas Standish of Duxbury and occupied by his mother Alice. Alexander Standish left 'Bradlehall' to son Thomas in 1622. Bradley Hall had five hearths in 1664.

(58) DAM HOUSE FARM SD554111
Fragment of small open hall of post-and-truss construction, possibly first half C16, fossilised within small farmhouse of late C17-early C18. Present building two-storey, three-unit baffle-entry plan, brick, with C19 barn added at right angles to N (rebuilt as dwelling 1998). Renovation in summer 1999 exposed in housebody one principal rafter truss with curved angle struts braced to jowled wallpost within E wall (figure 16). Corresponding post at other end removed. Similar truss also uncovered on N gable at junction with barn; this one closed, indicating other, which is open, may have been central to two-bay hall. Possibly late example of yeoman hallhouse. Reduced to present form and clad late C17-early C18, ceiling beams with tongue stops suggesting hall floored-in at same time.

(59) LANGTREE HALL SD561112
Manor house of Langtree family on moated site; modernised. Commonwealth survey 1653 describes range of eight bays and one of four, timber covered with slate. Former comprised hall, parlour, kitchen, brewhouse and upstairs, dining room (wainscoted) over hall, chamber over buttery, a chamber wainscoted, chamber over parlour with study in it; gallery leading to chambers. Four-bay part contained two larders and dairy, two dairy chambers, larder chamber and one other chamber (wainscoted), with study. Description suggests elements were a main range and service wing. Hall let to Roger Haydock of Bogburn Hall, Coppull (29) in 1653. 'Hall of Langtree' had seven hearths in 1664.
Porteus, (1927) p148-9.

(60) OLD SEVEN STARS SD555122
Unusual house of complex, piecemeal development, probably with timber-framed early C17 origins. Three-unit plan, main range with crosswing to L and outshut to front containing stair. Main range contains through-passage, section of scarf-jointed wallplate on rear wall and deep-chamfered beam in bay 3, indicating early and possibly timber-framed house of three bays and two storeys. Hearth presently on rear wall but position probably not original. Red sandstone wing added c1700 with cross-corner fireplace; may have had coupled porch originally, suggested by similar stone around entrance. Outshut added later in brick to end flush with latter. Rear wall clad in buff sandstone C18.
HISTORY: leasehold property referred to in 1707 and 1730, originally an inn.
Porteus (1927) p203.

LATHOM

Extensive plateau-like township of 8,694 acres stretching from lower reaches of Ashurst-Billinge ridge towards mosslands in west. Owned by Lathom family since C12, who founded nearby priory at Burscough in 1189. Manor subsequently passed by marriage to Stanley family in late C14, whose principal residence was at Lathom House (66) until its destruction during the Civil War after which it was replaced by Knowsley. Originally included Newburgh, founded by Lathoms in C14. Four recorded in freeholders list of 1600 and 171 households in 1664 Hearth Tax.

(61) ASPINWALL'S FARM SD471076
Demolished late C17 two-unit house, brick with porch leading to housebody; second bay subdivided with larger room (probably parlour) forming short projection also. Segmental-headed windows, string course and raised brick decoration in form of heart on W front. Close by and similar to Webster's Farm (73) of 1682.
Mercer, 1975, p182.

(62) BLYTHE HALL SD 439100
Gentry house on formerly moated site, mainly of C19 and C20 but containing earlier fabric possibly C16-17. Stone, two storeys, recessed centre and projecting wings, with principal rafter roof trusses, some above each element indicating this was original plan. Photograph of one over range (courtesy, Mr and Mrs Lee) shows kingpost, but originality uncertain.
HISTORY: Blythe freehold estate recorded in 1189 when

held by Geoffrey Travers whose son Henry took name de Blythe; Blackledge family acquired estate by marriage 1488. Evan Blackledge recorded as freeholder 1600; inventory of son John (LCRO WCW 1633, total £393 14s 2½d) records hall only with 'great chimney'.

(63) COCK FARM SD467077
Noteably early example of small double-pile house: 1708. Symmetrical front, central single-storey porch, gable chimneys; brick on stone base. Direct entry to housebody, parlour in bay 2, stair separating service rooms to rear. Load-bearing walls carry purlins at front, rear purlins rest on half-trusses on top of timber-framed walls flanking stair (as at Darbyshire House (15) of 1716 and Greenslate Farm (19) both Billinge). C18-19 addition to L, unusually with outshut to front.

(64) DARBYSHIRE FARM SD440071
Linear three-unit baffle entry house of c1700. Brick on tall stone plinth. Housebody with firehood, heated parlour in upper bay (unusually, not subdivided to create buttery), formerly unheated kitchen in bay 3. Purlin roof carried on crosswalls. Chimneys with raised brick decoration on rear wall, reset plaque with date 1577 (probably ex-situ).

(65) JUMP'S FARM (formerly AYSCOUGH'S) SD445100
Small, initially two-unit yeoman's house with crosswing, 1690. Brick; originally end-baffle-entry against housebody firehood. Third bay added subsequently (by 1709). Wing contains heated parlour, buttery and formerly stair (evidence of blocked stairlight). Fine ovolo-moulded housebody beams and cambered firehood bressumer. Principal rafter trusses midway along range and at junction with wing. Blocked single light windows front and rear suggesting former closets either side of firehood flue.
HISTORY: Ayscough yeoman family, leaseholders: datestone with cross calvary refers to recusant William Ayscough (1664-1709). Thomas Ayscough, father (?1636-1672), assessed on one hearth 1664; inventory (LCRO WCW 1672, total £27 10s 2d) names house and parlour only therefore predecessor of present house probably cruck-built. Inventory of William Ayscough 'of Blythe Moss within Lathom' (LCRO WCW 1709) totals £46 17s 6d and specifies firehouse, parlour (heated), buttery (each with chambers above) and kitchen, latter indicating 3rd bay added by this time.

(66) LATHOM HOUSE
Monumental classical country house in Palladian style, built near site of earlier fortified mansion largely destroyed during Civil War seige of 1644-1645. Built 1725-30, architect Giacomo Leoni for Sir Thomas Bootle; unforgiveably demolished 1929. Stone, main central block connected by curving Ionic collonades to twin flanking two-storey service wings. Three storeys plus attic within taller pedimented centre. North front of 13 bays, S front of nine, sides six deep. Ground floor service basement in rusticated stone, rest ashlar. Balustraded steps up to first floor *piano nobile*, windows on this level distinguished by pediments.

Interior rooms detailed in plans c1870 (LCRO DDHi; copy, figure 33). Basement had central large common hall with service rooms grouped around. Above, two-storey entrance hall ('grand hall' on 1870 plan) measuring 40 feet square and 37 high; on first floor, saloon to rear and twin staircases either side along with dining room and private apartments. Second floor contained bedrooms, attics had further bedrooms for maids and female guests. Kitchen later added to W end of main block.

Service wings in similar style: both had projecting pedimented centre, doors and windows with Gibbs surrounds, and cupola on roof. Only W, larger of two and containing stables, now survives; restoration began Autumn 1999. E wing, demolished 1960, contained brewhouse, store room and agent's room. Single gatepier of former pair survives at entrance, with pediment on rusticated pilasters.
HISTORY: investigation by Liverpool University archeology unit in 1996 found remains of what may be moat of previous house to rear of this site. Prior to Leoni building, 9th Earl of Derby said to have erected new front, but died 1702 before completion. Uncertain if any of this incorporated into later work.

(67) LEVELDALE SD435087
C17 house drastically remodelled c1800: exterior now mostly brick of that date. Re-used over entrance however is triangular arched lintel dated 1664. Of that date also are quarter-round beams on ground floor and mullioned windows on former rear wall of 1st bay. Original plan uncertain but wing at E end is indicated by blocked 2-light window in former return wall.

History: leasehold estate associated with Thomson family: initials on lintel represent Joseph Thomson of Ormskirk d 1670, described as 'clerk' in Ormskirk parish registers, 'gentleman' in inventory (LCRO WCW 1670; total £116 0s 02d). William Jameson of Ormskirk and Mary his wife, daughter of Joseph Thomson, conveyed Leveldale estate in 1682 to Henry Smith of Snape in Scarisbrick (LCRO DDcr, bundle 34).

(68) NEEDLESS INN SD446097
Tall, curious house of belated centralised plan on isolated site: probably c1720. Pebbledashed brick, two-and-a-half

storeys with narrow off-centre porch of two storeys only. Two-unit front range with housebody and parlour heated by end stacks which project anachronistically in C17 manner. Kitchen in range to rear of housebody. Horizontal windows, wooden mullioned originally, with segmental heads. Also referred to as 'All Woods' in 1804 (LCRO DDLm box 8/17).

(69) OTTERHEADS SD446082
Mature double-depth house of c1750-1770 on isolated, probably earlier, site. Flemish bond brick on stone plinth but more extensive use of stone to rear. Two-and-a-half storeys. Fine doorway with triangular pediment with pulvinated frieze and pilasters, tall sashed windows.

(70) TAYLOR'S FARM SD458107
Stone yeoman house of complex development. Now three-unit baffle entry plan with parlour wing and added kitchen with outshut. Core of housebody possibly early C17 and timber-framed; deep quarter-round beam and wallplate with pegholes remaining for wooden mullioned window. Crosswing added later C17 containing parlour heated by cross-corner fireplace, buttery and stair; roof has one spindly principal rafter truss. Window in front return wall of wing partly blocked by main range indicates latter was clad subsequently and quoins to R of now blocked entrance indicate form was then of two-unit baffle entry plan. Third bay containing kitchen added later (as at Jump's Farm, 65) but base of outshut to rear of this bay has differing masonry and quoins which may be plinth of earlier timber-framed wing at this end. Former thatch indicated by redundant water tabling on chimney of wing. HISTORY: Taylor yeoman family referred to in deeds which begin 1694 (LCRO DDLm). William Taylor of Lathom, yeoman, declared in his will (LCRO WCW 1733) that his lands were to be sold to the highest bidder when youngest son John reached age of 21.

(71) WAINWRIGHT'S FARM SD458108
Small brick yeoman house: double-depth but rear rooms in form of outshut, suggesting date c1710-1720. Redundant water-tabling on chimneys indicate roof formerly thatched. Later addition to N. Deeds (LCRO DDLm box 8/17) exist from 1724, which may date building.

(72) WATKINSON'S FARM SD455102
Brick two-unit house of centralised plan, probably c1720. Front range with two-storey porch and projecting gable chimneys, rear heated kitchen wing. Therefore similar to and contemporary with Needless Inn (67).

(73) WEBSTERS SD470077
Significant two-unit end-baffle-entry brick house dated 1682 with C19 additions to W and rear. Porch – unusual in house of small size – leading to housebody with firehood and firewindow; second bay subdivided into unheated parlour and buttery. Extensive raised brick decoration in English garden wall bond, with continuous storey band carried on projecting headers, segmental arches above ground floor windows linked to rectangle between. Noteably early use of load bearing walls throughout instead of roof trusses.

NEWBURGH

Low-lying village at base of Ashurst-Billinge ridge with floodplain of Douglas to N. As name indicates it was founded by lords of Lathom by early C14 as new market town: in 1385, Isabel, widow of Thomas de Lathom, had dower right of eight marks of the freeholders of Newburgh. Town however failed to grow; reference to burgage plots in C18 (see Greenhill Farm, 75) shows medieval origins evident. Several C17-18 buildings in centre, still occupying earlier sites. Newburgh assessed as part of Lathom, not separately, for Hearth Tax.

(74) DOE HOUSE SD482104
Unusual fragment of early C17 house, subsequently altered and extended, original form uncertain but possibly two-unit baffle-entry with 1st bay as receding wing. Single storey porch with segmental arched doorway also contains stair, an unconventional arrangement also found at Barker's Farm, Dalton, (35) and possibly Lower Wrennall, Wrightington (136); also, outside the area at Middle and Higher Moss, Darwen, of c1600 (surveyed by author 1986) and Sowerby Hall, Inskip-with-Sowerby, Fylde (surveyed by author 1989) of similar date.

(75) GREENHILL FARM SD486104
Compact double-pile yeoman house dated 1748. Flemish bond brick with sash windows and doorway with triangular hood on simple carved brackets. Front contains large housebody and small parlour, rear has buttery and unheated kitchen between dog-leg stair. Some fine doors of four or five fielded panels (plate 120).
HISTORY: Culshaw yeoman family. Initials are those of Henry Culshaw along with wife Alice and son Thomas. Will of Henry LCRO WCW 1761) refers to several messuages and tenements and burgage plots in Newburgh along with copyhold land in Wavertree, Liverpool, and property leased in Bispham from Earl of Derby. Family's gravestone in churchyard at Ormskirk parish church (plate 62).

(76) **IVY COTTAGE** SD482106
Two-unit house of C17-18 date with crosswing dated 1742. Original form unclear. Housebody may originally have had end-baffle entry against firehood, any evidence of doorway concealed by render. Quarter-round beam with stop buried in wall may suggest earlier timber-framed origin. One principal rafter truss at junction with wing. Latter dated 1742 at gable but probably earlier; fine stair of early C18 type. Possibly a two-storey timber-framed range to which stone wing was subsequently added and main range thereafter clad (as at Taylor's Farm, Lathom, 70).

(77) **KATHRY** SD469107
Small two-unit house with wing to rear of 2nd bay: date probably 1700-1710. First bay contains housebody formerly with firehood on W gable and firewindow (now blocked) on rear wall. Parlour in 2nd bay with cross-corner fireplace; wing to rear contains stair and buttery. External entrance now leads into parlour; original entry possibly in W gable wall (now rendered) beneath firehood. Outshut to rear of housebody, creating double-depth plan, is later. Purlins carried not on load-bearing crosswalls but principal rafter trusses of poor scantling.

(78) **LOWE'S** SD478093
Unconventional double-depth house of c1700. Stone, two-and-a-half storeys. Two-unit front range with housebody and parlour; twin service wings projecting to rear under coupled gables and containing heated kitchen and two unheated service rooms along with stair in unusual L-shaped lobby. Symmetrical front with windows originally of cross type in stone architraves. Doorway has Gibbs surround which must be later; similarly, tall sash windows to rear. Chimneys sited internally where range and wings meet. Fine staircase of dog-leg type with curved handrail at ground floor. Depth of plan results in hybrid roof, hipped over front range, with twin gables coupled at right angles over rear. At junction are two coupled upper cruck trusses, remarkable in an otherwise advanced building; timbers not re-used but of poor and irregular scantling. Similar in plan and use of upper crucks to Stone Hall, Dalton (48).

(79) **LYS COTTAGE** SD484103
Brick house of three-unit baffle-entry type with crosswing dated 1691: however a remodelling of timber-framed structure is likely. English garden wall brick with string course supported on dentilled headers. Wing, which carries date, probably added to two-storey timber-framed range of early C17, brick-clad at same time. Evidence of earlier build is principal rafter truss with collar above main range along with quarter-round beam with housebody beams and firehood bressumer with stops buried in wall. Wing has parlour with cross-corner fireplace; principal rafter truss with re-used cruck blade as tie.

(80) **MOORCROFT HOUSE** SD484103
Fine double-pile house in Flemish bond brick dated 1741 on rainwaterhead. Two-and-a-half storeys with semicircular hood on moulded brackets above doorway. Sash windows, but cellar at rear has two-light mullioned window.

(81) **ROSE COTTAGE** SD484102
Fragment of timber-framed house of late C16-early C17, remodelled and stone-clad C17-18. Present plan three-unit baffle entry with later outshut to rear. Original form uncertain: only framing that remains is on N gable with fine kingpost truss of herringbone form with straight bracing from tie to wallposts, and later brick infill; quarter-round moulding on tie. Housebody has quarter-round beam with mortices for brace to wallpost, but probably ex-situ. Firewindow uncovered in rear wall of housebody firehood indicates house was of end-baffle entry type after cladding, and bay 3 added later. Remains of unglazed wooden diamond-mullioned window found in N gable wall during renovation, now preserved ex-situ (plate 101). Outshut has principal made from re-used cruck blade.

(82) **WHITE COTTAGES** SD479106
Cruck-framed longhouse of at least C16, truncated: now of four bays. Three cruck trusses of medium scantling and low height. First two bays always domestic, third and fourth formerly stable and shippon. Original function of domestic bays unclear, but narrow 1st bay may have formed part of housebody, in which case building upper end probably lay further to W and now removed.

(83) **WOODCOCK HALL** (NEWBURGH HOUSE) SD484098
Substantial three-bay, double-depth upper-yeomanry house dated 1719 on rainwaterhead. Tall two-and-a-half storeys with three-gabled facade. Flemish bond brick with storey bands and wooden cross windows; doorway with semicircular hood on moulded brackets. Interesting interior arrangement whereby service rooms occupy almost as much floorspace as principal rooms. Central entry to housebody (hall) with dining room and parlour probably also occupying front. Service rooms to rear include heated kitchen, buttery and probably brewhouse. Extensive chambers recorded in 1723 inventory (below) indicate house mirrored gentry taste for first-floor living. Typical early C18 dogleg stair with closed string, turned balusters and newels with sunken panelling. Plain beams may indicate they were

formerly plastered. Similarities to Manor House, Upholland (120) of 1718 and Finch House, Shevington (99) of 1724.

History: built by James Spencer and wife Catherine, whose initials are on rainwaterhead. Inventory of former (LCRO WCW 1723, total £170 2s 2d) records hall, little parlour, dining room, great dining room (probably first floor) kitchen, buttery, white room, red chamber, children's room, nursery, serving men's chamber, brewhouse and chamber above, cellar.

ORRELL

Township of 1,617 acres sited on N slope of Ashurst-Billinge ridge and descending steeply to river valley at Gathurst. Manor acquired in C12 by Holland family of Upholland, and subsequently passed to Lovels; then to Earl of Derby in 1489 after Lovel estates forfeited for their support of Richard III; sold again to Orrell family of Turton in C16 and soon after to Bisphams of Bispham Hall, Billinge (13). Four freeholders in 1600; 30 households in 1664.

(84) ACKHURST HALL SD546068

Timber-framed minor gentry house of c1618, subsequently clad in stone and probably extended later C17. Three-unit plan with parlour wing and former lateral chimney stack in hall. Porch with semicircular-headed entrance which probably led originally into screens passage. Wing has five principal rafter trusses, outermost set against gable walls indicating original timber-framed origin; hall, with two similar trusses over, probably also timber-framed. First bay over kitchen has C19 kingpost truss. Wing contains large parlour with fine four-centred arched fireplace with graffitti date 1618 and initials A L, served by external stone stack; buttery and spiral stair with wooden newel. Date 1686 on porch may represent time of cladding, using massive squared sandstone blocks. Facade windows all have transoms, that in hall of four-plus-three lights divided by king mullion.

History: Ackhurst acquired by Leigh family c1616. Earlier, freeholders list 1600 refers to Whitfield family of 'Akarst'. Alexander Leigh (whose initials may be those on parlour fireplace); four hearths in 1664 Hearth Tax assessment; inventory (LCRO WCW 1675, total £383 19s 2d) identifies hall, parlour (both heated), buttery (all with chambers over), maids chamber and highermost rooms; will also mentions little chamber. Lack of reference to kitchen suggests this is addition of 1686.

(85) GATHURST FOLD SD539073

Stone house with two crosswings of differing date. Earliest component is E wing, probably 1670-1690, originally added to now-vanished main range which was presumably timber-framed. Originally comprised parlour (possibly unheated), buttery and stair (presence indicated by blocked stairlight). This demoted to service role when new housebody range and W wing added 1708. Former firehood in housebody now removed; fine stone hearths in new parlour and chamber above. Good dog-leg stair at rear of wing with closed string, moulded rail and chunky turned balusters. Windows mullioned throughout except for cross-window stairlight in W wing. Principal rafter trusses. Re-used beam in E wing has housing for former cruck blade. Datestone may indicate Birchall yeoman family.

PARBOLD

Upland township with Parbold Hill at 120m highest point, steeply descending to valley of Douglas; area 1,159 acres. Manor held from before 1242 by Lathom family, who later acquired fourth part of Wrightington and also manor of Allerton in Liverpool. As Catholics and Royalists, family's estates were confiscated by Commonwealth 1654; Lathoms eventually sold Parbold c1680 – if not earlier – to merchant John Crispe of London. No other freeholders in 1600; 39 households recorded in Hearth Tax 1664.

(86) DRAPER'S FARM SD519012

Early C17 timber-framed house of uncertain form; clad in stone last quarter C17 and remodelled to centralised plan. Two-unit baffle entry front range with central entrance and mullioned windows, divided by passage containing stair from rear wing with kitchen and outshut. Evidence of earlier build comes in form of doorways with nicked lintels and jowelled wallposts exposed on chamber floor between kitchen and outshut. Principal rafter trusses framing firehood area may indicate former smoke bay; further truss at junction of range and rear wing.

(87) MANOR COTTAGE SD498108

Small two-unit end-baffle entry house dated 1686 with addition of 1718 to E. Stone, two low storeys. First bay is receding crosswing containing parlour, buttery and dog-leg stair. Housebody has four-light window and quarter round beam. Above is upper cruck of poor scantling. Reset above former entrance is fragment of datestone with initials HL; this probably represents Lathom family.

(88) PARBOLD HALL SD512108

Dignified Palladian reworking – inspired by Leoni's Lathom (66) – of substantial c1600 gentry house of which hall and upper wing can still be partly identified. Evidence however suggests presence of earlier timber-framed building of at least C16. Present configuration may date from 1745 (date on rainwaterhead found c1958): double-depth plan, with two slightly projecting wings to S; two and a half storeys, hipped roof. Main north-facing entrance façade is seven-bay sash-window composition with pediment over shallow projecting entrance bay; Venetian windows over pedimented doorcase. Overall appearance of N front discordant however due to incorporation of earlier remains. Entrance and bays to R are in ashlar with sashes in moulded surrounds, string course and eaves cornice. To L, rubble masonry with taller sashes, attic windows and even mullioned cellar windows. S front by contrast completely symmetrical with uniform sashes (plate 107) and attic windows throughout.

Interior accessed via narrow entrance hall with garden hall (possibly former dining room) to rear. Latter contains fine plastered mid-C18 ceiling (plate 116), doors with Gibbs surrounds, rusticated dado and pedimented fireplace. E wing has service function with stair, kitchen and probable buttery to E. W wing has private accomodation with large room that was possible saloon, and two smaller rooms. Internally, E wing contains evidence it was formerly upper wing of extensive house of c1600, attached to hall of similar date. Incorporated within wing is former stair turret, with blocked 4-light transomed window: its location denotes upper end of house, and the two rooms in this wing were probably parlours (see below). Spanning range between tower and present S external wall is large fishbone-type kingpost truss indicating unusually large hall some 21ft deep; probably lateral hearth occupied present entrance hall area. Stub of quarter-round beam near stair suggests that beneath their plaster, beams in garden hall are of this type also and point to the hall also being of c1600. However fishbone truss itself suggests possible re-use from pre-1600 timber-framed building; furthermore, purlin with carpenter's mark CCCCCCC (implying seventh in series of frames); and fine broach-stopped cellar beams (ex-situ) are further evidence of large house of C16 at least. Present sash windows in E wing point to their insertion c1700, a minor refurbishment before major rebuilding of 1740s.

HISTORY: seat of Lathom family. Robert Lathom d.1516 holding manor of Parbold and fourth part of manor of Wrightington of Thomas, Earl of Derby, by knight's service, rent of a rose and 23d. Possibly c1600 rebuilding by Richard Lathom, who suceeded father Thomas in 1597; or his son Richard who suceeded 1602 aged 15. By time of latter's decease in 1623, some rebuilding had occurred as indicated by inventory (LCRO WCW 1623) recording following rooms: far chamber, brewhouse chamber, new parlour, little high chamber, dining chamber, 'dark' chamber, new chamber, inner lower chamber, outer lower chamber, servant chamber, buttery, 'backhouse', garner, dairy house, kitchen.

Thomas succeeded by son Richard, aged just 4 months; his estates confiscated for treason 1652 and ordered to be sold. Parliamentary survey of Parbold estate 1653 (PRO SP23/58) contains revealing description of house: a 'new building of two ranges and seven bays built with stone and covered with slate', and older part 'very much ruinated and ready to fall down'. By inference, latter was timber-framed. New building contained: hall 'paved with smooth stone, the west end thereof wainscoted', two parlours 'greater and lesser' at E end (probably the two rooms in the present E wing) another parlour on N side, stairs leading to gallery and dining room over first two parlours, chamber over 3rd parlour, two chambers over hall, one called 'Duke chamber'. Old building of one range and three bays 'bounding with the aforesaid new building west.' Contained buttery, kitchen and three chambers over, with one other range of two bays containing 'out parlour' with closet and two chambers over. This suggests c1600 rebuilding confined only to hall and east wing, leaving earlier west wing to remain in service role.

Lathoms sold estates to John Crisp c1680, but he may have been in residence at the hall in 1662: John Crispe Esq and two others were jointly assessed on six hearths in Parbold in that year. Crispe probably inserted the sash windows in E wing. Remodelling of hall carried out by his son Thomas (1690-1758), Sherriff of Lancashire 1715-6, MP for Ilchester 1727; his crest, a cameleopard, appears on N front central pediment. Will (LCRO WCW 1758) shows he also held land in Wrightington, Dalton, Newburgh and Suffolk.

Private report by Nigel Morgan and Garry Miller, 1988-1989. VCH VI, (1911) p178. Peter Fleetwood-Hesketh, Murray's Lancashire Architectural Guide (1955) p64-5. Pevsner, North Lancashire, 1969, p187-8.

PEMBERTON

Low-lying township west of Wigan with Douglas forming north-east boundary; 2,894 acres. Manor held by Pemberton family by early C13 and became subdivided from mid-C14 among several families. Eleven freeholders recorded 1600, 106 households recorded in 1664 Hearth Tax.

(89) HAWKLEY HALL

Stone gentry house of C17 or earlier upon formerly moated site, demolished 1960s. Symmetrical front: recessed centre between projecting wings, upper wing to R possibly of later date. Lateral chimney stack to rear of hall, entry to which probably via screens passage; projecting stacks on end walls of wings. All façade windows transomed, six lights to hall.

Stone on facade with letter M and date 1609.
History: Molyneux family, originally of Rainhill, near St Helens, held Hawkley estate from late C14 at least, acquiring fourth part of manor of Pemberton in 1578. Hawkley Hall referred to in 1561, and as a capital messuage in 1586. Richard Molyneux a freeholder 1600; another Richard Molyneux assessed on 10 hearths 1664.
*GMAU (1985) p190. WRO, 'History of Hawkley Hall' (anon). Pevsner, South Lancashire (1969) p430. VCH IV (1911) p81-82.

(90) WALTHEW HOUSE

House of wealthy yeoman freeholder Robert Walthew (d.1676), said to have been built 1650. Demolished. Inventory of latter (LCRO WCW 1676; total £474 9s 11þ) records extensive building with following rooms: hall, great parlour, little parlour, buttery, cellars, kitchen, brewhouse, milkhouse, chamber over hall with gallery next to it, parlour and closet within it, 'Mr Walthew's Chamber,' ceiled chamber, brewhouse chamber, kitchen chamber, chamber over milkhouse, garners, gallery at east end, malt loft, meal loft, uppermost rooms, gatehouse rooms. Also mentioned is 'old house' indicating predecessor may have remained. Walthew assessed on six hearths in 1664.
*Baggley, 1965.

RAINFORD

Extensive township of 5,872 acres, falling from Ashurst-Billinge ridge in east to mosslands in west. Lathom family of Lathom lords of manor by 1324, descending subsequently to the Stanleys, earls of Derby. Two freeholders 1600 and 85 households indicated by 1664 Hearth Tax.

(91) GUILD HALL (probably corruption of GILL'S HALL) SD512003

Handsome brick house of 1629 built by wealthy yeoman freeholder, but with evidence of earlier post-and-truss phase. Three-unit baffle-entry with parlour wing. Porch and later additions of 1688 in stone. 1629 work is in English garden wall bond on stone plinth; original door within porch has four-centred arch; stone mullioned windows of up to six lights, some with mason's marks of seven-pointed star (like Bispham Hall, Billinge, 13). Housebody has firehood with fire window, wing contains parlour with large external chimney stack and buttery to rear. Kitchen in bay 1 originally unheated; straight-flight service stair of splat baluster type. Principal rafter roof trusses with windbraces. Problematical rear extension to upper wing containing stair and dairy: mainly stone of 1688 but W wall timber-framed (with brick infill) suggesting a remnant of pre-1629 house.

Fine dog-leg stair, however, typical of 1688, suggesting earlier stair existed, probably within parlour wing. Also of 1688 is brewhouse to rear of kitchen; porch with triangular-headed door and wooden cross-window; fine panelling in entrance lobby.
HISTORY: home of wealthy Naylor family, recorded in Rainford since mid-C16 (Prescot PR); freeholders, but not recorded in 1600 list. Datestone 1629 refers to James Naylor, eldest son of William, who died 1628 holding freehold land in Rainford and Billinge (LCRO WCW 1629, total £464 16s 0d). James Naylor taxed on three hearths 1664. House and 12 acres subsequently acquired 1686 by Thomas Gill, gentleman, (d. 1708) who along with wife Deborah (d.1717) was responsible for additions of 1688. Inventory of Thomas (LCRO WCW 1708, total £264 17s 0d) identifies: house, parlour, kitchen, buttery, brewhouse – all with chambers over – milkhouse chamber, closet, closet over porch, passage, garrets.

(92) HYDES BROW FARM SD481018

Cruck house remodelled 1703 by addition of new two-unit baffle-entry main range at right angles to create more advanced centralised plan. Range comprises housebody and parlour and has symmetrical facade with horizontal sliding sashes. Remnant of former cruck range, with outshut to E, demoted to kitchen during remodelling: one truss survives at junction with main range, with much of E blade removed to allow access to chambers from stairhead. Lack of weathering on visible section of timber-framed wall between kitchen and outshut suggests latter also existed during cruck phase (similar to Bounty Farm, Upholland, 109). Joint in masonry shows cladding of rear wing occurred after 1703 remodelling; initially possibly W wall (facing prevailing winds) only, as E elevation is of differing stonework.

(93) MAGGOTS NOOK SD426027

Stone two-unit yeoman house of two builds. Earliest element is parlour wing, early C17; adjacent to large external chimney stack is blocked entrance to parlour with four-centred head beneath unusual triangular-shaped lintel. Wing added early C17 to vanished main range, probably cruck framed; replaced by present range c1700 with outshut to rear.

(94) SCYTHE STONE DELPH FARM SD473023

Stone yeoman house of advanced, centralised plan. 1682. Two-unit main range and rear service wing with outshut on N side. Chimneys at end gables and so the earliest departure in this area at this social level from traditional baffle-entry. Façade with low mullioned windows almost symmetrical, off-centre single-storey porch a later addition. Both house-body and parlour now heated by brick hearths but bearer in former suggests it originally had firehood. Staircase sited directly in front of entrance in housebody, leading to first floor lateral passage linking all chambers. In contrast to progressive nature of building, roof is carried on two upper cruck trusses of poor, irregular scantling, both showing signs of re-use.

SHEVINGTON

Township sited on N slope of Douglas Valley, to NW of Wigan; 1,728 acres. Manor greatly subdivided from early date and claimed at various time by several families. Three freeholders recorded 1600 and 41 households in 1664 Hearth Tax.

(95) CALICO WOOD FARM SD538088
Cruck house rebuilt c1710-1720 as small two-unit brick house with outshuts to rear. Solitary truss survives in cross-wall between bays 1 and 2: of medium scantling with later outriders, feet of blades removed below ceiling level. Also discovered during renovation was wooden mullioned window in former rear wall of cruck-framed building.

(96) COACH HOUSE FARM SD547089
Cruck-framed range of at least C16 with single-bay early C17 post-and-truss wing, containing parlour, added to front. One truss of medium scantling survives, lower portion of both blades removed. Photograph c1900 shows exposed principal rafter truss on gable of wing and square-framed panels on main range.

(97) CLUB HOUSE FARM SD547087
Early C17 yeoman's house of post-and-truss construction subsequently clad and extended, probably 1663. Present plan three-unit rear baffle entry with crosswing to W. However form during timber-framed phase was of wing and housebody only: former three-light wooden mullioned window by firehood reredos indicate this was once an outer wall. Window has diamond mullions with intermediate wooden glazing bars now removed. Entrance on N wall against stone spere of deep firehood: roof truss immediately above suggests former smoke bay between this and gable wall. Housebody has quarter-round beams and crosswall of square framing with sequence of carpenter's marks in arabic numerals, reading 33 to 37.

Wing has small heated parlour to front with service room to rear and formerly quarter-turn stair. One principal-rafter truss mid-way with doorway with nicked lintel set into tie beam; another similar truss immediately inside N gable wall.

Diamond-shaped pane of glass dated 1663 in five-light housebody window probably dates cladding. Third bay probably added at this time.

HISTORY: Prescott yeoman family. Initials on dated stained glass are those of Seth Prescott (1594-1679) wife Frances and eldest son Thomas. Prescott assessed on three hearths in 1664; inventory (LCRO WCW 1679) totalling £93 8s 7d lists following rooms: chamber at higher end of house, cheese loft, bed chamber, chamber over house, chamber over kitchen, kitchen, milk house, buttery. (Information courtesy of Miss Hilton).

(98) CROOKE HALL
Fine timber-framed minor gentry house built 1608; demolished 1937. Photograph c1900 shows central hall range between flanking projecting wings, that on R coupled to porch. Chimney at rear indicating lateral hearth. Ground floor brick (VCH): this may be later rebuilding. Jettied upper storey with herringbone bracing and quatrefoil panels on porch, fishbone kingpost trusses at gables. Two five-light transomed windows on chamber floor above hall suggests presence of gallery; attic level dormer above. Panel on porch read ANNO*DNI*1608*PEC*RR* IR*CARP with roses and figures. Hall contained flag floor, three moulded beams and table 18' x 3' with moulded legs, one inscribed 163(?) TC and another 'An Areloom (heirloom) to this hous for ever PC.'

HISTORY: built by Peter Catterall and wife Elizabeth (figures on panel may represent them): family held estates in Shevington since 1422. Grandfather Peter Catterall d.1583, leaving an estate of 8 messuages and 120 acres in Shevington, Wigan, Ince and Aspull to son and heir Roger, aged 33; lands in Shevington held of Edward Standish of Standish Hall at rent of 12d. Roger recorded as freeholder, 1600. Inventory (LCRO WCW 1602) records following: hall with chamber over (indicating pre-1608 building had been ceiled) great old parlour (also indicating some rebuilding), little parlour, kitchen, buttery, great chamber, parlour chamber, buttery chamber, kitchen chamber, closet, privy, 'goodwives closet', brewhouse, deyhouse, 'lower loft where servant lye' and 'entry between kitchen and brehouse' which may imply kitchen stood seperately. Grandson Thomas Catterall assessed on six hearths, largest number in Shevington, in 1664.
VCH VI, 1911, p202-3.

(99) FINCH HOUSE
Three-bay brick house of double-depth plan and two-and-a-half stories dated 1724. Demolished. Photograph (VCH IV) c1900 shows symmetrical three-gable front with recessed centre between two slightly projecting wings. Tall sash windows and storey bands, but cross windows in attics.

Compares with Manor House, Upholland (120) and Woodcock House, Newburgh (83).

(100) GATHURST HALL SD540075
Timber-framed yeoman's house of early C17, clad in brick late C17- early C18. Three-unit linear baffle entry with taller 1st bay (service) rebuilt probably C19. Third bay formerly subdivided to contain small unheated parlour and buttery; this and housebody have remains of stone plinth. Beams in housebody and parlour with deep chamfer and tongue stop. Three principal rafter trusses with angle struts and windbraces at junctions of bays 1 & 2, 2 & 3 and internally at E gable; all with wallposts remaining on N side. Later C17 brick extension, probably contemporary with cladding, to rear of bay 3, with quarter-round beams.

SKELMERSDALE

Township of 1,940 acres descending from western slope of Ashurst-Billinge ridge to mosslands in east. Manor held initially in C12 by Travers family then subdivided; that part owned by Yorkist Lovel family was forfeited by Henry VII in 1487 and subsequently granted to earls of Derby who acquired another portion in 1615. This subsequently sold to Ashurst family of Dalton in 1717 and to Sir Thomas Bootle of Lathom House (66) in 1751. Only one freeholder recorded 1600; 70 households in 1664.

(101) SEPHTON HALL SD495057
Demolished: timber-framed minor gentry house of C16 date, clad in stone early C18. Earliest remains were storeyed hall, possibly with through-passage to rear of axial stack, and W wing containing parlour and buttery. E wing contained no timber-frame but may have been contemporary. Further wing to N of hall, also framed, dated from C17.
HISTORY: Sephton family recorded from late C16. Thomas Sephton d.1593 holding the windmill in Skelmersdale and lands from Earl of Derby at rent of 5s 5d and Henry Eccleston at 12d. Other lands held in Ormskirk and Aughton. Son, another Thomas, was only freeholder in Skelmersdale 1600; d1601. Inventory of his son, again Thomas (c1587-1646, LCRO WCW 1647) records following rooms: hall, parlour (heated), buttery, kitchen, chambers over buttery, parlour and kitchen, also servants' chamber and little chamber by the hall. 'Boardes and joystes' valued at 12s implies building work (C17 wing N of hall?) recently took place. Also recorded was 'ould framed timber that formerly was a ten(a)nts house' valued at £3. 1664 Hearth Tax shows Mr Thomas Sephton (son?) assessed on four and Mrs Ellin Sephton three.
* Mercer (1975) p183; VCH III, p284.

STANDISH

Important township on spur of high ground descending towards Wigan and flanked to E and SW by meandering Douglas. Area 1,696 acres. Village centred round church of which fabric is largely C16 but mentioned in 1205. Manor owned by Standish family since at least time of Richard I until mid-C18; they were sole freeholders 1600. Hearth Tax 1664 records 54 households.

(102) GIANT'S HALL SD565078
Timber-framed yeoman's house of early C17, clad in stone 1675. Originally two-unit end baffle entry, with tall narrow parlour wing. Housebody has firehood with timber spere and jowelled heckpost, similar post carrying bressumer at opposite end. Accessed beneath firehood is small room, function uncertain. Quarter-turn stair to rear of housebody, separated by timber-framed wall with post supporting axial beam; these along with heckpost have quarter-round mouldings. Crosswall between housebody and wing has good sequence of carpenter's marks in arabic numerals. Two principal-rafter trusses, over wing and at junction with range. Former has re-used cruck-blades as principals; latter has vacant mortice for wallpost at S end of tiebeam, and remains of corresponding post at N end. This and vacant windbrace housings at both gables indicate previous external timber-frame, replaced by cladding of 1675. Lower, single-bay two storey addition to W, with former firehood, post-dates cladding of main building in 1675; uncertain whether it replaces former service end.
HISTORY: house of Lathom yeoman family. Richard Lathome a tenant in 1575; datestone refers to William Lathom, of Standish Wood, gentleman, d 1692 (will, missing). Peter Lathom in 1725 held farm of almost 29 customary (copyhold) acres of Ralph Standish of Standish Hall.
*Porteus (1927) p213 and (1933) p108.

(103) STANDISH HALL SD556091
Timber-framed gentry house built c1574, possibly originally of courtyard plan, on formerly-moated site; subsequently altered C17-C19. Mostly demolished 1920s and remainder by mid-1970s. Photograph c1900 shows two-storey hall range on stone base with decorative framing of quatrefoil panels and on upper floor large cusped saltires around huge 20-light mullioned window: latter suggests presence of gallery. Tall rear stack from lateral hearth, heating great hall measuring 36ft x 17ft; three chambers and corridor above with some oak panelling (VCH). N wing rebuilt late C17 in brick, several rooms with oak panelling, one also with plaster decoration above fireplace, displaying arms of Standish family. S wing rebuilt as chapel 1742-3, incorporat-

ing some moulded timbers from C16 wing it replaced. At right angle to W large three-storey brick wing built 1748, two and a half storeys, brick, with pedimented doorcase. This contained fine ex-situ panelling and two carved mantelpieces, one with royal arms and date 1603. Further extension to this in 1822 with wing containing dining and drawing rooms.

HISTORY: house described as 'nowe (new) Mansion House' in 1575; builder Edward Standish (d1610), was in 1577 'supposed to be a man of 500 marks yearly revenue and worth £1,000 in substance.' Succeeded by son and heir Alexander, then aged more than 50, in turn succeeded by his son Edward (1617-1682) around 1656; latter taxed on 17 hearths in 1664.

VCH VI, 1911, p195-7; Porteus (1933) p106.

(104) UPPER STANDISH WOOD FOLD SD563084
Timber-framed parlour wing of yeoman's house, early C17 and later clad in stone; presumably added to single-storey (timber-framed) main range subsequently replaced by present range. Wing contains parlour with external chimney stack and quarter-turn stair with splat balusters; buttery to rear. Section of fine timber-framed wall survives on chamber floor at junction with housebody with curved braces to wallplate. Lack of door in this wall indicates housebody was previously open. Principal rafter truss with angle struts and purlins with vacant windbrace housings to now-removed truss at E gable. Present range and service wing late C17-early C18 and of inferior quality with some mullioned windows at rear.

(105) UPPER WOOD FARM SD563085
Parlour wing of yeoman house, probably 3rd quarter C17, with main range of C18-19: latter replacing earlier range probably timber-framed. Wing in stone, with flimsy principal rafter truss mid-way, indicating timber-framed origin unlikely; remains of blocked wooden mullioned window in attic however. Contains parlour, probably buttery and stair lobby with fine dog-leg stair with unusual floor-to-ceiling newel with carved rosette decoration. Boarded door to parlour on ground floor, but later six-panel door to chamber above. Timber-framed internal wall surviving on first floor has sequence of carpenter's marks in arabic numerals. History: Possibly associated with Taylor yeoman family; Thomas Taylor assessed on five hearths 1664, which would indicate a sizeable property.

Porteus (1927) p209.

UPHOLLAND

Extensive and important township sited midway along Ashurst-Billinge ridge, totalling 4,685 acres. Village centred around church founded as Benedictine priory in 1317-1318; ground falls away north and east to Douglas and south and west towards mosslands. Manor held by Holland family from C13 and subsequently by Lovels; as Yorkists their estates forfeited by Henry VII and presented to Thomas, Earl of Derby in 1489. Manor sold to Ashurst family of Dalton in 1717 and subsequently to Sir Thomas Bootle of Lathom in 1751. Only one freeholder recorded 1600, which must be oversight as 14 named in 1605 (LCRO DDBa 10/8); 130 households assessed in 1664 Hearth Tax indicates thriving community.

(106) AMBROSE COTTAGE SD536031
Small main range of c1720-1730 added to low earlier crosswing of mid-to-late C17. Thin coursed sandstone throughout. Main range has symmetrical front and formerly stone cross windows but of single-depth only, with wing to rear of 1st bay. Replaced earlier and probably cruck-framed range on to which crosswing was initially grafted. Barn added laithe-house style to S, C18-19.

(107) BALCONY FARM (now QUALITY HOTEL) SD509041
Early yeoman's house of c1600 in imitation of gentry style. Housebody range with lateral chimney stack and stair tower and parlour wing with external stack. Unusually-placed porch to rear is mid-to-later C17 with semicircular arch on moulded responds; position at lower end of hall suggests entry to former through passage. Re-used lintel in later single-storey front porch of four-centred type. Housebody has segmental headed hearth, four-centred type in parlour and housebody chamber. Tower contains spiral newel stair; fine beams in housebody chamber and parlour have ovolo moulding and moulded soffit. Service wing is early C18, probably replacing something earlier and possibly timber-framed.

(108) BIRCH GREEN FARM (demolished)
Crosswing house of late C17-early C18, ruinous by late 1960s. Two-storey wing with what appeared to be truncated range at right angles. Latter originally single-storey on evidence of change in masonry, subsequently heightened, and similar therefore to Cicely's Cottage, Dalton. Main room in wing probably parlour, containing stair; fireplace in crosswall flanked by doors leading to two unheated rooms at rear of wing - unusual arrangement.

Mercer, 1975. Skelmersdale Development Corporation report, 1965.

Also: Cottage to S of Birch Green Farm (demolished). Small brick gabled cottage dated 1694; may have originated as crosswing added to range which were subsequently demolished.

Skelmersdale Development Corporation report, 1965.

(109) **BOUNTY FARM** SD537033
One blade only of former cruck house surviving within three-unit house clad in stone and altered C17-19; added stone C17 parlour wing to rear (possibly of 1667) containing upper cruck truss. Blade, of medium scantling, at junction of 2nd/3rd bays with windbrace housings in purlins providing evidence for second truss at N gable: however scarfed joint in wallplate here suggests building extended further N. Surviving section of square-framed wall between blade and gable has pegholes in rail suggesting presence of former wooden mullioned window. Lack of weathering on section of this wall suggests outshut preceded C17 wing; latter has firehood on end gable and datestone reading 1869 MB (Meyrick Bankes of Winstanley Hall) 1667. Named Rainford Bounty on 1846 OS map.

(110) **CARR LANE FARM**
Demolished c1972. Early two-unit yeoman house in stone dated 1660, with parlour wing and end baffle entry, outshut to rear of housebody. Initials RH IH on datestone probably those of Holland family; Robert Holland and John together assessed on five hearths 1664.

(111) **DEAN HOUSE FARM** SD526063
Three unit linear house, probably first half C17 with later addition. Probably fragment of once larger house. Earliest components are bays 1 (service) and 2 (housebody), latter with former baffle entry against firehood whose stone heck has moulded capital: door in E wall blocked. Plinth on W walls of these bays and ragged joint in masonry between 2nd and 3rd suggests latter bay is later addition. However internal timber-framed wall at this junction indicates something existed previously at this end. Possible therefore that bays 1 and 2 were early C17 addition to pre-existing upper end, perhaps timber-framed wing. Load-bearing crosswalls throughout. Window at N gable of five lights and plaque with initials TN and legs of Man (Earls of Derby crest) above.
HISTORY: copyhold estate of branch of Naylor family; Richard Naylor de Dene recorded as a copyholder in 1605 (LCRO DDBa 10/8, quoted Coney [198]) p108). Inventory of Richard Naylor (LCRO WCW 1647, total £134,10s 2d) identifies house, lower house, parlour, buttery, high chamber, chamber over parlour. TN on plaque refers to son Thomas. Thomas and Jane Naylor assessed on five hearths, 1666.

(112) **DIAL HOUSE**
Demolished 1960s: dated 1714 and late manifestation of parlour wing plan. Three units, entered via broad porch with separate doors to 1st bay (kitchen) and central housebody (similar to Mill Bridge Farm, Worthington, 127); latter formerly with firehood. Narrow wing to R contained originally-unheated parlour, stair lobby and buttery. Exposed kingpost roof truss over housebody; unusual, may indicate earlier, timber-framed origins or its re-use. Large C19 wing to rear.
*Mercer (1975) p183, with plan.

(113) **DIGMOOR HALL**
Demolished. Fine two-storey stone yeoman's house: photograph 1964 (Ormskirk Library) shows coupled porch and wing added to range which by masonry and details appears later. Position of stacks indicates baffle entry. Porch has semicircular arched entrance on moulded responds and looks c1670-1690; range c1700-1710.
HISTORY: James and William Smallshaw of Digmoor recorded as tenants-at-will (leaseholders) in Upholland 1605 (LCRO DDBa 10/8, quoted Coney (1989) p110.

(114) **DOUGLAS BANK FARM** (FISHER'S HOUSE) SD086522
Superior house of yeoman freeholder built in stone and brick in 1656. Three-unit baffle entry: central range between projecting parlour and service wings, latter coupled to full-height porch gabled separately. Two storeys plus attic. To rear, stair tower coupled with upper wing, also under its own gable. Unique combination of building materials: sandstone façade but brick (in predominately stone area) at sides and rear. Some raised brick decoration: east wall of service wing has diaper pattern, stair tower gable has cross. Housebody has firehood; parlour has large triangular-headed hearth. Staircase renewed but original probably of early dog-leg form. Beams in principal rooms quarter-round. Chamber over buttery has partition incorporating frieze of splat baluster style. Three principal-rafter trusses, one over main range (in front of stack, suggesting possible smoke bay originally) and one over each wing: fairly light scantling.
HISTORY: datestone has initials of Henry Fisher, yeoman (d. 1692) and wife Margaret (d. 1698). Family recorded in Lees area of Upholland from early C17: Peter Fisher, 'husbandman of the Lees' bought lands in Shevington in 1607 for £120. 'Henry Fisher of Shevington', recorded as freeholder in 1653 Parliamentary survey of Upholland (LCRO) is probably he who built the house. Fisher may have been an early financier of Upholland's grammar school. Hearth Tax 1664 shows he was assessed on four. Inventory (LCRO WCW 1692) records nine rooms: house, parlour, buttery, kitchen, buttery chamber, parlour chamber, red chamber, closet, kitchen chamber. Rainwater head dated 1715 on lower wing gable records Fisher's grandson, also Henry: who by 1747 had sold estate to

neighbour Lawrence Halliwell (grandson of he who rebuilt Halliwell's Farm, 115)
*Garry Miller, private report, 2000.

(115) HALLIWELL'S FARM SD517087
Prominent yeoman freeholder's house in stone: double-depth, centralised form created as a result of C18 additions to C17 structure. C17 work is porch and E wing with transomed windows on facade: originally added to pre-existing, probably timber-framed, main range. Latter replaced early C18 by single-bay double-depth addition to create more advanced layout. Porch, faced in distinctive orange sandstone, dated 1671, but wing itself may be earlier. Quoins on rear wall mark termination of wing, but at front, porch extends further W suggesting entrance into through-passage of vanished main range. Parlour wing contains parlour with stone semi-circular arched fireplace, ex-situ datestone RB 1649 above, along with stair and buttery. Latter projects slightly to E, creating unusual staggered gable on this elevation. Doorway to C18 bay on chamber floor by stairhead appears inserted, suggesting no access at this floor previously to vanished range: which by inference may have been an open hall. C18 work inferior, all window openings altered; probably originally mullion-and-transom crosses. Adjacent stone combination barn with shippon and stable, dated 1663. Roof trusses of principal rafter type, two containing re-used cruck material as principals; another re-used cruck blade as a beam inside.
HISTORY: datestone on porch refers to Lawrence Halliwell, gentleman, and wife Alice (d. 1693). Halliwell probably originated from family of same name at South Tunley Hall, Wrightington (140); in 1653 acquired freehold estate in Lees area of Upholland from Ralph Brownlow, gentleman. (LRO DDAl 117) whose initials are on the datestone now in parlour, discovered c 1982 in adjacent field. Upholland court book 1633 (LRO DDHI) states Brownlow's estate 'recently purchased of Thomas Orrell'; a Roger Brownlow recorded as freeholder in Upholland 1600. Halliwell, High Constable of West Derby Hundred 1667 and a financier of Upholland grammar school, assessed on six hearths 1664, jointly largest number in Upholland; fell to five 1671.

1649 datestone indicates earlier rebuilding by Brownlow, supported by memorandum on reverse of marriage settlement 1683 between Halliwell's son and heir Robert (LRO DDAl 102). This states Lawrence and Alice Halliwell were to occupy old parlour, chamber above, closet and cellar at west end of house. Impression therefore is that Brownlow may have rebuilt upper end which then lay to W, which was superseded by new parlour wing to E. C18 rebuilding removed everything to W. of 1671 phase.

(116) HEYES FARM SD503054
Dated 1685: two-unit end-baffle-entry. Stone, with first bay gabled in manner of crosswing at Cicely's Cottage, Dalton (39). Not surveyed internally.

(117) JOHNSON'S FARM SD523069
Yeoman's house containing fragments of open hall of possibly aisled form of C15 or earlier. Three-unit plan: low single storey central hall with two-storey upper wing containing porch dated 1647 and inferior service wing of late C17. Stone, rendered. Hall has deep roofspace swept down to low eaves in catslide manner. Inside, lower end of hall has posts set inward of outer walls, N one heavily moulded and S one with simple chamfer and thus possibly a replacement. Position at lower end may indicate they are remains of spere truss; manner of roof suggests space outward of these may have been aisles. Ceiling inserted probably late C16 (beams with broach stops) at same time as firehood at upper end; this has stone heck with moulded capital. Roof timbers above ceiling renewed so further analysis impossible. However fragments of former timber-framed firehood canopy remain outside of later brick flue. Added wing contains heated parlour to rear and small room to front, now heated, original function uncertain. Lower wing appears c1680-1700, hall probably clad when this was built.
HISTORY: occupied by Naylor yeoman family of copyholders (see Dean House Farm, 109); Thomas Naylor recorded as juror at Upholland manor court in 1423 (Coney [1989] p20). Initials on datestone may refer to John (d. 1673) and Ellen (d.1677) Naylor. Will of former (LCRO WCW 1673, inventory total £101 0s 6d) states his copyhold lands had been passed to son and heir Richard; inventory records house, buttery, kitchen and chamber above, garner, along with 'flagges and waleing stones' worth £1 implying recent building activity (lower wing?). John Naylor assessed on four hearths 1664.

(118) KNIGHT'S HALL SD517075
Timber-framed house of early C17, unusually rebuilt 1716 by Knight yeoman family. Three-bay plan. Main central block dated 1716 and containing housebody and rear service room projects between flanking bays of later date; asymmetrical with sashed windows, classical details and doorway at L end. Latter leads to entrance hall which may have been through-passage of earlier building; crosswall between this and bay 1 contains timber-framed wall with fine quarter-round moulded wallposts exposed indicating narrower range of earlier building on same axis as present one. Rail has vacant joist mortices indicating hall was ceiled, this plus quarter-round mouldings indicating date after c1600; beams of this type in present housebody also.

All roof trusses C19; masonry on façade of 1st and 3rd bays appears C19 also but of differing periods. Development problematical: possible that earlier bays stood at either end of housebody and were exempt from 1716 rebuilding and replaced only in C19 when structure re-roofed. Housebody façade windows sashed – earliest yeoman example in area and early for Lancashire as a whole – but mullioned at rear. Fine dog-leg stair at end of entrance hall/through-passage. Cellar contains well.

HISTORY: Knight yeoman family, presumed newcomers to Upholland early C18; initials on datestone those of Peter Knight and eldest son Edmund. Upholland PR records burial of Jane, wife of Peter Knight, latter described as 'carrier', 1715, and John, his son 1723. Will of Peter Knight (LCRO WCW 1723) leaves estate to Edmund.

(119) **LOWER TOWER HILL** SD518049

Small yeoman leaseholder's house of cruck-framed origin, rebuilt with crosswing 1684. Three-unit baffle-entry plan. One-and-a-half storey range now stone-clad but incorporating one mutilated cruck truss close to junction with wing; blades removed below ceiling level, probably when external walls clad in stone. Masonry of 3rd bay rebuilt subsequently, roof timbers renewed. Narrow two-storey wing, containing parlour, buttery and stair, has purlin roof with pointed gable finials. Similarity of details suggests main range was clad at same time as wing added. Doorway still has triangular-headed arch. Outshut added to rear of range is C18, in two phases. Two crucks in adjacent barn may have originated from house.

HISTORY: associated with Hooten yeoman family, leaseholders; datestone refers to Edward Hooten and wife Margaret (d 1694). 1653 Upholland survey records Thomas Hooten (d 1676) occupied messuage called Tower Hill and 31 acres by lease dated February 16 1631.

(120) **MANOR HOUSE** SD501031

Striking tripartite double-depth yeoman house of two-and-a-half storeys dated 1718. Idiosyncratic combination of advanced plan but regressive details. Symmetrical façade dominated by full height porch with semi-circular arched entrance, entablature above; one dormer window either side and three corresponding dormers at rear. Main façade windows of three lights with transoms, cross windows at attic level, all of square section with flat architraves; however rear has splayed mullioned and mullioned-and-transomed windows. Material is limestone, rare in area, with rusticated quoins. Interior walls however in brick with two massive brick multi-flue stacks on ridge. Porch opens into housebody with parlour to R and possibly dining room to L, all separated from service rooms by lateral passage leading from entrance in W wall. This and separate main and service stairs indicate strong segregation within, reinforced also by no communication on attic floor to rooms W of main stair; these probably housed servants. All first floor principal rooms, and kitchen chamber, heated; attics over housebody and parlour heated too.

No roof trusses: purlins carried directly on brick cross-walls. One of two three-bay, double-pile houses of similar date, others being Woodcock Hall, Newburgh, 1718 and Finch House, Wrightington 1722 (demolished). Restored 1990s after dereliction. Outbuilding to SW, of stone, dated C P 1668 on quoin, partly rebuilt; inside, two upper cruck trusses of good scantling. Further outbuilding to SE has relocated datestone 1727. Ex-situ gatepiers in front of house with fluted Doric angle pilasters entablatures and former ball finials, identical to St Aiden's church, Billinge, also 1718.

HISTORY: house associated with wealthy leaseholding family of Pennington in C17 and C18. John Pennington and Christopher of Pimbo recorded as leaseholders in Upholland 1605 (LCRO DDBa 10/8, quoted Coney [1989] p110). Datestone reading C P 1668 refers to Christopher Pennington, yeoman (c.1619-1671); inventory (LRO WCW 1671) totalled £201 10s 4d. 1653 Upholland survey (LCRO) records Christopher Pennington held messuage in Pimbo Lane with barn, shippon, kiln, carthouse, pigeon house and land totalling more han 88 acres (annual rent 18s 6 0d but yearly value assessed at £33.1s 6d) of William, 6th Earl of Derby, by lease dated January 15 1636 to John Pennington, husbandman, for lives of Christopher (aged 34 in 1653) and two others. House probably built by grandson, also Christopher (?1681-1740) whose initials, and those of wife Jane (d 1729) appear on 1727 datestone. His will (LCRO WCW 1740) records lands held in Rainford, Billinge and Upholland.

(121) **MILLETS** SD507031

Small double-pile house, early C18 (possibly 1725; relocated datestone now within adjoining barn) altered and extended in C19. Original entrance in S front blocked, most windows altered; but at rear mullioned windows remain in buttery and chamber above. Added at right angles to rear is two-storey extension of early C19, joined to barn beyond dated 1835.

(122) **NEWGATE FARM** SD508052

Stone yeoman's house rebuilt 1707 in conservative style with unusual plan, incorporating fragment of probably timber-framed building of early C17. Two-unit, end baffle entry originally with outshut to rear of housebody in 1st bay and 2nd bay treated as gabled crosswing: therefore confused attempt at double-depth form. Full-height porch has late use of semi-circular arch on moulded responds, and small oval window in gable. Earlier origins revealed in housebody where spere is timber-framed with jowelled heckpost, this and heavy unstopped spine beam suggesting this is remaining core of earlier structure nearer to 1600. Also closed truss with heavy principals directly above firehood may be from former smoke bay of this period. Wing contains heated parlour, buttery and typical early C18 dog-leg stair of closed string type with square newels, moulded rail and turned balusters. Load-bearing walls support purlins. Outshut built up to full two storeys in C18; original height indicated by quoins stopping halfway up wall. Further C19 addition at rear.

HISTORY: Newgate House bequeathed to Upholland Grammar school by Robert Walthew of Walthew House, Pemberton (90) in 1668. Several families referred to as being 'of Newgate' in C17 including William Smallshaw recorded as copyholder 1605. Datestone refers to William Rigby of Newgate (Upholland PR)

WIGAN

Market town with Roman origins sited in bend of Douglas around parish church with C12 remains. Largest settlement and commercial focus of district: borough status granted in 1246 and a market in 1258. Coal was being mined in the C16 and other manufacturing industries, including metal working and textiles, followed in C17 and C18. Sixteen freeholders recorded in 1600 and 606 households recorded in 1664 Hearth Tax indicates a sizeable population. Town was largely timber-framed until C19, but pre-C18 buildings are fragmentary.

(123) THE MEADOWS
Demolished. Dated 1689: photograph c1930 (WRO; plate 40) shows two-unit end baffle-entry house of brick on stone base with parlour wing and wing to rear of housebody: therefore early, idiosyncratic attempt at double plan similar to Newgate Farm, Upholland (122) of 1707. Stone mullioned windows of up to five lights.

HISTORY: Markland yeoman family. Ralph Markland assessed on six hearths 1664. Will of Robert Markland of The Meadows, 'gentleman' (LCRO WCW 1706) states he owned several messuages and burgages in Wigan.

WINSTANLEY

Township on eastern flank of Ashurst-Billinge ridge, area 1,859 acres, descending eastwards towards mosslands S of Wigan. Winstanley family owned manor from 1252 at least; in 1596 non-resident Edmund and Alice Winstanley sold it to London goldsmith-banker James Bankes under pressure of mounting debts. He was sole freeholder in 1600; hearth tax 1664 identifies 54 households.

(124) WINSTANLEY HALL SD545031
Stone manor house possibly c1596: similar to and probably modelled upon Birchley Hall, Billinge (12). Extensive remodelling 1780, 1818-1819, and 1843. derelist at time of writing. Engraving of 1817 (plate 25) shows original east-facing five-gabled façade, symmetrical and two-and-a-half storeys: recessed hall between projecting wings with smaller gabled projections in internal angles, both containing doorways. Most windows transomed including massive 16-light window illuminating hall and 14-light window above. Southern wing probably contained parlour, with services in northern wing divided from hall by through passage.

HISTORY: debate has occured over who built it, with some sources suggesting Winstanley family in 1570s. However James Bankes is most likely candidate as main branch of Winstanleys had lived in Wales since 1560s and style suits 1590s date, following Birchley. Will of Bankes (LCRO WCW 1617) mentions hall, parlour and great chamber over hall. Dower arrangement 1618 identifies kitchen and brewhouse (with chambers over), deyhouse, larder house and closet above - in all, probably entire service wing - for use of Bankes' widow Susanna. Son William assessed on 14 hearths 1664.
*GMAU report, 1998; VCH IV, p87-88.

WORTHINGTON

Diminutive township of just 659 acres. Owned by family of same name from probably before C13 to late C17; Thomas de Worthington's tenure already described as 'ancient' in 1212. They were sole freeholders in 1600. Hearth Tax 1664 records only 20 households.

(125) BLACK LAWYERS SDS74117
Demolished mid-1980s. Cruck-framed house of three bays, clad in English garden wall brick of late C17-early C18. Derelict by 1983, revealing three finely-shaped trusses of heavy scantling, suggesting significant non-gentry house of C16 or earlier. Blades halved above yokes (similar to Peel Hall, Ince, 53, and Kirklees Hall, Aspull, 7). Thatch roof beneath corrugated iron. Former datestone 1617 NX IX by window (X = F?) may not have been original; another read 1619 (Porteus). Initials possibly of Fisher family: a Henry Fisher paid for one hearth in 1664.
*Porteus (1927) p225.

(126) MANOR HOUSE SD579102

Single fine cruck truss contained within stone house of C17-C18. Four-unit baffle-entry plan with added parlour wing and adjoining porch dated 1671 under coupled gables and long inferior range. Cruck sited within housebody, formerly on high stone plinth. Blades of heavy scantling with moulding at base, and arch-braced collar: treatment indicating it was central to former open, two-bay hall. Lower height and narrow span suggests non-gentry origin and later date, perhaps late C15-early C16. Quarter-round beams carried on firehood bressumer suggest ceiling inserted early C17; original stair position may have been beneath firehood (like Giant's Hall, Standish, 102). Upper end rebuilt 1671 with addition of porch and two-and-a-half storey wing containing heated parlour along with buttery. Main range clad late C17-18.
HISTORY: leasehold estate part of the endowment of the Chantry of Holy Rood at Standish church, founded by Standish family of Arley in Blackrod, who acquired territories in Worthington 1362. In 1483 Peter Standish of Arley granted to the church the messuage and lands held of him by James Cauncey in Worthington and Blackrod. At Dissolution, Edward Rigby was tenant of lands forming part of endowment of Holy Rood Chantry at a rent of 21s. These were sold off and in 1574 were acquired by Standish of Standish family, James Rigby leasing tenement for lives of himself and wife Margery. Initials on 1671 datestone refer to Jolly yeoman family: leased by Ralph Standish to Seth Jolly in 1708 and 15$^{1/2}$ acres held 1715.
*Porteus, (1927) p225-227.

(127) MILL BRIDGE FARM SD581125

Brick three-unit baffle entry house with parlour wing and outshuts to rear of range. 1694, but possibly a remodelling of earlier timber-framed structure. Single-storey porch with unusual arrangement of twin doorways accessing housebody and parlour (similar to Dial House, Upholland, 112) Housebody has unusual beams of semi-round section; timber-framed wall with quarter-round moulding supporting bressumer at this end may be relic of earlier building. Outshuts contain stair and service rooms. Minimal raised brickwork in dogtooth pattern above windows in wing and rear. Eaves heightened C19 and roof trusses renewed. Datestone may refer to branch of Fisher yeoman family.

(128) WORTHINGTON HALL SD581109

Timber-framed manor house of 1577, subsequently altered and reduced in size. What survives of this date is now only tall two-storey hall range. Photograph c1900 (VCH VI) shows this with fine decorative panels and wooden mullioned windows and one seven-light mullioned and transomed window above hall. Upper end removed by that time and subsequently most of hall range rebuilt in brick early C20. Decoration now remains only above entrance, along with carved bressumer carrying jettied upper storey. Wide four-centred arched doorway inscribed EDWARDE WORTHINGTON 1577 leads to screens passage (now blocked by stair) backing onto which is deep axial firehood; unusual as lateral hearth more commonly associated with gentry houses. Added c1700 at E end is kitchen, in stone, formerly with cross windows (VCH photograph). This however probably replaced earlier structure to which 1577 range was added, as suggested by closed kingpost truss at this end of hall. Two principal rafter trusses with collars: one at present W gable has windbrace housings showing continuation to upper end which formerly existed (but in line with hall and not as wing). Most of rear rebuilt in stone C18.
HISTORY: seat of Worthington family, lords of manor from before C13 to late C17. Thomas de Worthington's tenure already described as 'ancient' in 1212. Edward Worthington, builder of hall, succeeded upon death of his father 1566, recorded as freeholder 1600. Inventory (LCRO WCW 1613, total £30 3s 10d) records following: hall, 'parlour in upper end of hall' (another indication that parlour was continuation of main range), buttery, larder, kitchen, great chamber, little chamber, chamber over parlour, chamber at stairhead, buttery chamber, highermost room (?). No mention of chambers over kitchen and larder suggests service end may have been single storey (and therefore cruck framed). House had four hearths in 1666, largest number in township.
*VCH VI, p222-224.

WRIGHTINGTON

Hilly township of 3,915 acres with Harrock (147m) forming highest point. Manor subdivided from early date leading to emergence of several landowning families, including Wrightington, Rigby of Harrock and Nelson of Fairhurst. Consequently, ten freeholders recorded in 1600. Hearth tax 1664 records 136 households.

(129) BANNISTER FARM SD500129

Unusual, complex stone C17 yeoman house containing cruck of C16 or earlier. Four units with long central range, divided into two by through passage, between wings of differing date. Cruck, to L of through passage, of medium to heavy scantling with tiebeam; concealed above ceiling height. Short housebody in 2nd bay has lateral hearth on rear wall with external stone stack and inserted ceiling carried on moulded mid-C16 beam with plaque with initials TN. First bay is added two-storey stone wing of early C17 date containing heated parlour and former buttery and stair tower on W wall. Similarity of details suggests main range was clad at same time as wing constructed. Third bay, unheated, probably had service function; said to be another, poorer, cruck in crosswall between it and fourth bay. Latter takes form of wing of later C17 date, but wallpost supporting principal-rafter truss implies possible timber-framed origin; subdivided with larger room to front heated by external stack. No communication between this and third bay suggests domestic industry or occupation by separate household.

HISTORY: name indicates connection with Bannister family, lords of fourth part of manor of Wrightington until c1536-1540 when sold to Nelson family later of Fairhurst Hall (133); initials on beam may represent Thomas Nelson, mentioned in 1568 as a lord of the manor. James Bannister recorded as freeholder 1600; Richard Bannister and James Bannister each assessed on two hearths in Hearth Tax 1664.

(130) CHARITY FARM SD530128

Two-unit yeoman house with crosswing, probably 1670-1690. Stone, with mullioned windows, that in hall largest at five lights. Segmental arched entrance with recess above, probably for datestone now missing. Round-headed single-light window in attic over wing. Added bay to L. Named 'Quaker Haydock's' on 1846 OS map.

(131) COPYHOLD FARM SD539138

Substantial yeoman's house of 1659: brick, three-unit baffle-entry with parlour wing and outshut to rear of service end. Most remarkable attribute is superb C17 plaster frieze covering most of crosswall at dais end of housebody (plates 121-122). Crude design consists of fleur-de-lys as centrepiece, with human faces, grotesque animal head, vines and cornucopiae. Exterior has decorative brickwork: lozenge pattern in raised headers on lower bay and lozenges in vitrified headers on porch and recessed centre. Front of wing refaced in stone C18-19; contains heated parlour, buttery and spiral stair. Service stair, also spiral type, contained in outshut to rear of bay 1 (kitchen) indicating strong segregation in household. Most windows altered but originally of mullioned type with some shaped brick mullions surviving.

HISTORY: isolated site suggesting medieval settlement following woodland clearance; name indicates land tenure. Occupied by branch of Halliwell yeoman family. Initials on lintel represent Oliver Halliwell, schoolmaster (d.1668) and wife Margaret. Inventory of Oliver Halliwell (LRO WCW 1668, total £82 14s 10d.) records following rooms: house, parlour, buttery, kitchen, (all with chambers over) milkhouse, brewhouse, closet and garetts. Halliwell assessed on six hearths in 1662 and four in 1664.

(132) COWLINGS FARM SD533136

House of linear three-unit baffle entry plan dated 1677. Rendered brick. Outshut to rear containing staircase of fine dog-leg form; quarter round beams. Not fully surveyed.

(133) FAIRHURST HALL SD489117

Substantial late C16 timber-framed home of Nelson gentry family, clad in brick mid C18 and altered C20. Fine sequence of roof trusses indicate original form: central hall range of three bays some 27 ft. long flanked by wings either end. Coupled to S wing, under own gable, was short projection which must have been stair tower perhaps at end of screens passage. Former lateral hearth on rear wall. All trusses of principal rafter type, except that at junction of range and S wing which has kingpost. Central truss of latter has heavy curved braces from tie to wallposts. Rear wall of this wing rebuilt in stone C17. Massive external stack serving large segmental-arched hearth inside suggests kitchen and therefore service role for S wing; latter has spiral wooden stair to attic.

HISTORY: Fairhurst estate owned by Catholic Nelson family since C16; this part of Wrightington manor originally owned by Banastre (Bannister) family, sold c1536-40 by Richard Banastre to Richard Nelson. Thomas Nelson one of lords of manor in 1568; Richard Nelson a freeholder 1600, d1618; first member of family described as 'of Fairhurst' in pedigree compiled 1664, so he possibly was bulder of house. Inventory of latter (LRO WCW 1619) totals £600 4s 9d and indicates substantial house – basis of present structure – with following rooms: hall, parlour, buttery, kitchen, larder, dairy, brewhouse, kitchen chamber, larder chamber, 'My Uncle Nelson his chamber', little closet, parlour and buttery chambers, chamber in the higher height, higher height. Heir, nephew Maxie Nelson, captain of foot in King's army, slain in battle of Marston Moor 1644. Son Thomas had estates sequestered 1653; he was assessed on five hearths 1664.

(134) HARROCK HALL SD508125

Minor gentry house of complex development, seat of the Rigby family since the C13: much altered, but core is c1600 with slight evidence for earlier timber-frame. Powerful two-storey façade: symmetrical, recessed hall range with central full-height bay window and at either end two-storey porches coupled with gabled wings. Style suggests date c1600, but E wing is C19 (rebuilt at rear c1980) along with W wing, porch and walling W of bay window. However W porch faithfully matches E one so therefore is probably a

C19 replica of what existed previously. Crenellated parapet on roof also C19.

E porch opens into lower end of hall, with opposing door in rear wall in manner of screens passage: crosswall to L has three blocked doors formerly leading to service rooms in E wing beyond. Bay window illuminates dais end of housebody with two doors in crosswall to upper wing. Lateral hearth on rear wall of hall flanked by stair turret and rear projecting wing that may have contained a parlour, with external stack: all this mainly c1600, but rest of upper wing C19.

Redundant coping in gable of crosswall at lower end of hall range indicates 1600 building was added to pre-existing service wing (probably timber-framed) subsequently replaced by present C19 structure. Restoration in 1990 revealed evidence of timber-frame to rear of crosswall at upper end of hall: plinth with substantial wallpost visible on chamber floor; probably fragment of earlier house on site.
HISTORY: Harrock owned by Rigby family since C13, tenants of the Hospitallers until Dissolution. Hall built probably by Nicholas Rigby (d.1629,)one of Lord Derby's officials. He succeeded to the estate in 1599 at age 37, recorded as freeholder 1600. Rental of 1540 shows his great-grandfather, also Nicholas, was second largest tenant in Wrightington, paying 5s.6d rent for Harrock. This Nicholas died 1557 holding 'capital messuage called the hall of Harrock'. Inventory of Nicholas Rigby (LCRO WCW 1629) totalled £638 5s 6d and recorded following rooms: hall, new parlour, parlour, closet beyond parlour, chamber over the buttery, middle chamber, study, buttery, kitchen, – house (part illegible), brewhouse. Another Nicholas Rigby, probably grandson, changed on six hearths for Harrock 1664, highest number in 'west side of Wrightington.' House described as 'very neglected and dilapidated' in 1911; extensively restored 1989-91.
VCH VI, p175. Pevsner, North Lancashire, 1969, p266. Nigel Morgan and Garry Miller, private report, 1991.

(135) HIGHER BARN SD515124
Complex C17-18 remodelling of earlier cruck-framed yeoman's house on isolated site. Present form three-unit baffle entry with stair tower and additions to rear. One remaining cruck, of medium scantling and probably C16, in crosswall between housebody and parlour. Blades removed above ceiling level: this occurred when when walls rebuilt in stone and structure heightened to two full storeys using principal rafter truss with blades of heavy scantling (similar to Harsnips, Dalton, 42). Initial form subsequent to cladding was two-unit end baffle entry with stair tower; indicated by ragged joint by entrance which shows 1st bay is later. Similar therefore to Stoney Lane Farm, also Wrightington (142). Location of stair tower suggests W front was principal elevation before additions to rear. Housebody firehood has heckpost with stone moulded capital similar to Johnson's Farm and Dean House, Upholland (113; 115) suggesting first half of C17. Rear wing added early C18 with ex-situ lintel (from outbuilding) dated NH 1678 incoporated in fireplace.
HISTORY: Initials may refer to branch of Halliwell family.
* *Nigel Morgan and Garry Miller, private report, 1991.*

(136) LOWER WRENNALL SD518138
Stone three-unit linear baffle-entry yeoman house dated 1673 on single storey porch. Upper bay subdivided into small parlour and buttery, with boarded doors. Doorway lintel in form of triangular arch; porch may formerly have contained stair; evidence of blocked doorway leading from it in chamber over housebody. Purlins carried on crosswalls. Associated with Wrennall yeoman family: a Hugh Wrennall recorded as freeholder 1600, but modest scale of this house suggests builder of lower status.

(137) NORTH TUNLEY SD528134
Early example of substantial yeoman's house, also displaying early use of brick: date possibly c.1620. Two storey, three unit baffle entry with parlour wing in bay 1, coupled with independently-gabled stair tower at rear. Narrow, full-height porch; at rear, outshut of two storeys added late C17- early C18. Stone plinth, brickwork in English garden wall bond. Back-to-back firehoods serving housebody and kitchen, but parlour unheated. Beams quarter-round moulding; door to spiral newel stair has nicked lintel. Chamber floor has passage from stairhead connecting chambers in wing and over housebody, an innovative feature heightening privacy. Principal rafter trusses of inferior scantling: three over range, central one immediately before flue may indicate former smoke bay.

Nearby large combination barn produced by complex rebuilding of two formerly independent cruck structures. Main range has two probably C16 cruck trusses, was extended in post-and-truss early C17 then subsequently stone-clad. Formerly free-standing stable at right angles has trusses of heavy scantling and may be of domestic origin; stone clad C18
HISTORY: medieval site; one of several farms participating in arable element of double-oval system on Harrock Hill. Robert de Nortunleygh referred to in 1309; later occupied by freeholding Rigby yeoman family. John Rigby d.1618 owning 1 messuage, 1 garden 16 acres of land one acre of meadow and three of pasture in Wrightington of William, earl of Derby by rent of 2d. Son and heir Nicholas aged around 30 in 1619; he may be builder of house. William Rigby assessed on three hearths in Hearth Tax assessment of 1664.

*Rylands, Inquisitions (1887) p117. Nigel Morgan and Garry Miller, private report for Mr W Ainscough, 1991. Porteus; 'Standish Deeds, p113.

(138) SANDERSON HOUSE SD513139
Complex, idiosyncratic product of staggered rebuilding. Present three-unit main range of early C18 with older rear comprising wing and stair turret of early C17. Wing – added along with tower to pre-existing timber-framed range – contains heated parlour (with external chimney stack) and buttery, formerly accessed by separate doors (now blocked). Further two-and-a-half storey service bay, at lower level, added to rear C17-early C18. This subsequently was incorporated into new main range (becoming 3rd bay) added c1700-1710 at right angles to line of former range. New range attempts classicism but fails at symmetry; has cross windows, storey band and three dormers at eaves. First bay contains parlour and dog-leg stair; housebody has stone hearth back-to-back with cross-corner fireplace in parlour. Stair tower became redundant: stair removed and hearth inserted to create small heated service room. Fireplace similarly inserted in 3rd bay, which became kitchen. Upper portion of stair tower truncated and roof became outshut-style continuation of 3rd bay. Principal rafter trusses over both wing and new range, latter with wavy principals of light scantling.

(139) SOUTH TUNLEY SD534123
Fragment of wealthy yeoman house initially built in timber-frame in 1622: latest dated post-and-truss building in area. Mostly rebuilt 1958 except for tall two-storey brick service wing to W on high stone base (probably 1667, date on rainwaterhead) and single-storey stone porch with triangular arched lintel dated 1622. However drawing prior to reconstruction (plate 22) shows timber-framed range and parlour wing to E and porch timber-framed on its upper storey. Wing has jetty with coving beneath, large external chimney stack on E wall and fishbone-type kingpost truss in gable; however latter apparently rebuilt 1896 due to decay (VCH). Ridge chimney indicates baffle-entry to housebody. Present service wing has stops buried in wall indicating previous timber-frame, so date 1667 represents cladding. Wing contains two service rooms, S one with wide firehood probably kitchen. Brick twin-flue stack on ridge has redundant water-tabling indicating former thatch. Stone over garden entrance dated 1671 appears to be re-used lintel; quoin in added porch on W wing is reused and has decoration in manner of round-headed arches.
HISTORY: South Tunley occupied by Wilson family, freeholders who held Tunley district along with Halliwells of South Tunley Hall (140); medieval site suggested by involvement in stock element of double-oval farming system on east slope of Harrock Hill. John Wilson assessed on lands in 1593 Lay Subsidy at rate of £1. Initials on porch are those of Thomas Wilson, gentleman, and wife Mary. Family crest, a demi-wolf, on rainwaterhead and brackets on downspout.

(140) SOUTH TUNLEY HALL SD535123
Stone upper-yeomanry house of C17, dated 1675 on single-storey porch: three-unit baffle-entry with central housebody range between twin flanking wings. Interior possibly contains evidence of preceding timber-framed structure.
HISTORY: seat of Halliwell family, freeholders who held Tunley along with Wilsons of South Tunley. Again, medieval origins suggested by participation in double-oval system. Family referred to in 1514, and Robert Halliwell of the hall of Tunley in 1578. Will of latter (LCRO WCW 1592) states wife Alice was to have the new chamber at east end of the house 'which her father did geeve the timber to me to erect and build the same.' This implies timber-framed wing at this end. Son Lawrence Halliwell d.1620 holding one messuage and 70 freehold acres in Wrightington. William Halliwell assessed on four hearths 1664; intials on porch refer to son Robert and wife Margaret.
*VCH VI, p176-177. Rylands (1887) p180.

(141) SPRING BANK SD526098
Curious fragment, possibly wing, of timber-framed house of early C17; now disused. Two storeys, lower of sandstone rubble, upper of square framing originally but mostly replaced by stone of C18-19 date; both gables rebuilt in stone throughout. Wallplate projects at S gable with mortice for former post, indicating structure once extended further in this direction. Also northernmost post on W wall has stub of former rail at right angles, indicating a projection lay on this side originally. Inside two bays divided by timber-framed wall capped by principal rafter truss on jowelled posts; wall has sequence of mason's marks in arabic numerals on first floor and doorway with nicked lintel. Beam between purlins at S gable has vacant stave holes in soffit suggesting former firehood canopy.
HISTORY: 1841 tithe map indicates a larger house, part of farming unit called 'Tanners'; 1892 OS map shows building reduced to present size.
*Singleton (1958).

(142) STONEY LANE FARM SD507118
Small, two-unit end-baffle-entry house: remodelling in stone c1700 of larger, possibly timber-framed early C17 structure. Stair tower to rear of housebody seems out of proportion for building of modest size. Timber-framed

origins suggested by doorway from parlour chamber to stair with nicked lintel and partly-blocked window with wooden surround in rear wall of housebody. Latter heated by firehood; parlour and chamber above have four-centred stone hearths served by extruded chimney stack. Subsequent C18 alterations: heightening by means of attic; further bay (non-domestic?) to E; outshut to rear of bay 1.
Private report by Datestone (1993).

(143) **TOOGOOD HALL** SD526134
House of centralised plan dated 1708. Two storey plus attic: front and sides stone, rear in brick. Two-unit front range with stair tower and later kitchen to rear of 2nd bay. Dates from later C19, but may replace earlier structure on evidence on remains of stone plinth and lack of windows in rear wall of 2nd bay. Front range symmetrical with moulded doorway and formerly stone cross windows; these survive on side walls. Dog-leg stair of fine style continuing into attic. Quarter-round beams (late use). Purlin roof. Formerly called Heskin House; associated with Heskin yeoman family.

(144) **WILLOW BARN** SD541144
C17 brick house containing evidence of earlier timber framing. Three-unit baffle entry with unusual short wing to rear of bays 2 and 3 which formerly contained stair; probably accessed beneath firehood in housebody. Back-to-back firehoods serving housebody and kitchen, latter unusual at yeoman level. Narrow first bay contains parlour and buttery with door to latter blocked. Present appearance dates from c1660-1690; English garden wall brickwork with lozenge pattern in blue (vitrified) headers. However heavy roof trusses (two comprising re-used cruck blades) parlour doorway with nicked lintel, kitchen beams with stops buried in wall, truss at W gable and wooden lintels above some windows point to origins as timber-framed house of early C17. Easternmost truss has carpenters' marks beginning at 7 in arabic numerals, suggesting building formerly extended further E, possibly with upper wing. Closed trusses above firehoods probably defined narrow smoke bay before brick flues inserted. Some original windows with mullions of shaped bricks.

(145) **WRIGHTINGTON HALL** SD530106
Timber-framed manor house possibly of C16, remodelled in stone probably late C17 and 1748. Sketch by Will Lathom (LCRO DP291) shows former north wing of post-and-truss construction with some decorative panels; but ground floor rebuilt in stone. Some rebuilding suggested c1700, with 'first sashed windows north of Trent' (Aitkin, 1795, p293). Principal east front dates from 1748, house largely rebuilt in C19 and timber-framed wing demolished C20.
HISTORY: Wrightington family held part of manor since later C13, John Wrightington a freeholder and justice of the peace in 1600; Dicconson family of Eccleston succeeded by marriage and Hugh Dicconson was assessed on 15 hearths in 1664, indicating extensive building.
VCH VI, p171-173.

Glossary
of selected architectural terms

Angle strut: Timber set between tiebeam and principals to strengthen a roof truss.

Arch:
- *Four-centred:* Shallow pointed form of late medieval or Tudor date.
- *Ogee:* Medieval form with double-curved S-shaped sides.
- *Triangular:* flattened, mid-late C17 degradation of four-centred form.

Architrave: Moulded surround for a doorway or window; originally the lower member of the classical entablature.

Ashlar: masonry of large, regular blocks with even faces and edges.

Attic: Room within the roofspace of a building.

Baffle entry (lobby entry): When external entrance leads into small lobby by side wall of housebody firehood; typical of C17 yeoman houses.

Balusters: Vertical pillars or posts supporting a handrail, such as that of a staircase.

Bays: Divisions of the interior or exterior of a building. Internally, bays are formed by rooms and externally by features such as windows.

Brickwork:
- *English Garden Wall Bond:* Pattern produced by alternating three or more courses (layers) of stretchers (the long face of the brick) with one course of headers (the short end side).
- *Flemish bond:* Where headers and stretchers alternate in the same course.

Brace: Curved or straight timber set diagonally between upright and horizontal members to strengthen a timber-frame.

Bressumer: Heavy beam spanning an opening, typically of a firehood or inglenook fireplace; also called inglebeam.

Casement: Window opening on hinges fixed at its side.

Chamfer: Where the square edge of a surface (such as a beam) is cut off at an angle. Types of chamfer include straight (planed off at 45 degrees), ovolo (a convex moulding) and cavetto (concave).

Cladding: Encasing of timber-framed structure in masonry.

Classical: Architecture of the ancient Greeks and Romans which subsequently became the inspiration for Renaissance architects in the C16.

Corbel: Stone or timber block used to support something above.

Cross-corner fireplace: Hearth built into the corner of a room

Cross-passage: Passage at the lower end of medieval and later halls, dividing it from service rooms

Cross window: Window with one mullion and one transom, typical of late C17-early C18.

Dais: Raised platform at the upper end of a medieval hall where the lord and his family were seated.

Double pile (double depth): House that is two rooms deep, typical of Classical planning.

Dormer window: Window that projects from a sloping roof.

Entablature: Collective term describing the three horizontal elements carried by columns in Classical architecture (architrave, frieze and cornice).

Finial: Decorative feature at apex of gable etc

Firehood: Large hearth in form of compartment spanned by heavy beam (bressumer) with flue (of wattle and daub in early examples) above; commonly called inglenook fireplace.

Gibbs surround: Embellishment of a doorway using alternating large and small blocks of stone; a C18 motif.

Gothic: The style of medieval architecture current from late C12 to mid C16, characterised by use of pointed arches.

Hall-house: Medieval house in which principal room extends full height of the building.

Heckpost: Timber post or stone pillar supporting one end of firehood bressumer.

Hoodmould: Projecting stone or brick moulding above a window to deflect rainwater from glass; typically has dropped and returned ends but occasionally is of straight monolithic form.

Jamb:	Vertical side of a doorway, window etc
Joist:	Subsidiary timber in a ceiling, used to support floorboards and usually carried by larger beams.
Keystone:	Central stone in an arch. Sometimes a false keystone is used in imitation over a doorway, window etc.
King mullion:	Mullion larger than the rest in window of this type.
Kingpost:	Vertical timber resting upon tiebeam of roof truss and directly supporting the ridge purlin.
Lateral stack:	Hearth on rear wall of hall, typical feature of gentry houses.
Lights:	Vertical divisions of a window by means of mullions.
Lintel:	Beam or stone spanning opening over a door, window etc.
Longhouse:	Primitive house with domestic and cattle accommodation under same roof.
Louvre:	Opening in roof of hall-house allowing smoke to escape.
Mullion:	Stone or timber upright dividing a window into lights.
Newel:	Timber post at the base, landing and top of a staircase.
Nicked lintel:	Debased form of ogee arch, of flattened four-centred form with vertical cut or 'nick' at apex; characteristic of late C16-early C17.
Oriel:	Bay window on an upper floor.
Pediment:	Classical feature taking form of triangular or segmental gable above a doorway, window etc.
Piano nobile:	Principal floor of a gentry house.
Pilaster:	Imitation column, typically supporting a pediment etc over a doorway.
Plinth:	Stone or brick base of a building, generally projecting.
Posts:	Main uprights in a timber-framed building
Principal rafter:	In triangulated roof trusses, heavy inclined member set into tiebeam that supports the purlins.
Purlin:	Timbers supporting rafters of a roof: the ridge purlin stands at the apex, with side purlins lower down.
Quoins:	Blocks of stone which demarcate the corners of a building.
Rails:	Horizontal members in a timber-framed building.
Rustication:	Where stonework is emphasised by using deeper joints; alternatively the face of the blocks may be decorated, ie in the manner of worm-casts (vermiculation).
Rubble:	Cruder form of masonry, with undressed stones as opposed to ashlar.
Settle:	Seat built into a corner of a firehood compartment.
Sill:	Lowermost rail of a timber-framed building, usually resting upon a plinth.
Solar:	Private room at upper end of medieval hall-house.
Spere:	Timber structure at lower end of medieval hall, acting as screen; alternatively, short length of wall forming side of firehood that is directly in front of entrance in baffle-entry houses.
Stair:	
Dog leg:	Parallel flights in opposite directions, with landings between them;
Open well:	One that rises around three sides of a compartment (well);
Spiral:	One that is enclosed within a circular compartment;
Newel:	Stair that rises around a central newel that supports the treads;
Quarter turn:	Type that rises to landing and takes a 45 degree turn.
Storey band:	Projecting course of brick or stone at storey level (also string course).
Studs:	Intermediate members in a timber-framed wall.
Tiebeam:	Horizontal timber that carries principal rafters of a roof truss.
Transom:	Member that divides a window horizontally.
Wallplate:	Timber that lies on top of a wall and supports the rafters.
Water tabling:	Projecting courses of brick, typically on chimneys, to deflect rainwater
Windbraces:	In a roof, straight or curved strengthening timbers connecting purlins and principal rafters.

Index

Ackhurst Hall, Orrell (84; pl 83, 119) 60,68,73,142,156,165,
    166,170,192
Addy, Sidney 44
Adlington 19
Adlington Hall (1; pl 70) 129,135,175
Ainsdale 172n
Alkrington Hall, Middleton, 124
Allanson Hall, Adlington (2) 60,68,146,175
Alston Old Hall, Longridge, 56n, 141
Ambrose Cottage, Upholland (106) 133,134,159,197
Anderton family of Birchley and Lostock, 61,73,84
Anderton's Farm, Bispham (23) 180
Architects 124-5
Ashurst family of Dalton, 61
Ashurst Hall, Dalton (34) 28,60,80,182
Ashurst Hill (Pl 1) 16,17
Aspinwall's Farm, Lathom (61) 147,188
Aspull, 31
Attics 119-120
Ayscough yeoman family of Lathom 42,92,95,97

Baguley Hall, Manchester 47,140
Balcony Farm, Upholland, (107) 91,98,99,101,144,166,197
Bankes family of Winstanley 29,61,64,66,68,73,93
Bannister Farm, Wrightington (129) 41,63,101,138,163,168,
    202
Barkers Farm, Dalton (35; pl 58, fig 31) 113-114,131,183
Barns 92-3
Beams 168-169
Belle Vue Farm (Scott's Fold) Dalton (37; pl 149)
    93,116,117,118,145,154,156,158,183
Bentham's Farm, Dalton (38) 105,183
Billinge 68
Billinge family 84, 96,153
Billinge Hall (11) 84,96,177
Billinge Hill (pl 2) 17
Birch Green Farm (108) 197
Birchley Hall, Billinge (12; pl 36) 60,73,74,76-7,80,83,100,108,
    123,144,150,152,158,178
Bispham family of Billinge 69,70,81,84
Bispham Hall, Billinge (13; pl 35,38,102, fig 19) 60,69,74,
    75,77,78,79-80,81,82,83,108,144,152,155,157,158,
    160,165,168,178
Bispham Hall, Bispham (24) 112,116,159,165,169,180
Blackbirds Farm, Dalton (36) 183
Black Death 40
Black Lawyers, Worthington (125; pl 12) 39,41,138,201
Blackledge family of Blythe Hall 69
Blackrod 17,68
Blythe Hall, Lathom (62) 68,189

Bogburn Hall, Coppull (29; pl 53,118, fig 10,28) 26,49,94,
    114,140,141,142,150,168,170,181
Bold Old Hall, St Helens 124,127-8
Bolton 29
Bootle, Sir Thomas 124
Bounty Farm, Upholland (109) 46,106,145,199
Boyle, Robert, Lord Burlington 124
Bradley Hall, Langtree (57; pl 16,18, figs 11-14) 48-9,50-51,
    55,187-8
Bradshaigh family of Haigh, 26,52,61,62,64.68,73,93
Bradyll, John, of Whalley 65
Brewhouse 117
Brick 146-8
Brickmaking 95
Brown family of Ince 40,60
Burleigh House, Northants 57
Burscough Priory 69
Butterfly Hall, Aspull (5) 106,176
Buttery 117

Calico Wood Farm, Shevington (93) 195
Carr House, Bretherton 146
Carr Lane Farm, Upholland (110) 106,198
Catterall family of Crooke, Shevington 71
Centralised plans 110
Classicism 108-114,123
Chambers:
    - gentry houses, 80-82,
    - yeoman houses118-9
Chantry of Douglas 65
Charity Farm, Wrightington(130) 106,203
Chester 35
Chimneys 71
Chisnall Hall, Wrightington (30; pl 39) 84,171,181
Chisnall family of Chisnall, Wrightington 62-3,84
Chorley 15
Cicely's Cottage, Dalton (39; pl103) 106,117,145,158,183
Civil War, 104
Clayton, Sir Richard of Adlington 130
Classicism 108-114,123
Clegg Hall, Littleborough 65
Club House Farm, Shevington (97; pl 42,105)53,55,92,93,118,
    120,155,158,160,164,165,195
Coach House Farm, Shevington (96)195
Coal mining 67-8,95-6
Cock Hall, Whitworth nr Rochdale, 172
Cock Farm, Lathom (63) 112, 154,166,189
Cockleshell Cottage, Windle, St Helens 152
Colliers Arms, Aspull (6) 110,112,176
Copyhold Farm, Wrightington (131; pl 10) 48,86,121,122,

209

fig 24) 29,20,96,104,115,116,117,118,147,150,154, 158,164,165,166,167,168,171,172,203
Coppull 17,19,63
Coppull Hall, Coppull (31) 21,23,60,146,181
Coppull Old Hall (32) 140,147,166,182
Copyhold tenure 29,91
Cowlings Farm, Wrightington (132) 203
Crank Hill 17
Crawshaw Hall, Adlington (3) 21,50,55,140,141,145,175
Crisp Cottage, Dalton (40) 183
Crisp, Thomas of Parbold Hall 128
Crooke Hall, Shevington (98; pl 32) 55,69,71,72-3,142,143,195
Crosswings 44-45, 100,106
Croxteth Hall, Liverpool 124
Crows Nest Farm, Billinge (14) 88,91,94,179
Crucks 36-8, 55-6
    - construction details 137-40
    - decline of 45-6,97
    - distribution and hierarchy 42
    - forms of cruck houses 42-5
    - upper crucks 45
Culshaw yeoman family of Newburgh (pl 62) 120

Dairy 147
Dam House, Langtree (58) 32,51,97,141,188
Darbyshire Farm, Lathom (64) 147,164,180
Darbyshire House, Billinge (15; pl 56,93) 96,112,113,117, 120, 131,144,150,151,159,170,179
Darbyshire yeoman family of Billinge 88,94,96,120
Darbyshire yeoman family of Dalton 95
Dean House, Upholland (111) 96,101,118,120,198
Douglas Valley:
    - agriculture 21-3,24,66-7,91-3
    - landscape features 15-17,19
    - place names 21
    - prosperity 30-1
    - settlement patterns 22-3
    - woodland clearance 20-1,35
Dial House, Upholland (120) 113,198
Digmoor Hall, Upholland (113) 155,198
Dinkley Hall, Ribble Valley, 45
Doe House, Newburgh (74) 190
Doorways 149-52, 169-70
Douglas Bank Farm (Fisher's House) Upholland (114; front cover, pl 47,90, fig23) 94,96,104,117,118,146,147, 150 164,168,198-9
Dower House, Ince (530 110, 186
Downholland Hall, Downholland 146
Drapers Farm, Parbold (86) 53,107,192

Eccles House, Bispham (25) 46,107,180
Elizabeth I 65
Elmers Green, Dalton 19, 22, 39, 106

Fairhurst Hall, Wrightington (134) 23,25,60,63,66,80,81, 83,165,166,203

Felton's Farm, Dalton (141)169,184
Feudalism 25
Finch House, Shevington (99) 131,132,195-6
Fisher family of Upholland 94, 96,104,117
Fir Tree House, Billinge (16; pl 110),111,112,115,117,150, 165,167,179
Firehoods 164-5
Fosters Green, Dalton 39
Freeholders 28-9,90-1
Furnishings 164-5

Gathurst 21
Gathurst Fold, Orrell (85) 160,165,192
Gathurst Hall, Shevington (100; pl 60) 53,117
Gawthorpe 65,171
Gentry class 25-28
    - decline of 83-4
    - prosperity 63-70
    - structure 59,63
Gentry houses 57-84, 123-130
Gerard family of Ince 59,61,64-5,93
Giants Hall, Standish (102; pl 46, fig 6,7) 45-6,53,55,91,101, 107,139,169,165,166,170, 196
Gidlow Hall, Aspull (7; pl 7, 100 fig 37) 24,49,50,55,63,64,65, 66,72,100,142,144,145,163,176
Gidlow family of Aspull 63,65,72,73,144
Glaciation 16
Great Houghwood, Billinge (18) 99,100,133,135,179
Great Rebuilding 31-33
Greens (grazing land) 22
Green Barn Farm, Blackrod (27) 110,112,131,180-1
Greenhill Farm, Newburgh (17; pl 74, 120) 115,117,120,133, 135,152,169,170,190
Greenslate Farm, Billinge (19; fig 38) 112,172,179
Guild Hall, Rainford (91; pl 115) 19,54,99,101,116,117,118, 146,152,156158,167,171,194

Hacking Hall, Billington 77
Haigh 117
Haigh Hall, Haigh (52) 30, 67,129,156,160,186
Halliwell's Farm, Upholland (115; pl 9) 28,116,145,154,156, 199
Halliwell family of Upholland 28,94
Halliwell family of Wrightington 96
Hall-houses, 37-9,49,53-5,78-9,97
Hardwick Hall, Derbyshire 57
Harrock Hall (133; pl 37,96 fig 20) 20,23,25,26,51,65-6,75, 78-9,80,82,83,153,154,155,156,203-4
Harrock Hill 17
Harsnips, Dalton (42) 97, 114,139,154,184
Hawkley 21,63
Hawkley Hall (89) 62,193-4
Haydock family of Bogburn Hall, Coppull 26,94,110
Hearths 165
Hearth tax, 30-1,32,33,42,46,55,68
Heaton gentry family of Billinge 61

Henry VII 59
Henry VIII 64-5
Hesketh gentry family of Rufford 59,61
Holt Farm, Coppull (33; pl 19, fig 5) 23,51,94,96,100-1,117,
 145,182
Heyes Farm, Upholland (116) 106,199
Higher Barn, Wrightiongton (135) 139,164,204
Holland's House, Dalton (43) 90,92,95,108,115,116,117-8,
 155,159,165,168,169,184
Holland yeoman family of Dalton 90,92,95
Holmes House, Blackrod (28; pl 73) 133,134,181
Holt, John 121
Hooten yeoman family of Upholland 92
Houghton gentry family of Kirklees, Aspull 26,40,63
Houghton Tower 59
Housebody (firehouse) 99,114,132
Hydes Brow Farm, Rainford (92) 44,110,169,194

Ince 16,31
Ince Hall (Peel Ditch) (55; pl 34) 72,187
Ince, Hall of (54; pl 33) 74,187
Ivy Cottage, Newburgh (76) 150,191

Johnson's Farm, Upholland (117; pl 20,21, fig 18) 52-3,91,93,
 95,96,100,102,164,165,169,199
Jump's Farm (Ayscough's), Latham (65) 42,92,95,96,106,115,
 117,118,161,189

Kathry, Newburgh (77) 115,116,191
Kirklees (Kirkless) Hall, Aspull (9; pl 14, 79, 123, fig 2) 24,26,
 40-1,47,55,60,63,76,138,139,159,163,176
Kitchens 37,82-3,117
Knights Hall, Upholland (118) 107, 142,145,160,168,199
Knights of St John of the Hospital (Knights Hospitallers) 25,
 62,64
Knowsley Hall, Knowsley 124

Landowners 25
Leasehold 29,91
Leyland, John 35,68
Longhouse 43
Lowe, Roger, 17,34
Lower Tower Hill, Upholland (119; pl 50)45,91,96,97,105,
 106,139,200
Lowes, Newburgh (78; pl 113, fig 9) 46,47,111-2,140,167,191
Lyme Tree House (Widdows), Billinge (20; pl 3) 19,105,152,
 158,179

Maddocks, Billinge (22) 133,134,155,167,180
Maggots Nook, Rainford (93; pl 91) 116,150,194
Manor Cottage, Parbold (87) 46,192
Manor House, Crawford, Upholland (120; pl 72,99; fig 35)
 46,127,131,132,152,153,154,160,167,169,200
Manor House, Worthington (126; pl 78, fig 3,4) 413,106,107,
 138,139,164,202
Martholme, Great Harwood 83

Martindale, Adam 87,102
Mawdesley 39
Milkhouse 117
Mill Bridge Farm, Worthington (127; pl 98) 116,153,202
Millets, Upholland 121) 133,200
Molyneux family of Hawkley, Pemberton 60,62-3
Molyneux family of Sefton 59
Monasteries, dissolution of 64-5
Moor (grazing land) 22
Moorcroft House, Newburgh (80; pl 76) 135,147,152,160,200
Moss Bank, St Helens 87

Nailmaking 68
Naylor yeoman family of Rainford 54,90,92,93
Naylor yeoman family of Upholland 93,95,96,97,120
Needless Inn, Lathom (68) 110,154
Nelson gentry family of Fairhurst, Wrightington 60,63,66,70,
 71,81
Newburgh 17
Newgate Farm, Upholland (122)113,116,154,159,164,200-1
New Hall, Clayton-le-Dale, 110
North Meols 44
North Tunley, Wrightington (137) 23,88,92,99,116,118,154,
 164,204

Open halls 37-9,97
Ordsall Hall, Salford 47-8
Otterheads, Lathom (69; pl 77) 135,147,152,190
Outshuts 44

Palladio, Andrea 124
Parbold 25
Parbold Hall (88; pl 67,68,107,11,116)21,23,25,51,60,65,66,
 74,78-9,80,81,83,128,132,145,152,160,161,165,166,
 168,169,170,171,192-3
Parbold Hill 16,17
Parlours (pl 1) 79-80,100,115-7
Parkers Farm, Rishton 164
Peel Hall, Ince (56; pl 13, fig 1) 24, 40-3,47,55,138,139,141,
 142,187
Pennington Hall (10; pl 89) 147,177
Piano nobile 127
Pilling 172
Porches 152-4
Plans
    - gentry, 76-8
    - yeoman 108-114
Plaster decoration (pl 116, 121,122) 171-2
Prescott yeoman family of Dalton, 97,105
Prescott yeoman family of Shevington 92,120
Prescott, Richard of Coppull, yeoman 94,96,117
Priors Wood Hall, Dalton (45; pl 60,68, 104) 20,97,105,116,
 117,118,119,154,158,159,168,185

Ridding (woodland clearing) 21
Rigby gentry family of Burgh, Chorley 61

211

Rigby gentry family of Harrock, Wrightington 26,62,65,6667, 69,84,92
Rigby House Farm, Adlington (4) 88,100,119,176
Rigby yeoman family of Adlington 88,119
River Douglas 16-17
River Ribble 16,20
Rose Cottage, Newburgh (81; pl 82, 101) 55,141,142,155,156, 165,191
Rufford Old Hall 35,47-8,140,142

Salmesbury Hall, Salmesbury 146
Sanderson House, Wrightington (138) 101,116,145,155,205
Scott yeoman family of Dalton 93, 105
Scythe Stone Delph Farm, Rainford (94; pl 54, fig 8,29) 46-7, 110,119,154,194-5
Sephton gentry family of Sephton Hall, Skelmersdale 60,66,67, 80,82
Settlement patterns 23-3
Shireburn family of Stoneyhurst, 59
Shevington 20, 31
Smiths Farm, Dalton (46; pl 43 fig 22, 25) 92,95,107,116,185
Smithills Hall, Bolton 47-8,140
Smoke bays 163
South Tunley, Wrightington (139; pl 22)23,54,101,142,143,205
South Tunley Hall, Wrightington (131) 23,108,205
Spencer yeoman family of Newburgh 132-3
Speke Hall, Liverpool 171
Spring Bank, Wrightington (141; pl23) 54,55,108,140,169,205
Stained glass 160, pl 105
Stainscomb, Goldshaw Booth 110
Stair towers 154-155
Staley Hall, Stalybridge 77
Standish 31,68
Standish gentry family of Standish 25,51,59,61-62,64
Standish Hall (103; pl 29,68) 30,49,1,72,129,130,140,14-3, 155,171,196
Stanley gentry family, earls of Derby, 26,29,55,59,94,102
Stannanought, Dalton (47; pl 106) 42,92,93,96,112,116,117, 118,159,160,163,165,167,185
Stannanought yeoman family of Dalton 42,92-93,96,116,118
Stock ovals 23,31
Stone 72-3
Stone Hall, Dalton (48; frontispiece, pl 55, 92) 46,111-2,115, 117,140,150,151,167,185-6
Stoney Lane Farm, Wrightington (142) 155,160,169,205-6

Tarleton 17
Taunton Hall, Ashton-under-Lyne 45,38
Taylor's Farm, Lathom (70) 106,117,190
Textiles 69,96,119
The Meadows, Wigan (128; pl 40) 88,113,201
Through passage 99
Timber-framing 35-56,72-3,107-8
Toogood Hall, Wrightington (143) 155,206
Tower Hill, Upholland 17
Towneley Hall, Burnley 124

Upholland 29,31,39
Upper Standish Wood Fold (105; pl 112, 117) 20,101,116,141, 166,169-70

Wainscoting (panelling) 171
Wainwright's Farm, Lathom (71)161,190
Wall painting 81, 172-3
Walthew House, Pemberton (90) 28,94
Walthew, Robert of Pemberton 28,93,94,102
Watkinson's Farm, Lathom (72) 117,190
Webster's Farm, Lathom (73; pl 87) 106,112,116,117,147,150, 190
West Derby Hundred 24
White Cottages, Newburgh (82)43
Widdows Farm, Dalton (50) 119,147,152,186
Wigan 68
Willow Barn, Wrightington (144; pl 52 fig 27) 45,55,107,117, 139,140,147,158,164,206
Windows 155-62
Winstanley 68
Winstanley Hall, Winstanley (124; pl 25) 28-9,61,73,74,77, 100,108,123,144,152,156,160,201
Winter Hill 16
Woodcock House, Newburgh (83; pl 71,94 fig 31) 131,132-3, 147,152,167,191-2
Woodland clearance 20-1,35
Worthington Hall, Worthington (128; pl 30, 85) 60,72,75,83, 129,132,40,142,143,150,160,202
Worthington gentry family of Crawshaw 63,67,84
Worthington gentry family of Worthington 59,67,69,84
Wrightington 25,39,63,59
Wrightington gentry family of Wrightington (pl 24) 59,60,66

Yew Tree House, Dalton (51, pl 5,51, fig 26) 32,107,115,116, 169,186
yeomanry 25-8
    - decline 120-1
    - houses of 88-91,97-121
    - income 91-6